TEAMBUILDING PUZZLES

Mike Anderson | Learning Works
Jim Cain | Teamwork & Teamplay
Chris Cavert | FUNdoing
Tom Heck | Teach Me Teamwork

Kendall Hunt
p u b l i s h i n g   c o m p a n y
4050 Westmark Drive • P O Box 1840 • Dubuque IA 52004-1840

D1158996

All rights reserved. No part of this book may be reproduced for distribution in any form or by any means without the permission of the lead author. We would like to make this material available for teachers and trainers to use for groupwork, teamwork and community building sessions. This use however does not include transferring these materials to internal documents, training manuals, websites, publications or other mass distributed documents, without permission. Write to us, we want to help, but please ask first. Thank you.

Inquiries for copy permission should be addressed to:

Jim Cain
Teambuilding Puzzles
468 Salmon Creek Road
Brockport, NY 14420 USA
Phone (585) 637-0328
Email: jimcain@teamworkandteamplay.com
Website: www.teamworkandteamplay.com

Background cover image © Carlos Caetano, 2009. Under license from Shutterstock, Inc.

www.kendallhunt.com
Send all inquiries to:
4050 Westmark Drive
Dubuque, IA 52004-1840

Published in 2005 as a FUNdoing publication

Copyright © 2010 by Jim Cain

ISBN 978-0-7575-7040-7

Kendall Hunt Publishing Company has the exclusive rights to reproduce this work, to prepare derivative works from this work, to publicly distribute this work, to publicly perform this work and to publicly display this work.

All rights reserved. No part of this publication may be reproduced, stored in a retrieval system, or transmitted, in any form or by any means, electronic, mechanical, photocopying, recording, or otherwise, without the prior written permission of the copyright owner.

Printed in the United States of America
10 9 8 7 6 5 4 3 2 1

**Teambuilding
Puzzles**

Contents

Teambuilding
Puzzles

Teambuilding Puzzles

Foreword

In addition to the hundreds of adventure-based learning books filling multiple bookcases in my office, there is a modest collection of about 300 puzzle and game books which have consistently found their way into my shopping bag at various bookstores, garage sales and airport newsstands. I just love puzzles, and every now and then I find a truly unique one that blends perfectly with the world of adventure-based and active learning. So here, for the first time, is a collection of interesting puzzles, games and activites that you can use with your teambuilding, corporate training, adventure-based and active learning programs. These puzzles require creative problem solving abilities, cooperation, communication and occasionally shear luck to solve. Some are straight forward and will yield to inquiring minds. Some provide a bit of the 'aha!' effect and often have a surprise solution, which in itself creates a wonderful teachable moment. Others are just plain tough and require the use of team skills to succeed. But no matter the level of difficulty, each of these puzzles offers a 'teachable moment' and some excellent opportunities for team discussion and reflection.

Working on a puzzle can be even more fun as a team, and writing a book like this one can be a bit of a puzzle too. So, with the team effort in mind, I called three of the most innovative and creative trainers I know and invited them to join me in this project. Chris Cavert, known for his Affordable Portables and 50 Ways to Use Your Noodle books, is the creative force behind his company, FUNdoing. Mike Anderson is an innovative educator and the Owner of The Petra Cliffs Group. Tom Heck is the President and Founder of the International Association of Teamwork Facilitators (IATF), creator of multiple teambuilding games which are sold worldwide, and the author of 12 multimedia teambuilding skills training programs.

We hope you enjoy this collection of puzzles, games, challenges and adventure-based education activities. We certainly have!

Jim Cain
Teamwork & Teamplay

The concept of a 'teachable moment' is actually very simple. Any situation that presents an opportunity for learning can become a teachable moment. Some of these moments occur randomly in our lives, such as learning which exit not to take from the expressway. Some have been carefully planned, such as enrolling in a college course to learn a specific new skill. The goal of this book is to present a unique collection of enjoyable and engaging activities that create teachable moments.

The activities chosen for this book consist of a wide variety of challenges and puzzles, many of which can be easily made from common household items or require no equipment or props at all. Others offer the opportunity for active learning, where participants learn to 'think on their feet' while accomplishing a specific task. Some puzzles are physically challenging, while others take more brain power than horsepower to complete.

The teachable moments explored in this collection include opportunities for creative problem solving, group decision making, group consensus building, goal setting, teamwork, working with limited resources, diversity, inclusion, giving directions, following guidelines and rules, dealing with change, integrity, clear communication and many other life skills that are valuable in the academic classroom and in the corporate boardroom.

Each puzzle is presented with some suggestions for teachable moment topics, including questions that can be used to stimulate conversations before, during and after the completion of each puzzle. In most cases, hints, clues and other suggestions are provided to assist facilitators, teachers and trainers in techniques which will help their participants successfully solve each puzzle, but without directly providing the solution. And for those puzzles that leave your players baffled, there are (of course) solutions in the back of this book.

In addition to more than one hundred different puzzles included in this book, The Great Puzzle Quest is presented to assist you in turning the simple art of solving puzzles into a wonderful community building and socially interactive group experience. Puzzle Golf and the Puzzle Party are also ways of making puzzles an interactive part of your next event or social gathering.

And finally, you'll find an annotated bibliography of additional puzzle and teambuilding resources, that should keep your teambuilding program filled with high energy and effective activities for years to come.

So, whether you are looking for methods to increase information retention in a corporate training program, exploring creative problem solving methods in the classroom, or leading a teambuilding program in the great outdoors, here are dozens of activities that create teachable moments that are sure to be remembered by your audiences, long after the puzzles have been solved.

Puzzles and Teachable Moments
Two Opportunities that Go Well Together

Puzzles are very much like life itself. They present challenges. They sometimes confound us. They teach us skills that work elsewhere. And, just when we figure out what is really going on, somebody changes the rules and we are forced to consider a new reality, and seek new solutions.

Learning how to solve puzzles then is not only a recreational pastime, but practice for real life as well. The skills required to solve challenges and puzzles translate to other portions of our lives. Patience, creative problem solving, determination, working as a team, perseverance... these are all useful skills that, when practiced are likely to improve the quality of our individual lives and our value as a member of a team.

Within the solution to a challenging puzzle comes a key moment when the facts and realities of the puzzle become increasingly clear. This unique moment, sometimes referred to as the 'aha!' effect, or even as a BFO (Blinding Flash of the Obvious), is the separation between challenge and solution, between a puzzle presented, and a puzzle solved. Within this moment come lessons that last long after the puzzle has been forgotten. This is what we refer to as a 'teachable moment.'

The puzzles and teachable moments presented in this book are designed to help you explore a variety of concepts with your students and team members. Sure, you can solve most of the problems in this book individually, but you would be missing a valuable opportunity. Each of the puzzles in this book present two possibilities:

1. To challenge teams in working together to find a solution to each puzzle, and

2. For the team to experience the learning opportunity or teachable moment presented in each puzzle.

Presenting one of these puzzles to a team while only seeking the solution is a bit like driving across the country to the Grand Canyon and never getting out of the car. You would be missing the second, and what some folks consider the best part of the experience altogether.

Another way of thinking about the value of puzzles and teachable moments incorporates a simplified experiential learning model*. This model suggests that there are three components to a successful learning process: activity, reflection and application. Consider these three essential elements as the legs of the stool illustrated here.

The puzzles presented in this book contribute more than one hundred different opportunities for the activity component of our stool. But this component alone does not create balance. We still need the two legs provided by the teachable moments to create a balanced stool. One leg is the opportunity to review and reflect upon the skills and experiences encountered during each puzzle. The final leg considers how to apply these skills to future real-life projects.

Incorporate all of these components and you will create a complete and valuable learning experience for your audience. Omit any single component and you will substantially limit the effectiveness of the learning experience.

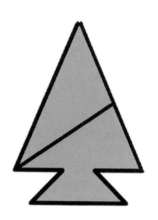

As an example of the value of teachable moments, consider Puzzle #5 from our collection. In this puzzle participants are given a collection of wooden pieces, that when properly assembled, will create a total of five arrowheads, all the same size. One arrowhead is already complete, and provides a size template for the remaining arrowheads. Most teams quickly discover that there are only six remaining pieces, which collectively create only three more arrowheads, for a total of four. The challenge of this puzzle is to use the four arrowheads in the proper configuration to create the outline of a fifth arrowhead, thus completing the task.

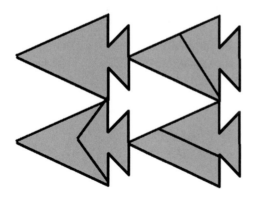

The teachable moment in this puzzle is for the group to realize that even though they feel they have been given inadequate resources, it is still possible to complete the task. In many cases, we all would like 'more stuff' to do our jobs. More time to complete the research paper. More employees to finish the construction project. More financial resources for materials. The arrowhead puzzle illustrates that we can do 'more with less' if we are willing to be creative and work together.

In order to bring out the teachable moment from this puzzle, the leader or facilitator can ask the team, at the completion of this project, "does this puzzle remind you of any other situations, and if so, tell us about them?" Or, "what other projects do you have limited resources with which to complete the task?" By exploring this line of discussion at the completion of the puzzle, participants are given the opportunity to transfer the skills learned from the activity back to their respective situations. This approach sometimes helps a team member solve not only the puzzle of the day, but potentially some additional challenges they are facing as well. One of the most important questions you can ask is, "what skills did you learn from this experience that can help you solve additional problems in the future?"

In some cases, the puzzles came first in this book. In other cases, the teachable moment. But in either case, both are essential parts of the whole. You'll find information on creating your own teachable moments in each puzzle description in this book. In addition, near the back of this book, you'll also find information on choosing the right puzzle for your group, and on modifying puzzles to meet the needs of your team.

We wish you the best of luck in your application of both components in this book; the puzzle solutions and the teachable moments they create.

* For more information about experiential learning, we invite you to read:

Experiential Learning - Experience as the Source of Learning and Development, 1984, David A. Kolb, Prentice Hall, Englewood Cliffs, NJ USA ISBN 0-13-295261-0.

Experience is a hard teacher.
It gives the test first,
and then the lesson.
Vernon Sanders Law

Teambuilding Puzzles

Challenging Your Assumptions
Thoughts About Solving Puzzles

While looking at a puzzle, any puzzle, you can reach the point where you realize that your first guess probably isn't the correct answer. Puzzles, by their nature, often lead us down the wrong path. They are designed to confuse us, to challenge our thinking, to require us to bend our thought process and consider alternative solutions. They are a test of our assumptions and our attention to details.

Many times, within the initial description of the puzzle, clues to the solution are also presented. But we are only human. We assume. We interpret the rules according to our own experiences and skills. We guess. We seek the obvious and often miss the subtle.

When this happens, there is one powerful technique that can bring us back to the path for success, and that is simply to ***Challenge Your Assumptions!***

There are dozens of stories in human history that end in failure, and with the phrase, "it seemed like a good idea at the time."** All of the truly unique solutions in our history, all of the innovative new technologies, the medical break-throughs, and the creative solutions to life-long challenges come forward once we began to challenge that which we already know to be true (but unsuccessful) and begin looking for other possibilities. And each new solution gives us more skills to apply to the next challenge. Solving puzzles isn't just a recreational pursuit. And it isn't just an activity that can fulfill educational curriculums or corporate directives. Solving puzzles builds valuable life skills. There are activities in this book that explore more than a dozen of these life skills, including: creative problem solving, creating consensus within a group, exploring diversity, creating an inclusive atmosphere, dealing with change, working with group decision making, meeting deadlines, setting goals, communicating clearly, working with limited resources, exploring leadership and teamwork.

One of these valuable life skills is the ability to meet adversity, and conquer it. Tenacity, perseverance, determination - these are the life skills that allow each of us to pick ourselves up after a failure, and try again. Solving puzzles as a team requires exactly these kinds of skills for success. These skills also transfer directly to other endeavors in life, from the classroom to the boardroom, and from the playground to the production floor.

Within this book comes more than a hundred different ways to engage your audiences, show them the power of working as a team, explore a variety of useful team and life skills, and build the kind of team that will not fold at the first failure, but continue trying, challenging their original assumptions, inventing new solutions, and never quitting until they have conquered the challenge.

** If you would like to explore more historical wrong-turns and learning from failure, we suggest you read:

You Did What? Mad Plans and Great Historical Disasters, 2004, Bill Fawcett and Brian Thomsen, Perennial Currents, New York, NY USA ISBN 0-06-053250-5

It Seemed Like a Good Idea. . ., A Compendium of Great Historical Fiascoes, 2001, Bill Fawcett and William Forstchen, Perennial Currents, New York, NY USA ISBN 0-380-80771-8

Failing Forward: How to Make the Most of Your Mistakes, 2000, John C. Maxwell, Thomas Nelson Publishers, Nashville, TN USA ISBN 0-7852-7430-8

To Engineer is Human - The Role of Failure in Successful Design, 1992, Henry Petroski, Vintage Books, New York, NY USA ISBN 0-679-73416-3

Design Paradigms - Case Histories of Error and Judgment in Engineering, 1994, Henry Petroski, Cambridge University Press, Cambridge, UK ISBN 0-521-46649-0

Why Buildings Fall Down, 1987, Matthys Levy and Mario Salvadori, W.W.Norton and Company, New York, NY USA ISBN 0-393-31152-X

Breakdown - Deadly Technological Disasters, 1995, Neil Schlager, Visible Ink Press, Detroit, MI USA ISBN 0-7876-0478-X

The puzzles, riddles and challenges presented in this section have been catalogued below by title, teachable moment, prop category and difficulty level. Prop categories include:

Simple	Puzzles with simple, easy to obtain or make equipment
Pencil	Pencil and paper puzzles - table top activities
Complex	Puzzles with unique or specialized equipment
None	Puzzles with no required equipment

Each puzzle is presented in the standardized manner shown on the first page after this list. A description of each puzzle, presentation suggestions, equipment and material recommendations, teachable moments, suitable variations, and useful hints, clues and suggestions, are provided. Solutions to nearly every puzzle can be found on pages 232 through 257 of this book.

No.	Puzzle Title	Teachable Moment	Prop Category	Difficulty Level
1	2B or Knot 2B	Building Consensus	Simple	Easy
1	Missing Link	Building Consensus	Simple	Easy
1	Not Knots	Building Consensus	Simple	Moderate
2	Handcuffs	Creative Problem Solving	Simple	Moderate
3	Three Cubed	Planning Comes First	Complex	Difficult
4	Labyrinth	Reflection, Discovery	Simple	Moderate
5	Arrowheads	Limited Resources	Simple	Moderate
6	People Movers	Teamwork, Problem Solving	Simple	Difficult
7	Tangrams	Physical Challenge	Simple	Moderate
7	Diversity Tangrams	Diversity, Inclusion	Simple	Moderate
7	G2G Tangrams	Choosing Best Qualities	Simple	Moderate
7	Tangram Quilt	Diversity and Unity	Simple	Moderate
7	Talking Tangrams	Communication, Listening	Simple	Moderate
8	Archimedes Puzzle	Variations of Tangrams	Simple	Moderate
9	Switching Corks	Teaching & Helping Others	Simple	Easy
10	Rock Around Clock	Simplicity, Problem Solving	None	Easy

No.	Puzzle Title	Teachable Moment	Prop Category	Difficulty Level
11	Room at the Top	Creative Problem Solving	Simple	Moderate
12	Building Connection	The Value of Connection	Simple	Moderate
13	How Deep?	Communication	Simple	Moderate
14	T.H.E. Puzzle	Versatility, Problem Solving	Simple	Easy
15	PVC Network	Teamwork, Problem Solving	Complex	Moderate
16	Plumber's Delight	Consequences	Complex	Difficult
17	Inside Out	Integrity, Rules, Ethics	Simple	Easy
18	Electric Box	Changing Environment	Simple	Moderate
19	Matchstick Puzzles	Creative Problem Solving	Simple	Easy/Moderate
20	Slow Burn	Fault Tree Analysis	Pencil	Moderate
21	Houses & Utilities	Thinking Outside the Box	Pencil/Simple	Moderate
22	Making Connections	Connection, Problem Solving	Pencil	Easy
23	Heads or Tails	Creative Problem Solving	Simple	Easy/Moderate
24	Drink Up!	Multiple Correct Solutions	Simple	Easy
25	Pigs & Pens	Multiple Correct Solutions	Pencil/Simple	Easy
26	Sheep & Pens	Creative Problem Solving	Pencil/Simple	Easy
27	Hieroglyphics	Linguistics, Perspective	Pencil	Easy/Moderate
28	A Quick Study	Seeking Rules & Patterns	Pencil	Easy
29	Pangrams	Linguistics	Pencil	Easy
30	Palindromes	Linguistics	Pencil	Easy
31	Magic Carpet	Identifying Goals & Barriers	Simple	Easy
32	Pencil Pushers	Physical Problem Solving	Simple	Moderate

Teambuilding Puzzles

No.	Puzzle Title	Teachable Moment	Prop Category	Difficulty Level
33	Bite the Bag	A Kinesthetic Challenge	Simple	Moderate
34	The 15th Object	Knowledge is Power!	Simple	Easy
35	Tower of Hanoi	Visual, Logical, Physical	Simple	Moderate
36	Just Passing Through	Creative Problem Solving	Simple	Moderate
37	Pipe Chimes	Auditory Challenge, Music	Simple	Easy
38	Pyramid Power	Multiple Solutions, Change	Simple	Easy
39	Golf Ball Pyramids	Learning Curve	Simple	Moderate
40	Paper Pyramids	Problem Solving	Simple	Easy
41	SNAP!	Reducing Stress	Simple	Easy
42	Blind Square	Common Vision, Tenacity	Simple	Difficult
43	Shape Up	Leadership	Simple	Easy
44	Corporate Maze	Teamwork, Trial & Error	Complex	Moderate
44	Chasing Sheep	Teamwork, Collaboration	Complex	Easy
45	Pentominoes	Geometric Problem Solving	Simple	Easy
46	Five Rooms	Creative Problem Solving	Simple	Difficult
47	True North	Consensus, Teamwork	None	Easy
48	Human Knot	Physical Teamwork	None	Easy
49	Line Up	Many Teachable Moments	Simple	Easy/Moderate
50	Paint Stick Shuffle	Problem Solving, Consensus	Simple	Easy
51	Seven Boxes of Bolts	Logic and Mathematics	None	Difficult
52	A Problem of Weight	Logic and Mathematics	None	Moderate
53	Count Six	Kinesthetic Teamwork	None	Easy

No.	Puzzle Title	Teachable Moment	Prop Category	Difficulty Level
54	The Coiled Rope	Kinesthetic Problem Solving	Simple	Easy
55	Whiteboard Puzzle	Get Acquainted Activities	Simple	Easy
56	The Giant Jigsaw	Communication, Tenacity	Complex	Difficult
57	An Unusual Puzzle	Active Learning, Movement	Complex	Easy
58	The Whole Story	Listening, Piecing Together	Simple	Easy/Moderate
59	Tongue Twisters	Linguistic Puzzles	None	Easy/Moderate
60	Shaping the Future	Adapting to Change	Simple	Easy
61	Word Puzzles	Listening Carefully	None	Moderate
62	A Strange Day	Abstract Reasoning & Logic	None	Moderate
63	Changing Sides	Thinking on Your Feet	Complex	Moderate
64	Classic Knot Theory	Kinesthetic Problem Solving	Simple	Moderate
65	Placemat Puzzle	Visual & Tactile Puzzles	Simple	Easy
66	Making Contact	Making Connections, Unity	Simple	Easy
67	Nothing Divides Us	Mathematical Information	None	Easy
68	Where Do You Stand?	Thinking on Your Feet	Simple	Easy
69	Adapt or Extinct	Adapting to Change	Simple	Easy
70	The Fence	Geometric Problem Solving	Pencil	Easy
71	Land of Lakes	Geometric Problem Solving	Pencil	Easy/Moderate
72	Sharing Connections	Knowing Others	Simple	Easy
73	The Bridge	Tactile Problem Solving	Simple	Moderate
73	The Balance	Tactile Problem Solving	Simple	Moderate
74	3 Kinds of Memory	Visual/Auditory/Kinesthetic	Simple	Moderate
75	Matchmaking	Memory, Teamwork	Simple	Easy

Teambuilding Puzzles

No.	Puzzle Title	Teachable Moment	Prop Category	Difficulty Level
76	Changing Directions	Adapting to Change	None	Easy
77	Island Hopping	Problem Solving & Change	Pencil	Easy
77	Close All the Doors	Team Problem Solving	Pencil	Moderate
78	Line Up the Glasses	Creative Problem Solving	Simple	Easy
79	Mathematical Magic	Problem Solving & Math	Simple	Easy
80	Parking Cars	Changing Plans	Simple	Moderate
81	The Tower	Creative Problem Solving	Simple	Easy
82	Single Drop of Water	Assumptions & Estimates	Simple	Easy
83	Extreme Origami	Assumptions & Estimates	Simple	Easy
84	Arm Wrestling	Collaboration & Competition	None	Easy
85	Finding Your People	Unity Community & Inclusion	Simple	Easy
86	I'm In Games	Linguistics & Culture	None	Easy
87	63 / 64 / 65	Analyzing the Truth	Simple	Easy
88	The Parade	Kinesthetic Problem Solving	None	Moderate
89	First Flight	Problem Solving, Teamwork	Simple	Easy
90	Your Move	Collaboration & Competition	Simple	Moderate
91	Inuksuit	Balance, Collaboration	Complex	Moderate
92	The Big Cover Up	Communication	Simple	Easy
93	Circle of Connection	Unity & Connection	None	Easy
94	The Square	Simplicity, Problem Solving	Simple	Easy
95	Team Labyrinth	Cooperation, Teamwork	Complex	Moderate
96	The Puzzle Cube	Kinesthetic Teamwork	Complex	Moderate

No.	Puzzle Title	Teachable Moment	Prop Category	Difficulty Level
97	Jumping George	Kinesthetic Problem Solving	Simple	Moderate
98	Just One Word	Listening, Assumptions	Simple	Easy
99	Concentration	Visual/Auditory/Kinesthetic	None	Easy
99	Categories	Visual/Auditory/Kinesthetic	None	Easy
100	Ciphers & Codes	Logical Reasoning	Pencil	Moderate

"We are at the very beginning of time for the human race. It is not unreasonable that we grapple with problems. But there are tens of thousands of years in the future. Our responsibility is to do what we can, learn what we can, improve the solutions, and pass them on."
Richard Feynman

"An old puzzle asks how a barometer can be used to measure the height of a building. Answers range from dropping the instrument from the top and measuring the time of its fall to giving it to the building's superintendent in return for a look at the plans. A modern version of the puzzle asks how a personal computer can balance a checkbook. An elegant solution is to sell the machine and deposit the money."
Jon Bentley

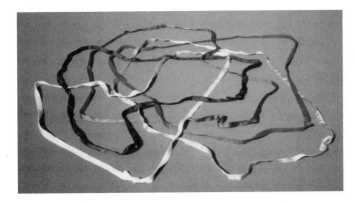

1. 2B or Knot 2B,
The Missing Link and Not Knots
Building Consensus With Rope

Here are a trio of teambuilding activities that you can present with only a few pieces of colorful rope or tubular climbing webbing. Each of these activities presents a visual puzzle for a team to solve. But the solution is only part of the puzzle. Achieving consensus within the team is the ultimate goal and the teachable moment for these unique puzzles.

2B or Knot 2B, (left) shows an arrangement of four colorful pieces of rope or webbing that have been joined together by a fifth piece. This puzzle is presented in such a manner that it is not immediately obvious which rope is the one holding the other four together. The challenge for the group is to discover which rope is holding the other ropes together, and to achieve consensus on this selection, before touching any of the ropes.

The goal of **The Missing Link** (pictured left), is for a group to decide if the two segments of tubular climbing webbing (often called Raccoon Circles, see below for details) are linked together (like links of a chain) or unlinked, by visually checking them and without touching them.

While the actual solution may be simple or complex, the real value of this activity comes from a team working together to achieve a group consensus, listening to each other, and learning the skills that it takes to get everyone on the same page. We like to begin this activity by a process called *'pairing and sharing'* which involves everyone working with a partner in an attempt to convince one other person before trying to convince the entire group.

A natural consensus building activity to follow 2B or KNOT 2B or The Missing Link is **Not Knots**, shown below. In this activity, which can be accomplished with only a single piece of rope or webbing, a "doodle" is constructed and the group is given the choice of whether this doodle will create a KNOT or NOT A KNOT (i.e. a straight line), when the ends of the rope are pulled away from each other.

The object here is to provide the group with some tools to use when they cannot easily form aconsensus. Typically, upon analysis, about half of the group thinks the doodle will form a knot, and the other half a straight line. If this is the case, ask participants to partner

with another person that has a different viewpoint (i.e. one partner from the KNOT side, and one partner from the NOT A KNOT side). By learning how to listen to a person with a different viewpoint, group members learn how to cooperate. After this discussion, ask participants to choose sides, with the KNOT decision folks on one side of the knot doodle and the NOT A KNOT folks on the other side.

At this point, it is likely that there will still not be a complete consensus within the group. Prior to slowly pulling the ends of the knot doodle, let the members of the group know that you will pull the knot doodle slowly, and that they can change sides at any time during the unraveling of the knot doodle (this illustrates the ability to make an initial decision, but still be flexible as more information becomes available).

Supplies 2B or Knot 2B requires five different colors of rope or tubular climbing webbing. Each rope segment should be about 10 feet (3 meters) in length.

The Missing Link requires two different colors of rope or tubular webbing. Each rope should be 10-16 feet (3-5 meters) in length.

Not Knots requires just a single piece or soft, flexible rope or webbing. This rope should be about 6 feet (2 meters) in length.

Teachable Moments In addition to the visual problem solving skills required to success fully complete each of these activities, the highlight is often exploring the tools required to achieve consensus within a group. Pairing and sharing is a very powerful technique for 'building consensus.' So is the concept of pairing with a partner that doesn't necessarily agree with you at the outset. Finally, the concept of making a decision and then being allowed to alter it when new information becomes available (as is the case in Not Knots) has been well received in corporate settings in relation to topics such as personal accountability and decision management.

Variations In addition to the multi-colored version of 2B or Knot 2B shown above, these five ropes can also be constructed with striped ropes (for a greater degree of visual difficulty), or five ropes that are all the same color. The size of this activity can also be varied by making each rope much longer, say 100 feet (30 meters) in length, or much smaller, such as the size that would fit on a microscope slide. While a collection of five ropes is optimal for most groups, four ropes can be used for simplicity, and a greater number of ropes, 6 to 8, for a higher degree of difficulty.

The Missing Link works best with 2 ropes, and the size and length of these ropes can vary as desired.

Not Knots generally begins with a configuration prepared by the facilitator. After solving this challenge, present short ropes to each participant and invite them to create their own rope 'doodle' which the rest of the group can analyze.

A unique consensus technique for Not Knots includes forming a partnership with another participant that initially does not agree with you, and then working together to convince each other and to achieve a paired consensus.

Hints and Clues For 2B or Knot 2B, consider not only which rope appears to be the correct rope, but also which ropes can be eliminated from the choice because they are obviously not the correct rope. Also, look for the 'hint rope.' Any rope that is only attached to one other rope indicates which rope is the correct one.

For The Missing Link, counting the number of times each rope passes over or under another rope may provide some insight.

Some team members create their own model of the rope doodle in Not Knots, by using a shoelace or belt.

Raccoon Circles have been named by Dr. Tom Smith and Dr. Jim Cain for their collection of tubular climbing webbing and the many, many activities that this equipment can be used to present. You can find a free collection of Raccoon Circle activities at the Teamwork and Teamplay website (www.teamworkandteamplay.com), and the extensive 272 page book, written by Tom Smith and Jim Cain, filled with more than 200 Raccoon Circle team activities from Kendall Hunt Publishers at 1-800-228-0810 or visit their website: www.kendallhunt.com

Additional Raccoon Circle activities have been compiled by Tom Heck. A multi-media CD entitled "The Group Loop Activity Guide - 27 Fun Team Building Games with Webbing" includes a 140 page printable document, video clips and color photographs of each activity. Contact Tom at (828) 665-0303 or www.teachmeteamwork.com.

Chris Cavert has also compiled his favorite Raccoon Circle activities, under the title of "Lines and Loops - Community Building Activities with Webbing." 22 pages of activities, illustrations and references. Contact Chris at: chris@fundoing.com or www.fundoing.com

*"Life is not a problem to be solved,
but a reality to be experienced."*
Soren Kierkegaard

If you are looking for an activity that requires close teamwork, here it is.

Partners stand facing each other. One person places the rope handcuffs over both of their wrists. The second person places one hand into their handcuff, and before placing their other hand into the wrist loop, they pass the middle of their rope through the other person's rope. The two are now connected together.

The challenge is for both partners to become separated from each other, without untying the knots, and without pulling their hands out of their own rope loops. Additional restrictions can include without cutting through the ropes, rubbing them back and forth until they catch fire or wear through, and of course, without biting through them. The challenge is completed when everyone in the group is free.

Supplies You'll need cotton rope (often used for clotheslines and available in most hardware stores) to make your handcuffs. Six feet (2 meters) of rope per person, with loops at each end. Yarn, monofiliment fishing line and small diameter strings are not recommended for this activity.

Teachable Moments The concept of working through a problem that seems to have no obvious answer is a valuable work skill. Creative, out-of-the-box thinking is required. Retracing the steps between the initial formation of the puzzle, and finally solving the puzzle, provides a roadmap for future investigations and solutions to other problems and puzzles. Finding the answer as part of a group investigation and then sharing the solution is also a living lesson of an abundance mentally towards information sharing.

You can use Handcuffs and Shackles, and many other puzzles in this book, as an object lesson to clarify your role as a facilitator, trainer, teacher or group leader. You can say, for example:

"There are times when you might reach an impasse during one of these puzzles. At these times, one of my roles as a facilitator might be to ask questions for you to explore. For example, how many holes can you find within this puzzle right now? Which holes are you using? Which holes have you overlooked? Look for a solution that does not require you to move your feet. My role, in most cases, is not to give you the answers, but to help you discover the answers for yourself."

This simple lesson will help your participants understand what they can expect from you, as a facilitator, as you work together on this and future puzzles.

Variations Handcuffs and Shackles is often performed by partners working together. One of the more unusual variations is to circle an entire team so that everyone is handcuffed to the person on both sides of them. The solution is exactly the same as it is for pairs.

You can also handcuff groups of two, three and four people together. One technique for making this activity more cerebral than physical is to handcuff participants together through a chain-link fence. You can also use string instead of rope and connect participant's handcuffs together by passing the string through the keyhole of a door.

For participants with limited mobility, you might want to increase the length of rope used to make the handcuffs for ease of movement.

Hints and Clues Handcuffs and Shackles provides the perfect situation for explaining that giving someone the solution and helping someone find the solution for themselves are two different things. Encourage participants to consider two things: what is working, and what is not. By eliminating the kinds of attempts that have already proven not to lead to success, and focusing on those techniques which appear to hold the best hopes for succeeding, we learn to prioritize our efforts.

As a further clue, you can also tell participants that they are looking for a 'window of opportunity' in the rope handcuffs, and to focus their attentions there.

Planning is Everything

If you want to encourage your team to plan before doing, here is just the activity. Three Cubed requires some advanced planning, anticipation of coming events, and starting in the right place. Even with an outstanding workforce, skilled participants and a boatload of luck, it is nearly impossible to complete this simple task without starting in the right place. The good news is, even attempts that are unsuccessful provide helpful hints that will lead your team on the path towards success.

Three Cubed is just that - 3 raised to the 3rd power, or better yet, 27 golf balls stacked in our cubic box. Begin by showing the box, with lid in place, to the team, now located in the planning zone. Open the lid and spill the contents (all of the balls) onto the ground, floor or table (you might want another container so that the balls do not roll away). Then hand the box and lid to a member of the group. You can now explain the task (as shown below), or have this information printed on the lid of the box, or written on an index card for the group to read themselves.

Your team task is as follows:

1. Place the lid and box a short distance away from your present location. This new location is called 'the building zone.'

2. Each member of the group, <u>one at a time</u>, is to travel from the planning zone to the building zone, and place one ball into the cubic box.

3. This continues until all the balls have been placed. A 'correct' placement of all 27 balls by the team allows the wooden lid to be placed on the box.

4. No member can move or alter the position of any ball, box or lid placed by another person. In fact, none of these objects can be moved by anyone, after they have been placed. Good Luck.

After each attempt, the box and balls are brought back to the planning zone, the contents removed, the box replaced in the building zone, and the team encouraged to try again.

Supplies You'll need 27 small solid balls (and it is a good idea to have a few in reserve, just in case you happen to lose a few). Golf balls are about the right size, and they are incompressible too. Foam balls, soft rubber balls, and ping pong balls are poor choices because they can be easily compressed. Next you'll need to create a box that is exactly the same size cube as the 27 balls, with a lid that covers the top of the box.

Teachable Moments   Depending on the orientation of the cubic box, stable place-ment of even a single ball is difficult (as the balls tend to roll away from where they were originally positioned). In the case of Three Cubed, even a single ball in the 'wrong' location eliminates the opportunity for success.

Sometimes, members of the group would like to alter the position of a previous member's contribution (their placement of a ball). Perhaps this ball has rolled from its original placement. Or perhaps it was incorrectly placed to begin with. In either case, this 'rework' of another group member's contribution is a topic for discussion. How can such rework be eliminated?

Using each of the unsuccessful attempts as learning experiences will help the group to focus on moving towards success, rather than dwelling on their mistakes. Encourage additional planning after each attempt to identify contributors to success and failure.

Variations Although there is to be no 'practicing' in the planning zone, you can inform the group that there is time to repeat this activity, until the team is successful. To this end, you may ask the team to estimate the number of attempts they will need to achieve success.

Hints and Clues   Encourage the group to identify causes of failure during the early attempts of solving this puzzle. After each round, invite them to form new strategies that avoid these known contributors to failure. Finally, if necessary, ask the group to consider what the 'first' task is, during each attempt. The placement of the cubic container (the box AND the lid), is an essential contributor to the success, or failure, of this activity.

For additional mathematical information on stacking spheres, we invite you to read: Kepler's Conjecture - How some of the greatest minds in history helped solve one of the oldest math problems in the world, 2003, George G. Szpiro, John Wiley & Sons, Hoboken, NJ USA ISBN 0-471-08601-0.

Here are two versions of labyrinths that can be used by your group. The first version is a team challenge, and involves finding a way out of a maze or labyrinth. The second version is a peaceful construct, and creates a quiet place for personal reflection.

The Team Labyrinth - In this version, a strong cord or rope has been stretched between a dozen or more small trees to form a labyrinth or maze. Participants are led blindfolded into the maze, and left standing with their hands holding onto the perimeter rope. The task of this team challenge is for the entire group to find their way out of the maze, while remaining blindfolded throughout the activity. Talking is allowed. Participants are encouraged to plan first and then begin working through this plan. For example, they may want to decide whether to stay together as a team, or break into smaller groups to examine the maze.

For safety reasons, participants are required to maintain contact with the rope at all times, and to follow the rope without ever passing underneath it.

An 'exit' path must be created in the rope maze. When participants have found this exit, their blindfolds are removed, but so is their ability to communicate with the members of their team remaining inside the maze.

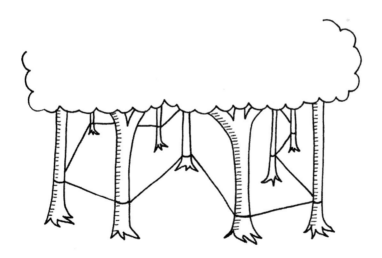

A Reflective Labyrinth - This second version of the labyrinth creates a quiet place for personal reflection and thought. You can create your own design based upon corporate logos, academic mascots, historical and cultural images or traditional folklore. The labyrinth shown in the illustration was temporarily constructed as a reflective space for a conference center program. Although this path fits within a space roughly the size of a tennis court, walking the complete path, at a reflective pace, takes a full ten minutes or more.

Supplies The Team Labyrinth is constructed using a soft rope and requires a dozen or more trees, poles or fence posts and a flat surface with any tripping hazards removed. Use a rope at least 1/4 inch (6 mm) in diameter. <u>Do not</u> use string to construct your labyrinth.

The reflective labyrinth can be constructed of nearly any available materials, including: stones, sand, living plants or trees, logs, rope or flagging tape (as shown above). See the books below for additional ideas about creating a reflective labyrinth.

Teachable Moments Finding your way, especially without sight, is substantially easier if you don't go it alone. Communication and feedback may not be necessary for your personal plan, but this information may be essential to the success of others. Consider the possibility of having those who find the exit act as mentors or coaches to those participants still within the maze.

Variations You can alter the difficulty of the team labyrinth by changing the size and complexity of the maze pattern used. You can begin the team labyrinth by placing individual team members alone along the rope. You can also place a small bell near the exit location, to alert other participants.

Hints and Clues Communication between team members is essential in the team labyrinth. Encourage team members to at least work with partners, rather than setting out alone.

For additional insights about mazes and labyrinths, we invite you to read:

The Art of the Maze, 2000, Adrian Fisher and George Gerster, Seven Dials, London, UK ISBN 1-84188-025-6

Labyrinth: A Guide for Healing and Spiritual Growth, 2000, Melissa Gayle West, Broadway Books, New York, NY USA ISBN 0-7679-0356-0

The Worldwide Labyrinth Project, San Francisco, California www.gracecathedral.org/veriditas

*"No problem is so formidable
that you can't walk away from it."*
Charles M. Schultz

5. Arrowheads
Pointing in the Right Direction

Here is a challenging puzzle for exploring the concepts of limited resources. If your team needs to successfully complete a task when there seems to be insufficient resources to do so, then this is the perfect puzzle for you.

Using the seven puzzle pieces shown here, simultaneously assemble five arrowheads. One arrowhead is already complete, and provides a size template for the remaining arrowheads. Each of the four remaining arrowheads will be the same size as this one. When you are finished, you will be able to see all five arrowheads at the same time.

Supplies You can create your own arrowhead puzzle using heavy paper, card-stock, cardboard or plywood, by dissecting the pattern shown at the end of this activity.

Teachable Moments This specific puzzle is used to illustrate the connection between teachable moments and puzzles in the first chapter of this book.

Understanding how to get things done, especially when limited resources are available, is a valuable life skill. In this case, how was your team able to identify how to accomplish the task? How are the limited resources of this situation like other situations in your life, work, institution or corporation?

In this puzzling activity, four arrowheads can creatively be used to make five. How many arrowheads can be made from sixteen arrowheads? Would you believe twenty-five?

If you follow the team output charge on the next page, more team members should produce more output. But, that is not always the case. What sorts of behaviors and efforts in your team produce synergistic team output? Which behaviors and efforts create detrimental team output?

Arrowheads is the perfect puzzle to help your team understand the value of synergy. Synergy can be described metaphorically as: 1 + 1 = 3. Synergy exists when the output of a team is greater than the output of each individual combined. The graphic shown illustrates this point. If one team member can produce one unit of output and we hire nine additional team members, we expect to be able to produce a total output of ten units. If our team members work synergistically, they can actually produce more than ten units of output. Conversely, if our team members do not work synergistically or even worse, reduce each other's effectiveness, less than ten units of output will be produced. From this simple analysis you can see that teams operating synergistically have a substantial advantage over teams that do not.

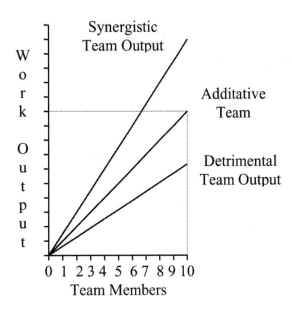

Variations These arrowheads are part of a collective family of 'tessellations' which repeat indefinitely. You could provide two more cutout arrowheads, for a total of six, and ask the group to create eight arrowheads in total. If your group is knowledgeable on environmental issues, you can replace the arrowheads with pine trees, which will also fit together in a similar fashion.

Hints and Clues You already have enough pieces to complete the five arrowheads required. Sometimes you need to get all your people (arrowheads) moving in the same direction. A two by two organization can be helpful.

"The best way to escape from a problem is to solve it."
Alan Saporta

Teambuilding
Puzzles

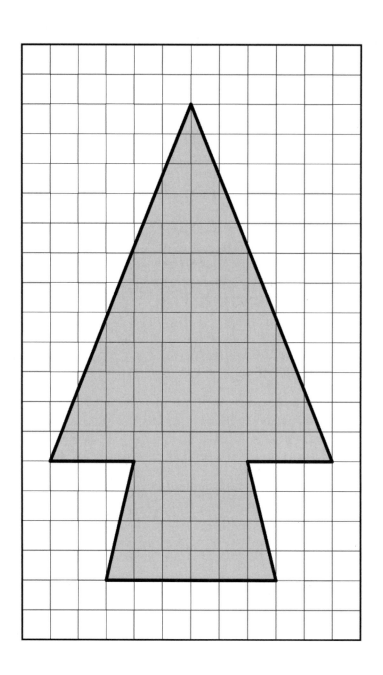

6. People Movers
Working Together to Find the Right Path

Here are a few puzzles that encourage 'thinking on your feet.' Each of the puzzles shown below incorporate creative problem solving skills for every member of the team, not just a few key members.

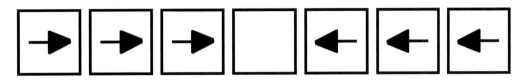

PM1 - Our first people mover puzzle is actually a classic 'shuttle' puzzle that has been performed with human participants, and also as a table top puzzle with wooden pegs or coins. Start with the stepping stone pattern shown above, consisting of seven spaces. Three participants stand on the left end of the pattern, facing the center, as do three other participants on the right end of the pattern (also facing the center). The challenge is for each group to pass the members of the other group, and find themselves at the opposite end of the pattern. A few rules apply to changing places:

1. The goal is to have both groups change places.
2. You can move into any open space.
3. You can jump over (around) a member of the opposite group, into any open space.
4. You cannot pass a member of your own group.
5. You cannot back up.
6. If you reach a position from which you cannot move forward, and the system becomes 'locked,' the entire group must return to the beginning and try again.
7. There is no penalty for trial-and-error solutions, but try to be as efficient as possible and learn from any mistakes that happen.

It takes a minimum of 15 moves to complete the above challenge. Groups achieving success to this challenge can be further challenged by demonstrating that they can repeat their performance, but this time, without talking. As a final, high level challenge, invite your group to complete this activity efficiently without breathing! That is, asking everyone in the group to simultaneously take a breath and hold it, start and complete the relocation, before anyone needs to breath again. Good luck!

A corporate version of this activity, presented as an internal company memo, is presented on the last page of this activity description.

Supplies For most of these 'people moving' puzzles, it is helpful to have some type of space marker to identify the available locations. This can be a piece of paper, paper plate, gym spot marker, sidewalk paving stone, stepping stones, carpet sample or any other small object about the size that will support a single person.

Teachable Moments   Leadership is a bit easier when the people you are leading also know where they are going and how to get there. These puzzles encourage self-direction and the need for group vision and execution. Individual competency and account-ability are also necessary. Themes of recovering from failure, learning from mistakes, continuous improvement and adapting to new challenges can also be presented using these puzzles.

Variations One of the best variations for PM1 above is to place the seven stepping stones in a curved pattern (similar to a smile or letter C). This allows all participants to see each other during the challenge, compared to the straight line version which allows for only limited vision.

Here are a few additional 'people moving' puzzles.

PM1.5 The number of team members on each end can vary from 2 to 4, but we encourage the same number on each end, for simplicity. For groups that are larger than eight team members, we recommend splitting the group into half, each with their own pattern, rather than attempting to complete the task with such a large group. Some of these people mover puzzles increase in difficulty exponentially with the number of participants. Teams of three to four participants per side is ideal. Four participants per side will require 24 correct moves to complete, while five participants per side would require 35 correct moves.

"The problem with any unwritten law is that you don't know where to go to erase it."
Glaser and Way

PM2   Rather than a two-ended puzzle, create a three-way shuttle puzzle with a T or Y formation. As an additional challenge to this formation, have each team choose their final destination leg in advance. In order to change the location of all three teams in this formation, you'll need to move some (or all) teams twice.

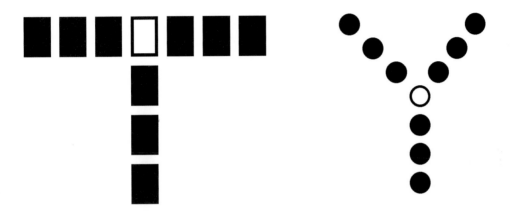

PM3 You can model people moving activities after nearly any wooden peg shuttle puzzle. However we encourage you to use only those puzzles where ALL participants stay in play during the challenge (rather than eliminating some in the course of the game). You can modify the above style of people moving puzzles to the Big M or E formations found on the next page. The E formation is a bit more difficult and is typically solved in 31 to 43 moves. For these two puzzles, there is no 'jumping,' but rather only sliding into any open space. Also, a participant can move any number of spaces in 'one turn,' as long as they only slide through open spaces and along the lines connecting each location. The Big M formation allows a choice in the triangular central region, where the E formation does not. The goal remains to have each team of four trade places with the other team of four participants.

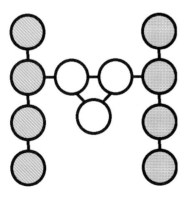

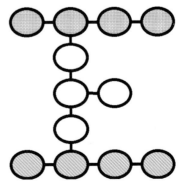

PM4   Our next variation is the Double Diamond formation, as shown below. In this configuration, two groups attempt to change locations. Each 'move' consists of sliding into any open position, or jumping over (around) any other person. Team members can jump members of their own group or members of the other group. This level of people moving puzzle requires a minimum of 46 moves to complete. If you would like to simplify this style of puzzle, and utilize less than the 16 people required for the Double Diamond formation, consider using the Double Cross (10 people), or Double Square (6 people) formations.

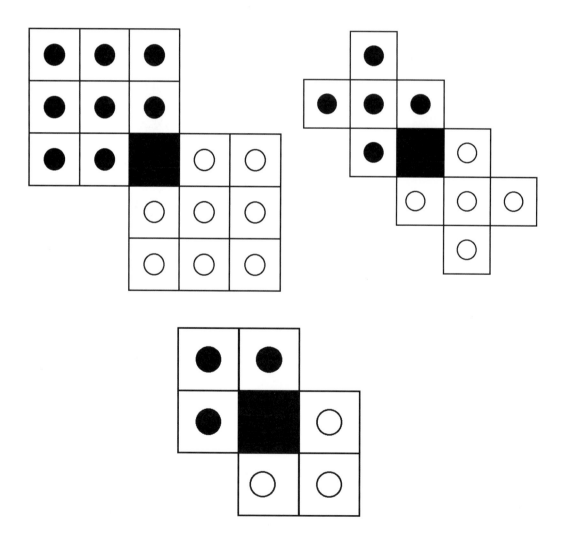

PM5 Our final version of people moving puzzles is one we call 'Sorting Things Out.' In this puzzle, eight players are positioned as shown in the starting sequence with several empty spaces on each side of their position. These players fit into two distinct groups which can be based on gender, those wearing hats and those without, shirt color, with shoes and without, etc. The challenge is to sort out the individual members of the group in four 'moves,' and produce the final sequence shown, somewhere within the available space. Each 'move' requires moving two side-by-side partners at a time to a new location. The final sequence has each of the categories of participants grouped together.

You can also perform this operation in reverse, beginning with participants grouped together, and ending with alternating group members, if you like.

Starting Sequence (begin here)

Four 'Moves' (move four pairs of people)

Final Sequence (should look like this)

Hints and Clues Each of the puzzles presented here can be used to encourage trial and error solutions, learning and adapting from our mistakes. You can further encourage the concept of an experimental laboratory by offering the group 10 minutes to make as many attempts (and mistakes) as possible before a final trial for all the marbles. The concept of 'failing forward,' that is learning from our mistakes, improving our processes, and becoming better as a result of trying, is well supported by using these puzzles. You can learn more about this concept by reading: Failing Forward: How to Make the Most of Your Mistakes, by John C. Maxwell, Thomas Nelson Publishers, ISBN 0-7852-7430-8

The following page is photocopy ready as a self-directed work team activity similar to the PM 1 version on page 27.

Corporate Memo

The Team Puzzle Group

Todays Date

To: Management Team Members from Region Six.
From: Mr. Big
Subject: Congratulations and a Change in Management

Dear Region Six Management Team Members,

Your management team has been so outstanding in meeting the needs of our organization, that the board of directors have personally asked that you all be reassigned to another region in need of the success your methods provide. The goal is for both management teams to change places as efficiently as possible.

Instructions for Management Team Relocation

Begin with both teams facing the middle of the 'stepping stones' with one empty location in the center. The goal is to have both teams change place. You can move into an open space. You can jump over (around) a member of the opposite team. You cannot pass a member of your own team. You cannot back up. If you reach a position from which you cannot move forward, the entire team must return to the beginning, and try again. There is no penalty for trial-and-error solutions during the first 10 minutes, but try to be efficient and learn from any mistakes that you may make along the way. At the end of ten minutes, your management team will be asked to demonstrate your ability to relocate efficiently.

From Teambuilding Puzzles, *by Anderson, Cain, Cavert and Heck, 2009*

7. Tangrams
Exploring Diversity, Community and Problem Solving

Here are several different techniques for using Tangram puzzles to create teachable moments. You'll even find a Tangram on the cover of this book!

Simple Tangrams - Tangrams, those seven geometric shapes that form hundreds of objects, figures and patterns, can be used by teams to create specific shapes. See the reference book listed at the end of this activity description for additional Tangram shapes.

Walking Around Tangrams - A rather interesting team version of Tangrams can be produced by taking a very large scale set of plywood Tangrams, and placing a foot strap in the middle of each piece. Now team participants can move around, with one piece attached to one of their feet, and attempt to find the correct location for their contribution to the puzzle. You can use this version for 'Speed Tangrams' where teams compete to complete their Tangram shapes as quickly as possible.

Underwater Tangrams - While this activity actually takes place on dry land, it does require some underwater skills. Begin with the entire team standing around the perimeter of a long rope, 100 feet (30 meters) in length. In the center of the circle, seven very large Tangram pieces have been placed in random order. The task for the group is to correctly assemble these Tangram pieces into a shape described by the facilitator. The challenge is that team members can only enter the circle one person at a time, and they must hold their breath for the duration of the time they are inside the circle. The circle is essentially an imaginary swimming pool, and the Tangram pieces are 'underwater.' Since participants cannot hear underwater, communication can only occur on dry land (outside the perimeter of the circle). By requiring participants to only stay inside the circle for as long as they can hold their breath, facilitators encourage all group members to become involved in the solution process, not just a select few.

Tangrams for Exploring Diversity and Uniqueness - Shown below is the traditional Tangram puzzle followed by three other variations for your enjoyment. Make each of these shapes from a different color and you'll have the opportunity to discuss diversity issues as part of your puzzle solving.

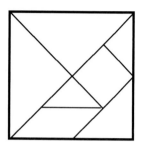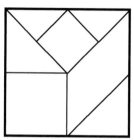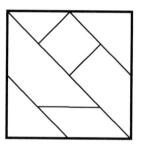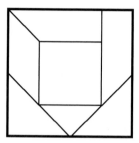

After providing each group of four to six participants with one of the above collections of geometric pieces, ask them to create various shapes, and see how many of these same shapes can also be made by each of the other groups, using their own unique pieces. You can ask some of the following questions to your group.

What shapes or patterns do we all have in common?
What shapes or patterns can each group uniquely make?
Is it important that all groups are the same?

Notice that each of the four patterns, though different, do have several pieces in common with each of the other patterns.

A Few Extra Pieces - If you would like to explore teachable moments related to making good choices, choosing the best seven pieces from a collection of ten or some of the 'good to great' principles mentioned by Jim Collins in his similarly titled book, you can add a few geometric pieces of the same color to your Tangrams, and then ask groups to select the best choices to complete each of the patterns you provide. You can also write key words, corporate value statements, or other concepts on each piece as clues for which pieces are most essential.

Good to Great - Why Some Companies Make the Leap...and Others Don't, 2001, Jim Collins, Harper Business, New York, NY USA ISBN 0-06-662099-6

The Diversity Quilt Tangram - Using the four different patterns illustrated above, with each pattern made from a different color material, demonstrate that it is possible to assemble a square four times the size of each individual Tangram, simply by bringing each puzzle together. The challenge however, is to reconstruct this same four-times larger square, without any pieces of the same color touching each other. The finished result will look a bit like a patchwork quilt.

While the 'four color map theorem' guarantees that it is possible to color any map geography with only four colors, this same theorem does not guarantee that any geometrical figures will go together to fill an enclosed space. This proof is up to you to resolve. Good Luck!

For more mathematical background on the four color map theorem, we invite you to read: Four Colors Suffice - How the Map Problem Was Solved, 2002, Robin Wilson, Princeton University Press, Princeton, NJ USA ISBN 0-691-11533-8

Tangram Communication - As a communication activity, you can provide one person or small group with a Tangram pattern already assembled. Their task is to verbally communicate to other participants or groups how to recreate this same pattern using their own Tangram pieces. Initially, try this version with one directional information only (that is, with only the presenter talking). Next, try another pattern, but this time allowing feedback and two-way communication between presenter and Tangram builders.

Supplies For teams, we recommend making very large Tangram puzzles from colorful materials. While paper, foamboard, or cardboard can work, flexible plastic or plywood are a bit more durable.

Teachable Moments   Creative problem solving, kinesthetic problem solving, exploring diversity, cultural sensitivity, inclusion, making good choices, and clear communication. If you enjoy the inclusion activity above, you are encouraged to see Puzzle #85, Finding Your People.

Variations   You can make Tangrams from a variety of materials (wood, plastic, paper, foamboard, cardboard, magnets, cloth, leather, stained glass, and yes even food (if you choose to cut your square desert cakes or gelatin desserts just right). With the right forethought, you can assemble your Tangrams on the ground, on tables, on walls (using spray adhesive or tape), on the ceiling, on a refrigerator (using magnets), on overhead transparencies (for projecting to a large audience) or anywhere else you can find the right combination of Tangrams and space.

There are a variety of methods for dissecting a square into seven geometrical shapes. Four examples were shown previously. You can also create your own unique tangram-like shapes by dissecting the first square shown below. We recommend that you create straight lines following each of the grid lines, for simplicity in cutting and building other shapes. Two examples from this grid system are also shown.

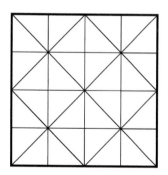
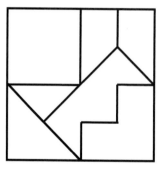
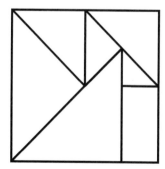

Hints and Clues   One of the requirements of successfully assembling Tangrams is to know when you have the right pieces in the right places. If you reach a point where you lack the necessary pieces to complete the puzzle, you most certainly have used a wrong piece in the wrong place. Knowing when you've reached this point is a skill which is helpful at the game table and the board room table.

One of the most helpful techniques to assist a team solving a Tangram puzzle is to offer to place one or two pieces in the correct position, at the team's request. You can also provide an outline or framework to further identify the space the Tangram puzzle will fill.

If you would like to see more Tangram patterns, we invite you to read:

Tangram Puzzles - 500 Tricky Shapes to Confound & Astound, 2002, Chris Crawford, Sterling Publishing, New York, NY USA ISBN 0-8069-7589-X

An Internet key word search for 'Tangrams' will yield hundreds of results. Many of these sources have downloadable activities. Visit the following websites for more Tangram shapes and information:

http://tangrams.ca
http://www.johnrausch.com/PuzzlingWorld
http://www.sdv.fr/;ages/casa/html/tangram.html
http://www.sportime.com/

Possible shapes with traditional Tangram shapes.

Sportime offers a Tangram activity entitled Puzzling Moves. This activity was created by Tom Heck. Visit the Sportime website for more information. (www.sportime.com)

We also invite you the visit www.seriouspuzzles.com/index.html. This site sells a wide variety of puzzles, tavern style, brain teasers, books and the tangram game called Tangoes. They even have some variations of stackable games found here in Teambuilding Puzzles.

8. Archimedes Puzzle
Exploring the Oldest Puzzle in the World

If you enjoy the Tangram puzzles featured in the last section of this book, try the Archimedes Puzzle for a higher challenge alternative. It is an interesting variation to the Tangram puzzles, with double the number of pieces.

The Archimedes Puzzle is generally regarded as the oldest recorded puzzle in history. In addition to its rather advanced age, it is also beautiful in its simplicity, mathematical organization and utility.

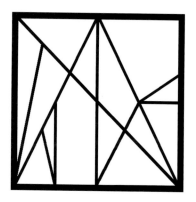

The Archimedes puzzle can be used as a kind of super-dissection puzzle, capable of creating hundreds of shapes, patterns, letters and numbers.

Team challenges for the Archimedes Puzzle include creating squares and other geometric shapes that use all fourteen pieces. As a variation, you can request teams to produce shapes and patterns that require less than the fourteen possible pieces, leaving the team to decide which pieces are the right choice.

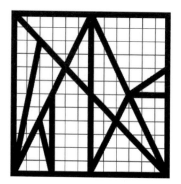

Supplies You'll need to create the 14 pieces of an Archimedes Puzzle on paper, plywood, cardboard, foamboard or some other durable material. A pattern for this puzzle, superimposed upon a square grid, is provided here. It can be helpful to have a grid pattern as a work surface when constructing shapes and patterns using the Archimedes Puzzle, as shown in the example below. You can create your own collection of shapes and profiles by experimenting with the puzzles pieces yourself. We also encourage you to conduct an Internet search using the keyword 'Archimeded Puzzle' and you will find additional patterns to create.

Teachable Moments With more pieces than a Tangram, the Archimedes Puzzle is perfect for larger groups where you would like each person to have control of their own puzzle piece.

In the corporate-focused book Good to Great by Jim Collins (see next page), there is considerable energy devoted to 'getting the right people on the bus. The wrong people off the bus. And then getting the right people into the right seats.' You can use the Archimedes Puzzle to create various patterns that reinforce this principle. Begin by writing corporate concepts, phrases and words on each of the fourteen puzzle pieces. Next, assemble shapes or patterns that do not require all of the pieces, but rather, only the RIGHT pieces to complete the task. The discussion of what the RIGHT pieces are alone is of considerable value.

Variations As a mathematical problem, calculate the area of each piece of the Archimedes Puzzle. You'll find that they are all integers! Another interesting activity is to give two groups each half of the puzzle pieces (seven each), and ask them to create the same shape or pattern. This is an excellent opportunity to show that there is more than one plan that will produce the same results.

Hints and Clues Providing a grid sheet or framework with outlines of the shapes or patterns you wish to create is helpful.

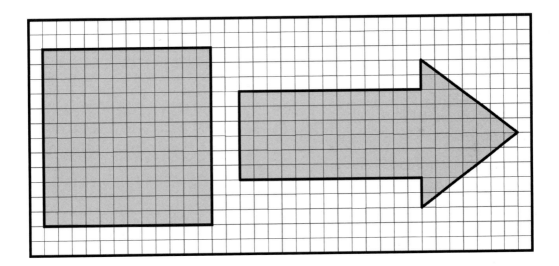

Good to Great - Why Some Companies Make the Leap...and Others Don't, 2001, Jim Collins, Harper Collins, New York, NY USA ISBN 0-06-662099-6

9. Switching Corks
Slight of Hand and Teaching Styles

You can learn a lot about teaching styles from this magical puzzle.

Begin by passing two corks out to every member of your group. Instruct them to hold up both hands, palms facing you, fingers slightly spread. Each person will place one cork between the thumb and index finger of their right hand and another between the thumb and index finger of their left hand. The challenge is to switch the cork held in your left hand to your right hand and the cork held in your right hand cork to your left hand using only your middle fingers and thumbs, in one quick movement.

The facilitator can demonstrate this task. On the first attempt, typically less than 50% of the audience will be able to replicate this task, which builds a great case for the teachable moment that soon follows. Demonstrate quickly changing the corks again. At this point, encourage your audience to help each other work through the challenge. After a few minutes of additional practice, it is time for a 'proficiency examination.' Even at this point, there are likely to be participants that have not yet mastered this skill.

This time, walk the participants through every step and hand movement slowly, using visual demonstrations and plenty of information. Discuss how this style of teaching actually educates more participants than the initial attempt. How does this presentation reinforce or refute other learning situations that you have experienced?

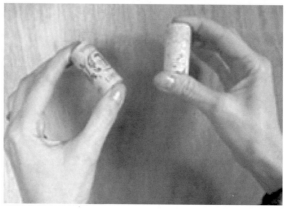

Supplies You'll need a supply of wine corks, new or used, but in good condition. If you would like to substitute a 'non-alcoholic' puzzle prop, you can use short segments of round dowel rods, wooden spools, or even real eggs (although the plastic kind are potentially less messy). It is often helpful for beginners to use two different color corks (or other props).

Teachable Moments   Even when demonstrated in front of a group, this puzzling challenge is difficult to replicate. Encourage participants to work together to help each other be successful. Next, change your own teaching style, and walk participants through each step and hand movement. Finally, teach in a one-on-one fashion for students that require that level of instruction.

You can also use this activity to explore various 'learning styles' and how teaching styles can be altered to meet the needs of students with these different learning styles. We encourage you to read the book: Multiple Intelligences in the Classroom, 2000, Thomas Armstrong, ASCD, Alexandria, VA USA ISBN 0-87120-376-6. Read this book to explore other training, teaching and learning styles appropriate for your audiences. You can include a homework assignment for this activity where students are asked to create various methods of presenting the activity that explore each of the various learning styles. The activity can be presented via pictures, text information, videotape, hands-on demonstrations and many other techniques. Each of these multiple intelligence techniques becomes a potential alternative for you, when presenting other activities as part of your training programs.

Variations   Try presenting this same activity, using different learning style techniques, as mentioned above. If you enjoy this style of a magical puzzle challenge, be sure to read: Presenting and Training With Magic - 53 Simple Magic Tricks You Can Use to Energize Any Audience, 1998, Ed Rose, McGraw-Hill, New York, NY USA ISBN 0-07-054040-3.

For a mathematical explanation of Switching Corks, read: Games, Set & Math - Enigmas and Conundrums, 1989, Ian Stewart, Basil Blackwell, Cambridge, MA, USA ISBN 0-631-17114-2 See Chapter Seven, Parity Piece.

Hints and Clues   The solution is all in the wrists. Also, you can try working backwards.

"Always bear in mind that your own resolution to succeed is more important than any one thing."
Abraham Lincoln

10. Rock Around the Clock
Creative Problem Solving

Rock Around the Clock requires no equipment at all. Making it the perfect kinesthetic puzzle for your group when you need to pack light.

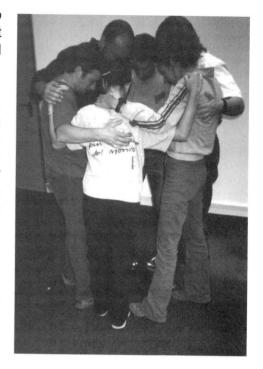

With your group standing in a circle, invite participants to stand so that each foot is in contact with the person's foot to each side of them. Next, identify one person to be the hour hand in the twelve o'clock position. The challenge is for the entire group to rotate so that the person in the twelve o'clock position moves to the six o'clock position, without anyone in the group breaking foot contact with their neighbors. Obviously each member of the group will need to rotate 180 degrees from their starting position to accomplish this task. Moving to a new location is not all that difficult, but remaining in contact with other team members while accomplishing this task is very challenging.

Supplies None.

Teachable Moments While some groups brainstorm potential techniques at the initiation of this activity, one of the most significant teachable moments comes from the difference in difficulty between the techniques often chosen and the one listed in the solution list for this activity. The teachable moment then becomes, "why didn't we see this as a potential solution?" A discussion on the creative problem solving process is appropriate at this time.

You can also discuss personal accountability, integrity or quality control analysis by the group in reporting mistakes or loss of contact during this activity. Did participants feel free to speak up when an error occurred? What was the reaction of the group when a mistake was identified? How is this process similar to one that happens in the workplace or the classroom?

Here is an interesting observation. For any size group, the closer the members of the circle stand to each other, the easier this activity becomes. Edward Hallowell presents a strong case for the value of connection in our lives, in his book, simply titled Connect. The stronger our feeling of connection, the healthier we become.

Connect - 12 vital ties that open your heart, lengthen your life, and deepen your soul, 1999, Edward M. Hallowell, Pantheon Books, New York, NY USA ISBN 0-375-40357-4. Connection improves the quality and length of your life, and here is the information that proves it!

Tom Rath's book *Vital Friends* (ISBN 1-59562-007-9) provides some very helpful numbers quantifying the effect that positive relationships have within a work group. 96% of employees with at least three close friends at work reported that they were *extremely satisfied* with their lives. 56% of employees with a best friend at work are *engaged*! That is more than double the average of employee engagement across all categories (29%) and a whopping eight times the engagement of those without friends (8%) in the workplace. For more about this study and the value of workplace relationships, visit www.vitalfriends.org

Protecting Adolescents From Harm: Findings From the National Longitudinal Study on Adolescent Health, Michael Resnick, Peter Bearman, Robert Blum, et.al., *Journal of the American Medical Association (JAMA),* Volume 278, Number 10, September 10, 1997, pages 823-832.

Variations Nearly any activity that takes place in a straight line can be modified to work in a circle. In this case, the same challenge, moving with your feet always in contact with a partner, can be altered from a circular format to a straight line. We like the circular format best since everyone can see all members of the group in this configuration.

Hints and Clues Groups often make mistakes or lose contact during initial trials of this activity. At some point in this process, especially after a recent mistake or loss of contact, encourage the group to have a seat right where they are standing, and brainstorm some other possibilities from this position.

11. Plenty of Room at the Top
Making the Impossible Possible

This is one of those cases where the challenge seems impossible at first. To stack as many nails as possible onto the head of a single nail without using any other materials. Even with exceptional balance and skill it is difficult to stack any nails, let alone a dozen or more.

Supplies A visit to your local hardware store will provide the nails and wood blocks necessary for this puzzle. Larger nails (3-6 inches in length) are a bit more interesting. You'll need approximately 12-15 nails and one block of wood per puzzle. For large groups, you might consider one puzzle for every 3 to 4 participants and one very large puzzle for the group to complete at the end. Bolts can also be used if you wish to eliminate the sharp points typically found on various types of nails.

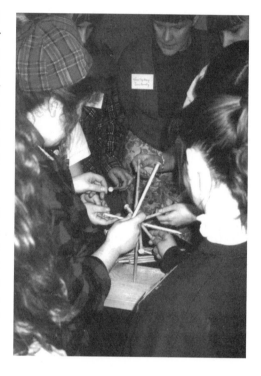

Teachable Moments   Sometimes we create things in our lives which are precariously balanced. One small vibration and everything comes crashing down. Our goal is to create structures and patterns which will be strong against the other forces in our lives. After completing this puzzle, ask group members to identify all of the components of their lives which must be balanced. How precarious is this balance? How could you make this balance a bit more stable?

Another teachable moment occurs when the group considers a path or process necessary to begin with a single nail at a time and works towards building a stable structure before placing this on top of the vertical nail. How did this process evolve? How can we use this same process to address other challenges in our work? Is there a way to shorten this evolution? How can we apply this process to our next task?

A third teachable moment possibility is to create a 'think tank' with your team. Divide the group into smaller sub-groups of 2-4 participants and provide each sub-group with one nail puzzle. Inform everyone that they have 5 minutes to experiment and to come up with a plan for successfully completing this project. At the completion of 5 minutes, pull the entire group together to share results, agree on a plan, and then present them with a much larger version of the puzzle to complete as a whole group.

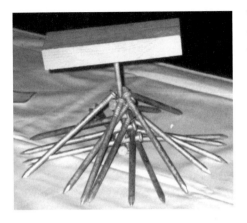

Variations While it is hard to beat the simplicity of this puzzle (a single block of wood and 12-15 nails), there are a few possibilities for other designs. For example, you can modify the number of nails used in this activity. It is possible to stack 30 or more nails if you have the right technique. Next, you can provide a variety of nails for this activity. Using a random collection of nails from 2 to 6 inches in length leads to some interesting solutions. You can also provide 'finishing nails' for this activity, which are 'headless.' This version may seem impossible to solve at first, but even finishing nails can be balanced if you know how to use them correctly. Finally, you can create a larger version of this activity by using baseball bats (yes, they really work) instead of nails. See puzzle #73 The Bridge, for another version of this puzzle, called The Balance, that you can make with wooden dowel rods.

Hints and Clues The answer lies in creating a structure which in itself is stable, even before placing it on top of the vertical nail. Think of familiar structures you have seen, perhaps even one in the building you are in right now. Hint: Think about a bridge, roof truss or the rafters in a house.

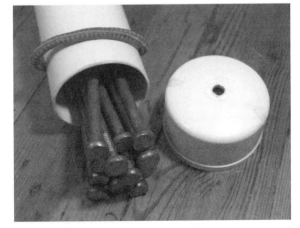

Thanks to John Berkeley for sharing his portable PVC nail puzzle capsule design.

12. Building Connections
Building Unity, Community and Connection

For the past year, Jim Cain has been working with Kirk Weisler to create the content for a corporate focused book related to building unity, community and connection in the workplace. In need of the perfect activity to demonstrate the major concepts presented in this book, Jim invented the following puzzle. You can learn more about this book project from the information presented at the end of this activity.

Building Connections is the perfect follow-on activity to the previous nail puzzle, Plenty of Room at the Top. Once you know a technique for stacking a dozen or so nails on top of a single nail, you are ready for Building Connections.

Our puzzle begins by placing the two nail stands within the square locators on the board shown in the illustration. Next, pass out about 30-40 large nails. Instruct the team that their goal is to use these loose nails as resources, and with them, create a connection (build a bridge) between the two single nail towers. Ready, begin!

Supplies You'll need a flat board with two pockets for retaining the nail tower bases and 30-40 large nails. You can also purchase equipment similar to that shown in the illustration from Training Wheels, Inc., at www.training-wheels.com or call 1-888-553-0147.

Teachable Moments The 'ah-hah!' effect in this puzzle comes from realizing that the option to move the nail towers and their wooden block bases is always possible. When this occurs, it is possible to create a 'bridge' between the two towers using only a single nail. Teachable Moment - it takes less materials and less time to create a connection between the two 'groups' when the first thing you do is bring the groups closer together.

Variations You can vary the size of nails used for this activity. Consider using very large deck nails.

Hints and Clues Encourage participants that the nails provided are company resources. Is it possible to create a bridge between the two towers using only a few nails? How about using only a single nail?

The Value of Connection - In the Workplace, <u>You</u> can become the catalyst for building unity, community and connection and creating a positive environment in your corporation, Jim Cain and Kirk Weisler. Visit the Teamwork & Teamplay website at: www.teamworkandteamplay.com for information about the availability of this publication.

"An undefined problem has an infinite number of solutions."
Robert A. Humphrey

*"I have yet to see any problem,
however complicated, which, when you look at it in the right way,
did not become still more complicated."*
Poul Anderson

*"Good management is the art of making
problems so interesting and their solutions so constructive that
everyone wants to get to work and deal with them."*
Paul Hawken

13. How Deep is the Well?
Communication and Problem Solving

Our third Nail Puzzle comes from Luca Santini of the Management Adventure Program (MAP) of Milan, Italy. This activity incorporates both problem solving and clear communication skills.

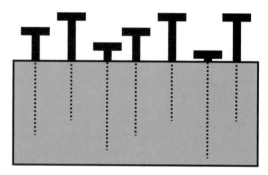

How Deep is the Well? begins with a block of wood that has several holes of various depths drilled along the top edge. A collection of modified nails or bolts is also included. Each of these fasteners is a different length. The challenge of this activity is to place each of the bolts in the correct 'well' or hole so that when complete, each of the heads is at exactly the same height above the block.

The puzzle shown here consists of seven nails and seven holes. Initially, all team members are allowed to view the wood block and nails in their initial configuration. A two minute planning period is allowed, after which the entire team is asked to move a short distance away from the puzzle. This distance should be sufficient to block the direct viewing of the puzzle by the team, but close enough so that a person near the puzzle could still verbally communicate with the rest of the team.

One person at a time is allowed to approach the puzzle and can remove any two nails from the wood block. These nails however must be replaced in any available holes in the block before this person leaves. Team members rotate visiting the puzzle until a final configuration is achieved.

Depending on the teachable moment you wish to explore with this activity, you can include some straight forward markings on the wooden block, such as a measuring ruler, number for each hole location or other useful hints. You can also supply unusual markings, hieroglyphics, pictographs or symbols. You can also inform the group that one of the nails or bolts is already in the proper location. As an additional clue, you could provide a depth guage or some other device for quickly determining the height that each nail or bolt should be placed at.

Supplies You'll need a block of wood, several bolts (that have been purchased in different lengths) or nails (that have been cut into different lengths, removing each pointed tip). Drill holes in the block of wood to different depths. We recommend that the difference in depth between any two holes be at least 3/8" (10 mm). Nails should similarly be cut to various lengths (or bolts purchased in various lengths) that differ by at least 3/8" (10 mm). The king size version shown here can be made from PVC tubes that have been cut to different lengths.

Teachable Moments   Beginning a project with some uncertainty is a real life situation. Learning how to investigate a challenge, make some assumptions, attempt a best guess, and learn from your mistakes is also a valuable experience. In this puzzle, it is as much about working together as a team, overcoming adversity, building new skills and growing together, as it is about solving the puzzle.

You can also discuss the difference between 'process' and 'product' in this challenge. The product is obviously the final configuration or solution of this puzzle, while the process is the technique or method by which the group identifies the final configuration. Which comes first, the product or the process? Which is more important? Where does the initial effort need to be placed, on the product or process?

Variations   You can vary the number of nails or bolts used to accommodate the size of your group. You can also vary the size and shape of the wooden block. If you would like to create an activity that discusses 'making the best choices,' you can drill more holes than necessary, and suggest that the group choose the best hole locations possible, rather than just a random selection. You can ask each team to set a goal of how many team members will visit the puzzle before reaching a final configuration.

Hints and Clues   In the final configuration, the heads of each nail or bolt will not be touching the wood block. Suggest to the group that creating a system of describing each nail and/ or hole location might be of value to the solution of this challenge.

The king size version of this activity shown in the photographs above were provided by the Management Adventure Program (MAP) of Milan, Italy. www.mapsrl.com info@ mapsrl.com

14. T.H.E. Puzzle
The Alphabet Squared

Here are a few dissection puzzles that will test your alphabetic and geometric skills.

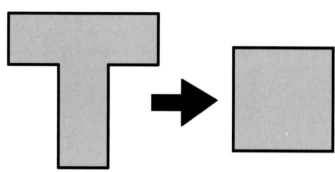

For starters, see if you can slice this capital letter T into five pieces, and make a perfect square from these same five pieces.

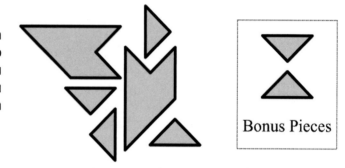

Next, see if you can assemble the pieces shown to create the capital letter H. If you add the two bonus pieces, you can also create a square from this collection.

Bonus Pieces

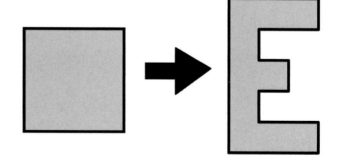

Finally, see if you can take a square and cut it into five pieces so that it will produce the capital letter E shown.

Supplies A piece of graph paper or a computer graphics program can be very helpful in accurately creating these puzzles. Heavy cardstock, sheet plastic or plywood are good choices for constructing each of these puzzles.

Teachable Moments Transformable puzzles are similar to other transformable products in our lives. Suitcases that expand, roll, and open in a variety of ways. Household products that unfold for use, and refold for storage or transport. Interchangeable appliances that use a common base or power supply. Each of these objects teaches us about product design and the occasional need for transforming or morphing these products for transport, storage or utility.

What products do you use everyday that are transformable? Can you think of other products that transform, fold, retract or provide more than one function? Can you think of products that need to be small during transport and then unfold or extend during use? On a scale of one to ten, how effective is our team at adapting and morphing?

Variations Dissection puzzles are designed to intentionally create two distinct shapes from the same pieces. The classic dissection puzzle uses familiar shapes (letters, numbers, household objects) as one puzzle solution, and a geometric shape (circle, square, triangle, hexagon) as the other. See if you can make other dissection puzzles from letters of the alphabet.

To make the solution of these puzzles more of a team challenge, here are a few suggestions:

1. Make each puzzle from plywood and attach foot straps so that participants need to walk around to find a potential placement for their piece.

2. Use foamboard, cardboard or lightweight foam to make each puzzle, and build the solution on a wall or ceiling using loop and eye fabric strips (available at hardware and fabric stores), magnets, or spray adhesives.

3. Build each puzzle from study materials and attach gloves or handholds on the back of each piece for a mid-air solution.

Hints and Clues Dissection puzzles are generally created using straight cuts. Some pieces may need to be flipped over to complete a puzzle.

15. The PVC Network
An Alternate Design for the International Space Station

If you enjoy visiting your local hardware store as much as we do, then you are sure to enjoy this creative puzzle made from PVC tubes and connectors.

The PVC Network is easy to describe, but a bit harder to actually solve. Using all of the PVC tubes and connectors provided, create a single, interconnected structure, so that no holes are left open.

A 'self-guided' information sheet is provided for this activity so that you can use the PVC Network to explore leadership issues. The first page provides basic instructions, along with several hints (which are only provided at the request of the group). The second page is a self check sheet which allows the team to analyze their own leadership performance. We recommend that you allow the group to discuss several of these questions, but there is no need to discuss every one of them. This second page can actually be used for nearly all of the puzzles in this book.

Supplies You can purchase these PVC tubes, under the name 'Teamplay Tubes', from Training Wheels, Inc., at www.training-wheels.com or call 1-888-553-0147. This unique collection of PVC tubes consists of fifty specifically selected and modified PVC tubes and connectors.

Teachable Moments   There are several opportunities for teachable moments with the PVC Network. Reading for comprehension and following the rules, organizing your workspace and equipment, taking inventory, working as a team, using all the available information, taking care of the team vs. getting the job done, starting over if necessary, empowering other team members, and celebrating a job well done are just a few possibilities.

Variations Teamplay Tubes can be used to present over two dozen additional teambuilding activities. Here are a few of our favorites:

Blind Artist - Have one group assemble any 15 pieces from their kit into some shape, and then invite a second group (wearing blindfolds) to reconstruct the same shape with their own collection of pieces.

Tallest Tower - Using any 10 (or 20 or 30 pieces) create the tallest tower possible, with only 3 points of contact with the floor. If you are limited by vertical ceiling height, require each tower to hold something (like a roll of duct tape) at the top. This added weight will require a shorter, stronger tower. For a final test of the engineering of this tower, use an electric room fan to see which towers can hold up to a strong wind.

Statue - Create a variety of human or animal shapes (sitting, running, riding a horse, lying down, standing at attention, swimming, surfing, cycling, throwing a boomerang, cooking an omelet, playing hockey, throwing a baseball, etc.).

The Goal Post - Construct a football style goal post, or a soccer goal, or a basketball hoop and stand, and then launch a balloon, lightweight ball or paper airplane towards the goal. Personal or team goals can be written on masking tape and then attached to balloons or balls.

Spelling Bee - Using as many pieces as possible, construct letters of the alphabet. Once all available parts have been turned into letters, use these letters to spell as many words as possible.

Two Way Bridge - Begin this activity by locating two groups on the opposite side of a folding wall or curtain so that they may talk to each other, but not see what the other group is creating. Each group is instructed to build one half of a bridge structure, so that when the divider or curtain is removed, the bridge will easily come together. This task requires clear communication and two sets of PVC tubes.

A Tree in the Forest - Using only 10 parts (tubing and connectors) create the tallest "tree" possible. Trees compete for sunlight and water, and must withstand wind to survive in a mature forest.

Matchstick Puzzles - Many puzzle activities using matches or straws can also be performed using the PVC Teamplay Tubes. For example, can you make four equilateral triangles simultaneously by using six Teamplay Tubes of approximately the same length?

Hints and Clues Clues to the PVC Network are provided on page one of the information sheet that follows.

On the following pages you will find two reproducible self-guided instruction sheets for the PVC Network.

The Leadership Network
Page One

1. The Project. Your group has been asked to create a complete "network" using **ALL** of the PVC tubes and connectors. Just like any hardware, electronic or water system, a good network will have no "leaks." For this activity, no open tubes or connector "holes" can be left. This means that each tube will be inserted into two connectors, that each connector will have a tube in each opening, and that the whole system will be interconnected. Your network design is a "stand alone" architecture, so for this activity, you are asked not to collaborate with other groups (they are attempting to solve the same problem with exactly the same pieces).

2. Some Valuable Information. First attempt to build your network without looking at the following three hints. If you are having some problems after ten minutes, feel free to check the information below. When you are finished, ask several members of your group to read the Leadership Evaluation questions on the back side of this sheet and answer them as a group.

Clues

A. Connectors Have Priorities. Which of the connectors should you attempt to use first, second, and last? Count the number of openings and start with the highest first.

B. Diversity Works Throughout the Process. By using some long and some short tubes in the beginning, you'll have a supply of long and short tubes at the end.

C. Stress Levels. Connections that fall apart are trying to tell you something! Networks that contain too much "internal stress" from unusual angles, connections that are forced, and designs that are based more on brute strength than finesse, are likely candidates for reorganizing (so try to lessen the stress level of the network!)

From Teambuilding Puzzles, *by Anderson, Cain, Cavert and Heck, 2009*

Leadership Evaluation
Page Two

1. What types of team behavior were demonstrated by each member of the group? (i.e What was the role of each team member: decision maker, creative genius, worker bee, problem solver, etc).

2. Was there an obvious leader in the group, or did the group share leadership?

3. How was leadership decided, shared or avoided?

4. Which of the following styles of problem solving were used by your group (circle one):

    1. trial & error   2. analyze, plan, perform   3. a really good guess & a whole lot of luck

5. After your group decided on a plan, did the group change the plan during the activity? If so, why?

6. How many ideas were considered during the early stages of the activity? Was each idea, and each person, given an opportunity to be heard?

7. Describe how each member of the group was given an opportunity to contribute to the group's success?

8. How would you rate your group's overall completion of this task?

9. In general, were the participants in your group more concerned about completing the task, or in caring for the members of the group? On the "American football field of leadership" below, mark where your team stands.

Completing the Task Endzone	10	20	30	40	50	40	30	20	10	Care for the Members Group Endzone

10. If you had the opportunity to perform this task again, what would you suggest to do differently?

11. If you were asked to give advice to a new team trying to accomplish this assignment, what information would you provide to help them be successful?

12. If you were going to hire an employee to complete this task, what skills would you look for?

13. If you were chosen to lead the next group in successfully completing this activity, what style of leadership would you employ?

From Teambuilding Puzzles, *by Anderson, Cain, Cavert and Heck, 2009*

16. Plumber's Delight

Decisions Have Consequences

Here are two collections of PVC tubing that require analysis. The goal in each case is to determine the appropriate valves to close to achieve the desired result.

The first version of this activity comes from the creative minds of Mary and Rodney Emerson. Mary's goal was to create a hands-on tool for encouraging water conservation, and her husband Rodney assisted with his plumbing skills. The result is an educational, two dimensional puzzle that was the spark for the more extensive three dimensional version also shown.

The PVC house consists of dozens of PVC tubes, connectors, faucets and valves. A few livestock number tags (available at livestock or feed and seed stores) can be used to assist team members in identifying each of the various valves. The team challenge of this puzzle, is to identify the minimum number of valves necessary to turn off the water to one of the exit faucets (which is connected to a lawn sprinkler that is positioned very close to a member of the management team). You'll find a description of how to present this style of puzzle to a corporate audience in the variations section of this article.

Supplies You'll need a rather extensive collection of PVC or CPVC tubes and connectors, valves and faucets, pipe joint compound or cement and plenty of creativity to create your own version of Plumber's Delight. A two-dimensional version, such as the one shown above, is a bit easier to assemble than the more complicated three-dimensional house. Both of these versions are provided simply as examples. Construct a unique version for your audiences.

Teachable Moments The ability to analyze a difficult situation and to make the right choices promptly are essential leadership qualities. The 3-D version provides definite consequences for errors (the water sprinkler turns on).

Variations An alternative technique, sometimes referred to as the mousetrap technique, is to take one of the above devices and begin with ALL the valves in the closed position. The challenge is to open a set number of valves, with the goal of NOT turning on the water to the outlet.

A second variation is to present this style of puzzle as a pencil and paper challenge. Participants identify which valves should be turned off by crossing them out on a sketch or illustration.

The following story is an example of how you might present the Plumber's Delight puzzle to a corporate audience:

"Sometimes employees can be real lifesavers! This activity begins by requesting a 'volunteer' for a hazardous mission. The mission is to inspect a potential leakage in the company water system, one that could cost thousands of dollars in water damage if not corrected. The volunteer takes along a bucket filled with an umbrella, a pair of safety glasses, a towel and a sponge, and stands inside of the hoola hoop placed near a lawn sprinkler.

The rest of the team is allowed to approach the perimeter of the emergency water system shut-off network, which just so happens to have been installed prior to standard zoning laws so it is a bit unique to say the least. Team members are asked to stay in the position they are presently in, and to identify up to six valves they think should be turned to the off position to stop the flow of water to the sprinkler system. After reaching consensus on this decision, the facilitator will turn off the valves identified, and then turn on the main water supply. If no water flows to the sprinkler, mission accomplished. If water flows to the sprinkler, the group can choose a different valve to turn off every 60 seconds."

Possible reviewing questions for the group include:

> Did having 'different points of view' assist in the solution, or was this an additional problem?

> Was there a true consensus, or did the group just 'hope for the best' at some point?

> Did it make a difference that a member of the team was in a compromised situation?

> Would you have wanted to change places with the employee nearest the sprinkler?

> Did the level of activity increase when the water began to flow? Why or why not?

> How does this situation remind you of a situation from your own workplace?

Hints and Clues While you can eventually turn off all the valves in each of these designs, the goal is to turn off the 'right valves first.' Encourage team consensus and involvement. Your decisions have a real life consequence.

*"The engineer's first problem in any design situation
is to discover what the problem really is."*

*"If you don't ask the right questions, you don't get the right answers.
A question asked in the right way often points to its own answer. Asking
questions is the ABC of diagnosis. Only the inquiring mind solves problems."*
Edward Hodnett

17. Inside / Out
Creative Problem Solving and Following the Rules

Here is a challenge that explores concepts of ethical behavior in the workplace, following the rules, and personal and professional accountability.

Inside/Out is a simple team challenge that opens the door for meaningful discussions about professional issues of integrity. The initial challenge doesn't appear very difficult. The teachable moment and its message however, are sure to last a long time after the activity has concluded.

We begin Inside/Out by placing a tubular webbing (or rope) circle on the ground, and inviting a team to stand inside the perimeter. The challenge is for this team to go from the inside of the circle to the outside of the circle by passing underneath the circle. This is to be accomplished without anyone in the group using their arms, or shoulders, or hands.

To encourage planning before action, request that the team leave their circle to plan 'offsite.' When they have a plan and each member of the group understands their contribution, they can return to their circle and begin.

After completing the task, inform the group that they are 'half done' with the challenge. Now that they are outside, the second part of the challenge is to go Outside/In.

Supplies You'll need a piece of tubular climbing webbing or rope, that has been tied with a knot into a circle. A 15 foot (4.6 meter) long segment of rope produces a circle sufficient for a group of 5-7 participants. If you have more participants, we recommend using multiple circles rather than placing everyone within a single circle.

Teachable Moments Facilitators always have a series of questions ready for team challenges. Questions such as, 'who was the leader, and why,' and 'did you have a plan, and if so, did the plan change during the activity?' can add additional insight into a team's performance. For Inside/Out however, there are some specific questions which lead to two rather dramatic teachable moments. First, how much time did the group spend planning Inside/Out and Outside/In? Why is the planning period for the second task so much less.

Next, and here is the major point of this activity, 'how do you feel about getting the job done and staying within the rules?' 'Did all of you manage Inside/Out and Outside/In without using your arms, or shoulders, or hands?' At this point, most folks are agreeing 'yes, we did a great job.' Now the facilitator can question the group further. 'So, I shouldn't have seen anyone crawling on the HANDS and knees on the floor, or using their arms to maintain their balance, or hold up their leg, or help another member of the group? The rules stated, 'without using your arms, or shoulders, or hands.' But what did you HEAR?'

At this point, a discussion about personal interpretation of the rules is appropriate. Discussing getting the job done vs. getting the job done within the boundaries of the rules is also possible. You can also bring up discussions related to helping each other follow the rules, running your own internal quality control, being personally accountable for your actions in the group, and taking responsibility for your actions.

Variations You can focus on any of the various learning points with this activity. Ethical behavior, creative problem solving, group involvement, following the rules, advanced planning and personal accountability are all possibilities. If you want to include communication, coaching or mentoring in this activity, you can blindfold a portion of the team. This will necessitate sighted members of the team communicating the vision, leading those with limited vision, and providing information and guidance.

Hints and Clues Rather than provide any additional information, we recommend just restating the original challenge - to go from the inside of the circle, to the outside, by going underneath the circle, without using your arms, or shoulders, or hands.

For more activities, challenges and puzzles using tubular climbing webbing, we invite you to read:

The Revised and Expanded Book of Raccoon Circles, 2007, Jim Cain and Tom Smith, Kendall Hunt Publishers, Dubuque, IA USA www.kendallhunt.com (1-800-228-0810) ISBN 0-7575-3265-9. Over 200 different activities using only a single, simple prop.

The Ropework and Ropeplay Kit, from Training-Wheels, Inc. Over 400 different activities, challenges and games that you can play with a unique collection of ten different ropes. Visit www.training-wheels.com or call 1-888-553-0147.

Raccoon Circles Facilitator Guide, Jim Cain, Teamwork & Teamplay website downloadable PDF document www.teamworkandteamplay.com/raccooncircles.html

The Group Loop Multi-Media CD, Tom Heck www.teachmeteamwork.com

18. The Electric Box
Reacting to a Changing Environment

Adapting to a changing environment is challenging, especially when the environment changes continuously. The Electric Box provides just such a challenge. Thanks to Patrick Caton for sharing this activity.

The Electric Box is made from a 15 foot long segment of tubular climbing webbing that has been knotted into a circle. This flexible circle can be used to create each of the shapes shown here, one for each member of the group. The goal is for each participant to pass through one of these rectangles, without touching the webbing. The challenge is for the group to adapt to the changing shape of the Electric Box and anticipate how to work within this changing environment.

The activity begins with the entire group on one side of the Electric Box. Two members of the team are initially asked to hold the webbing loop and create a flat rectangle, about 3 feet (1 meter) off the ground, as the starting shape of the Electric Box. Before each member of the group passes through, the two participants holding the webbing alter the size of the rectangular opening, building to a square and finally ending with a tall vertical rectangle. Each configuration is unique, just like the members of the team. Don't forget to include the two team members holding the Electric Box. For safety and to discourage anyone from jumping through the Electric Box, require that anyone passing through the box be in contact with at least two other team members at all times.

Supplies A 15 foot long segment of tubular climbing webbing (known as a Raccoon Circle - See the references of this book for more information) that has been knotted into a circle. You can substitute a colorful segment of rope or ribbon for this activity. You can also use a 15 foot long length of duct tape, which provides instant feedback if a member of the team makes contact with it.

Teachable Moments Adapting to a changing environment isn't easy. Some may believe that it isn't fair to ask different members of the team to perform different tasks. "Why does

Bob get to go through the easy square and I have to struggle through the narrow rectangle?" The opportunity here is to discuss exactly these concepts, and how the overall success of the group depends upon this level of commitment.

Another teachable moment exists in the preparation for this activity. Did team members anticipate the configuration of the Electric Box in advance and plan accordingly? Or did they only react to the configuration they were presented with and struggle through as best they could? The concepts of pro-active vs. reactive apply here. Which is best? What skill is needed for our future success on the next project we undertake as a team? How can the skills we have learned be used on our next assignment?

Finally, for each person passing through the Electric Box, the box changes shape. This is a great activity to reinforce the concepts found in the book Who Moved My Cheese, by Spencer Johnson (1998, Penguin Putnam, New York, NY USA ISBN 0-399-14446-3)

Variations Utilize tubular climbing webbing, rope, ribbon or even duct tape to make the rectangle. You can also use an electrical extension cord (not connected to power, of course) to further reinforce the Electric Box concept. Another alternative is to use a hoola hoop that does not change size, but rather changes orientation (from vertical to horizontal to angled). And finally, you can perform a variation to this activity by using a small diameter length of shock (bungie) cord or elastic to form a geometric outline that can change shape, size and location. For more on this possibility, read the activity description for 'The Worm Hole' found on page 206 of the book Teamwork & Teamplay.

In addition to individually passing through the Electric Box, consider having couples, or parents and children working together to pass through. Partnering can include coaches and players, mentors and new employees, therapeutic assistants and patients, or campers and counselors. Individuals can also take objects through with them. A five gallon bucket of water can represent a significant burden.

Finally, the configuration of the Electric Box can be random, so that each participant has limited time for strategy or preparation before passing through their assigned opening.

Hints and Clues Anticipating the configuration of the Electric Box in advance is helpful in planning the order of team members passing through. Allowing individuals to communicate their own comfort level with the opening size they have chosen is preferable to having the group choose for them. Careful spotting of each group member as they pass through is important, even for individuals that appear to be confident or have a relatively easy configuration to pass through.

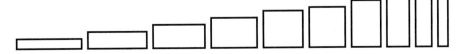

19. Matchstick Puzzles Galore
Thinking Outside the Matchstick Boxes

Teambuilding
Puzzles

In the classic style of matchstick puzzles, the following challenges are presented. But rather than presenting these as table top amusements for after dinner, we have modified them for teams using a few of the supplies listed below.

Supplies   Instead of matchsticks, you can use a wide variety of larger household or hardware store items for the following puzzles. Unsharpened pencils, drinking straws, coffee stirring sticks, chop sticks, toothpicks, large paperclips, rulers or yardsticks, dowel rods, paint stirring sticks, 2x4's, cardboard and PVC tubes, uncooked spaghetti or foam noodles are just a few possible options.

Teachable Moments   Creative problem solving, teamwork and thinking outside the box are just a few of the teachable moments possible with this activity. For more information about the paperclips shown on the following pages, read: The Evolution of Useful Things - How Everyday Artifacts, From Pins to Paperclips, Came to Be as They are, 1992, Henry Petroski, Vintage Books, New York, NY USA ISBN 0-679-74039-2.

Several of the puzzles presented here have multiple solutions. This can be a great opportunity to compare solutions and build new solutions based upon other suggestions.

Variations   In addition to presenting these puzzles with groups during teambuilding sessions, consider using them as 'homework assignments' or during breaks. You can also present these puzzles as paper and pencil challenges instead of three-dimensional activities with actual props.

Hints and Clues   Many matchstick puzzles provide misguided and occasionally even misleading or vague clues or directions. Encourage participants to agree on their interpretation of what the puzzle is suggesting before proposing solutions. After clarifying the puzzle's directions, brainstorm and physically demonstrate several possible solutions. Then seek team consensus before choosing a final configuration.

When solving these puzzles, encourage team members with helpful insights or suggestions for potentially correct solutions, to assist other team members in finding the solution as well, before communicating this information out loud to the entire group. By following this simple suggestion, more team members will have the opportunity to analyze the puzzle for themselves, rather than simply waiting for another member of the group to provide a solution.

"Each success only buys an admission ticket to a more difficult problem."
Henry Kissinger

For each of the puzzles below, rather than using the word matchstick, PVC tube or some other item, we will simply refer to the components of each puzzle as 'sticks.' You are welcome to substitute any of the suggested items in the 'supplies' section above.

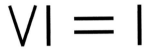

A. Add one more stick to the following equation to make it true.

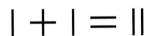

B. While the following equation is already true, relocate one stick to make the new result 130.

C. Begin with three sticks side by side. Add two sticks to make eight.

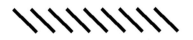

D. Without breaking any, use nine sticks to make ten. Then use the same nine sticks to make twenty-eight.

E. Starting with the configuration shown below, move three sticks to create five equilateral triangles. Then remove three sticks, and moving only three of the remaining sticks, make four equal sized equilateral triangles. (This is a great puzzle to use exceptionally long sticks, such as 10 foot (3 meter) lengths of PVC tubing).

F. From the configuration below, take one, move one, and leave one square.

G. From the configuration below, remove two, move two, and leave two.

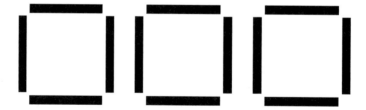

H. This time (in Spanish) remove two, move two, and leave two.

I. Begin with 12 large paperclips and form the four squares shown below. Now give back one paperclip from each square, and using the remaining paperclips (and without bending or deforming them in any manner) create four similar sized squares.

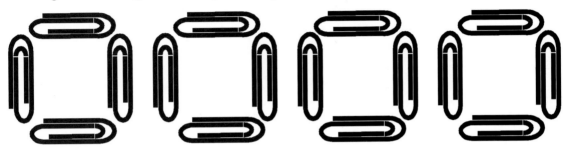

J. Start by holding sixteen sticks in your hands. Next, take away any five sticks and with what you have left, make nine.

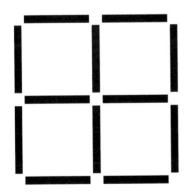

K. The configuration shown here contains twelve sticks. Relocate four sticks in this pattern, and create ten squares.

L. Each house below faces in the opposite direction. Relocate two sticks in each house, to make them each face the opposite direction.

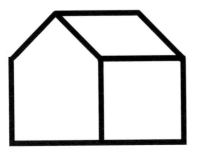
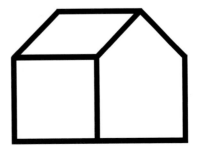

M. Use nine sticks to make seven equal sized equilateral triangles.

N. Relocate only two sticks and make the dog look the other way.

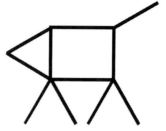

O. Using eight sticks, simultaneously make two squares and four triangles. Next, using these same eight sticks, make two squares and eight triangles. Finally, add another stick, for a total of nine sticks, and make three equal sized squares and two equilateral triangles.

P. Bonus Puzzle - Here are five squares made from four sticks each. Relocate any four sticks and leave six squares.

(Hint: This one has a solution that is neither outside the box, nor inside the box. It is, in fact, the box itself.)

Q. Double Bonus Puzzle - Here are another five squares, made from four sticks each. Remove any eight sticks, and with the remaining sticks, make six squares.

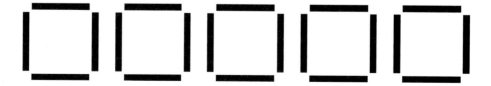

20. The Slow Burn
Creative Problem Solving Under Fire

Making a decision under fire isn't easy. Here is a puzzle that explores this real life concept, and provides an elementary example of fault tree analysis.

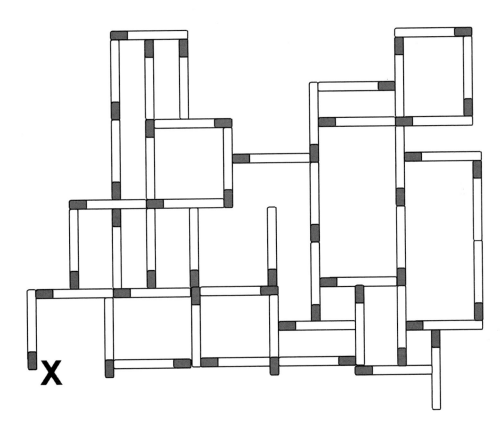

Consider the collection of matches shown above. If the match marked with an X ignites, and begins to burn along its length, it will ignite those other matches with their striking head near this match. All matches burn at exactly the same rate. All flames ignite other matches at the tip, midpoint or end of the burning match only. What match will be the last to catch fire and burn to completion? How many matches will burn before the last one ignites? Are there any matches which will never catch fire?

Supplies This puzzle is best, and safest, when presented as a pencil and paper challenge. ***Do not attempt this puzzle with actual matches.***

Teachable Moments   This puzzle is a simplified example of a 'critical path' scenario, sometimes referred to as fault tree analysis. By defining the path traveled by the flame, including branch points and dead ends, teams learn to critically analyze or recommend concepts ranging from individual decisions to multi-level possibilities.

Variations   You can use a different configuration of match illustrations to reinforce corporate decisions, fire department training scenarios, outdoor living skills, or other relevant situations. Rather than using a burning match analogy, consider using a computer software or decision tree analogy where the decision at each junction alters the path of the impulse traveling throughout the pattern. You could also present a similar problem as a series of hallways with choices to be made at each intersection.

Hints and Clues   Start with the first match, and draw a line through each match along the path of ignition. Similarly identify each junction location along the path. Return to each junction to check for other possible paths originating there.

"The problem is not that there are problems. The problem is expecting otherwise and thinking that having problems is a problem."
Theodore Rubin

"I know that most men, including those at ease with problems of the greatest complexity, can seldom accept even the simplest and most obvious truth if it be such as would oblige them to admit the falsity of conclusions which they have delighted in explaining to colleagues, which they have proudly taught to others, and which they have woven, thread by thread, into the fabric of their lives."
Leo Tolstoy

21. Houses & Utilities
Thinking Inside and Outside the Box

One of the classic techniques employed in puzzles of all kinds is to create one line of reasoning that seems to be working, only to have this technique fail for the final challenge in the puzzle. And that is exactly what is happening here.

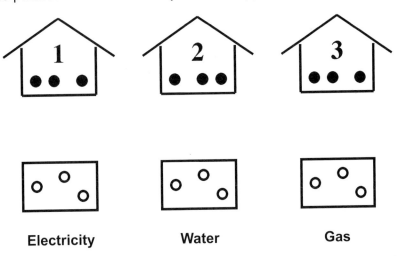

In the illustration above, three houses need to each be connected to three utilities. Local zoning laws prohibit utility lines crossing each other. Draw paths that connect a black dot on each house to a white dot on each of the three utilities without crossing the path of any other utility line.

Supplies You can present this puzzle as a pencil and paper activity. You can also use books for each house and utility and string or rope to connect them. Finally, your team can build a PVC connection (our favorite version) between each house and utility. This version turns a cerebral activity into a more kinesthetic and active learning opportunity.

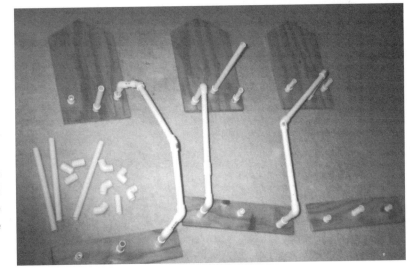

Teachable Moments   Carefully listening to the rules and guidelines, challenging our assumptions, and thinking outside-the-box are essential skills to solving this puzzle. Encourage participants to ask questions, to clarify information, and to try as many different techniques as they can. You might implement a 'failure zone,' where the goal is to identify, within a five minute time frame, as many techniques as possible that would fail. Afterwards, discuss which techniques do not produce success, and encourage the team to avoid repeating these same mistakes over and over and over.

The following teachable moment works well with the PVC tubing version of this puzzle.

Just as building contractors employ architects to create drawings and plan their work in advance, you can provide your participants with paper and pencils to plan their work. You can also suggest that once connected, each utility will be turned on, and it will be impossible to change this connection in the future - so plan carefully. Another way of presenting this additional challenge is to mention that utility connections are typically made with a fast setting adhesive. This means that once a pipe and connector are joined together, the connection is permanent!

Variations Rather than labeling the three lower boxes as utilities, they could be services or organizations which would benefit these three homeowners or families. From a corporate perspective, these could be three divisions and the vendors that support them. For schools, there are an elementary, middle and high schools that each need access to athletic fields, libraries and classrooms.

You can consider adding a fourth house, or utility, or both. Or perhaps a three-dimensional placement of each establishment.

Hints and Clues If you always do what you've always done, then you will always get what you've always gotten before. If you keep reaching the end of this puzzle, without being able to complete it, start searching for what works and what doesn't, and change what doesn't seem to work.

Teambuilding
Puzzles

22. Making Connections
Finding a Way to Join Us All Together

Instruction #1: Connect Point A to Point B.

Making a single connection is tough enough, but making many connections at once is very challenging. Here are a few different styles of connection puzzles. Good Luck!

For each of the puzzles below, the task is to draw a line between each of the paired locations (A to A, B to B, 1 to 1). The correct solution allows each of the pairs to be connected without crossing any lines. Puzzles are presented in order of increasing difficulty.

Each of the circular vehicles shown to the right must exit the triangular parking lot through the square toll booth with the same number. See if you can find a way, without crossing the path of any other car.

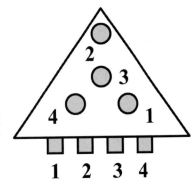

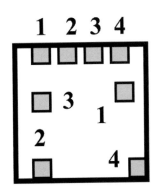

Help each of the teams above find their way to their locker room, without crossing the path of any other team.

IT Services is a bit busy just now, so you will need to route your own computer printer cables from each workstation to the network connection, without crossing any lines.

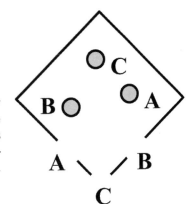

Each of the switches must be connected to the correct light, without any of the wires crossing.

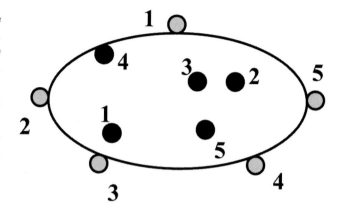

Supplies These puzzles can be presented using pencil and paper. You can also use additional props, including rope (to connect the two objects), and people (in place of the squares and circles shown).

Teachable Moments While it is possible to connect any one of the paired objects in each puzzle with a straight line, this procedure only satisfies one of the connections required and may actually ruin the possibility of successfully completing each of the other connections. Making Connections is a perfect puzzle for illustrating how important it is for every member of the team to succeed, not just a few key players. It also shows that sometimes we need to go out of our way to insure the overall success of the team, even if that means working harder or traveling a longer path ourselves.

These puzzles lend themselves to exploring goal setting and attainment. In each puzzle teams must find a way to make connections, from 'here' to 'there.' Life is very much the same. Getting to where you want to be, and making connections along the way can seem impossible at times. What skills that you utilized in these puzzles can you transfer to your current life?

Variations You can create your own version of these puzzles, by using an outline shape similar to your corporate logo, school emblem, or some other familiar shape or symbol. We also recommend using appropriate metaphors related to 'making connections' for your audience. You can alter the difficulty level of these puzzles by reducing or increasing the number of objects which need to be connected.

For a different style of connection puzzle, see Puzzle #21, Houses and Utilities.

Hints and Clues If your first attempt is unsuccessful, try starting with a different pair. You can also try to make connections in both directions, from circles to squares, and also from squares to circles.

23. Heads or Tails
Coin Puzzles in Many Styles

Here are a variety of coin puzzles that you can make a part of your teambuilding programs or as creative problem solving homework activities.

Supplies Coins work just fine, and the bigger the coin the better. You can even find giant imitation coins (about 3-4 inches in diameter) at craft stores, or use dinner plates, poker chips, hoola hoops or flying disks. You can also cut foam 'noodles' into colorful macro-sized chips (as shown below) and use these as lightweight coins.

Teachable Moments   Creative Problem Solving, Listening Skills, Thinking Outside the Box.

Variations   Rather than presenting these puzzles to groups during teambuilding sessions, consider using them as 'homework assignments' or presenting them as activities during breaks. You can also substitute paper and pencil versions of these problems instead of using real coins.

Hints and Clues Sometimes coin puzzles can be solved by manipulating the coins until a successful configuration is obtained. This means having enough coins for the entire group to work with.

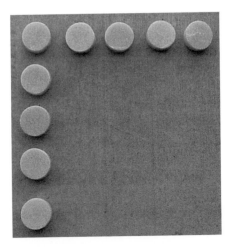

A. Move two coins to produce two rows of six coins each

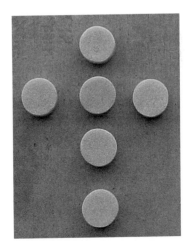

B. Move one coin to produce two rows of four coins each.

C. Here is a square with four coins each side. Use these 12 coins to produce another square with five coins on each side.

on

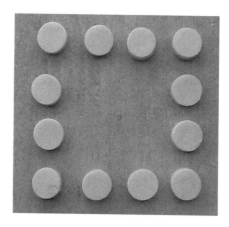

D. Use 14 coins to make a square with five coins on each side. Now use only 13 coins. Then only 12 coins.

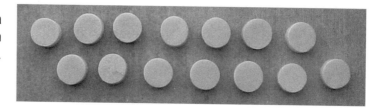

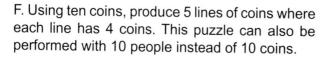

E. Arrange 3 coins about the line so that there are two heads showing on the left side of the line and two tails showing on the right side of the line.

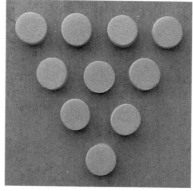

F. Using ten coins, produce 5 lines of coins where each line has 4 coins. This puzzle can also be performed with 10 people instead of 10 coins.

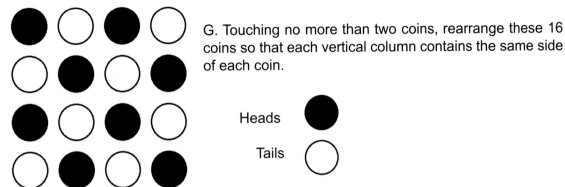

G. Touching no more than two coins, rearrange these 16 coins so that each vertical column contains the same side of each coin.

Heads

Tails

H. You can perform each of the activities in the People Movers section, using coins instead of people. For example, in puzzle #6 PM5 Sorting Things Out, you will need to move coins in adjoining pairs (two at a time), four times, to create the alternating pattern shown.

Start Like This

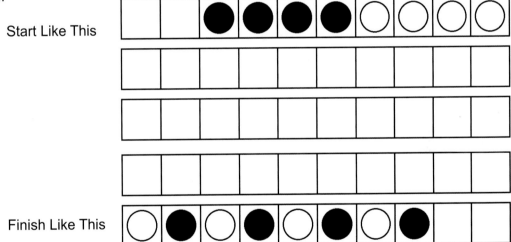

Finish Like This

For more activities with foam noodle chips (and the whole noodles too) see:

50 Ways to Use Your Noodle: Loads of Land Games with Foam Noodle Toys, by Chris Cavert and Sam Sikes. Learning Unlimited Publications. ISBN: 0-9646541-1-3

50 More Ways to Use Your Noodle: Loads of Land and Water Games with Foam Noodle Toys, by Chris Cavert and Sam Sikes. Learning Unlimited Publication. ISBN: 0-9646541-5-6 (Both books are also available at www.fundoing.com)

24. Drink Up!
Creative Problem Solving with Bottles and Straws

Teambuilding Puzzles

The next time you finish a bottle of soda pop in one of those old fashioned 16 ounce (0.5 liter) glass bottles, save the bottle and try this challenge. Using only a standard drinking straw, lift the bottle from the table and hold it in the air for at least 10 seconds. You are welcome to touch the straw but you cannot touch the bottle.

Supplies A glass soda pop bottle and a standard drinking straw. You can use a plastic soda bottle if necessary.

Teachable Moments The simplest techniques are sometimes the best. How many different solutions can you find for this challenge?

Variations In our initial presentation of this problem, you can touch the straw, but not the glass bottle. You could modify the activity by allowing only one hand to touch the straw. You can also limit where the straw can contact the bottle. For example, the straw can only touch the inside of the bottle. Finally, you can touch the straw, but cannot tie a knot in it.

Hints and Clues How many sides does a bottle have? (Inside & Outside) Which side is the best choice? What shapes could a straw have that would be helpful in this situation?

"Where there is a will there is a way," is an old and true saying.
He who resolves upon doing a thing, by that very resolution often scales the
barriers to it, and secures its achievement. To think we are able, is almost
to be so - to determine upon attainment is frequently attainment itself."
Samuel Smiles

25. Pig & Pens
Puzzles from the Farm

Enjoy this challenge that combines rural farm living skills with mathematical recommendations.

After visiting the local county extension office, Farmer Bob learns that pigs that grow up in pens with an odd number of total pigs grow faster and are healthier than those growing up in pens with an even number of pigs. He also learns that four pens is often regarded as the optimal number of pens to have on any farm. Although he is not exactly sure if these two factors go together, Farmer Bob is determined to try and place his nine pigs into four pens, with an odd number of pigs in each pen. Can you help him?

Four Pens

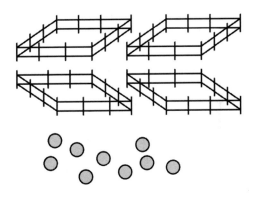

Nine Pigs

Supplies While you can conduct this puzzle as a pencil and paper activity, it can be more fun to use toy pigs and toy fences. You can also make model pigs from empty bleach or liquid laundry detergent bottles, and use short sections of rope for the fences.

Teachable Moments A puzzle with multiple correct solutions is a beautiful thing. With so many choices and possibilities in life, presenting a puzzle with only one exact solution is not only unrealistic, but certainly less than ideal for building necessary life skills. This puzzle has several possible solutions and a few more opportunities for creativity. It is also a great puzzle for demonstrating the power of brainstorming without evaluating. The goal here could be to find as many solutions as possible. This encourages teams to not only find the first solution, but also the ones that follow. Some of secondary solutions may be better analyzed or even superior to the first solutions proposed.

Hints and Clues If placing an odd number of pigs into each of four separate pens is difficult, try combining the pens in some fashion. If Farmer Bob has the materials to build four pens, what possible configurations for these pens can your team design?

Variations You'll find another fencing challenge on the next page. Here is an activity you can post on a website and conduct via emailed responses. You could also present and solve this puzzle via telephone or fax potential solutions to a central number. What about a 'real life' version at your school or summer camp where real animals and fencing are part of your rural farm experience day?
Introducing mathematical concepts and rural living skills together is quite a combination.

If you would like a corporate version of this puzzle, you can replace Farmer Bob with a regional vice-president and trade the twenty sheep for twenty technicians. The livestock pen then becomes an office floorplan with nine cubicles. We know that employees perform at a higher level when they have a window in their office, so the task becomes assigning each of the employees to the eight outer cubicles so that there are six employees on each side.

"Within the problem lies the solution."
Milton Katselas

26. Sheep & Pens
More Puzzling Situations From Farmer Bob's Farm

Farmer Bob decided to take his entire herd of twenty champion sheep to the country fair. He spent a whole day building a portable pen system for his sheep (as shown in the illustration). While performing his inspection of the livestock at the fair, the county health inspector stopped by to see Farmer Bob's champion sheep. "I think your sheep, especially the ones in the center pen, would be happier and healthier if you would place six sheep on each side of the pen system, and empty out the center pen." Bob thanked the inspector for his visit, and then began to think about how to follow the inspector's recommendation. Can you think of a way to relocate the 20 sheep in Farmer Bob's livestock pens so that six sheep are on each side and no sheep are in the center pen?

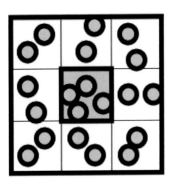

Supplies You can perform this puzzle using pencil and paper, or collect 20 coins or tokens to represent the sheep and draw a larger version of Farmer Bob's livestock pen system (a copyable version of the pen is available on the following page). By moving around these coins or tokens, see if you can find a method for following the inspector's recommendations.

Teachable Moments Many problems and challenges in life have limitations. The amount of money available is limited. Or the total time to find the solution is finite. Or we only have so much of compound X to solve the problem. Learning how to work with insufficient resources, physical limitations, and other system constraints is a fact of life. Doing more with less requires efficiency and skill. In this case, Farmer Bob needs to do something different with the same amount of materials. And time is running out. The fair opens tomorrow!

This puzzle also celebrates alternative solutions to a given problem. Farmer Bob constructed his livestock pen system with one idea of how to populate each individual pen. The inspector offered an alternative concept with some merit. Rethinking his original concept is a mind-expanding task for Farmer Bob, and for you too.

Hints and Clues Start with a drawing of Farmer Bob's livestock pen system. There should be eight total pens available for the twenty sheep in his herd. Begin adding sheep one at a time, until you have a total of six sheep on each side.

Variations Try presenting this puzzle using a grid pattern large enough for 20 team members. Allow two minutes for group planning followed by 30 seconds to execute this plan. Allow additional two minute planning sessions, until the group succeeds in finding a workable solution.

As another variation, can you think of other livestock pen patterns or herd sizes that can be used to create a new version of this puzzle?

**Teambuilding
Puzzles**

27. Modern Hieroglyphics
Words that say one thing, and mean another

We hope you enjoy these word puzzles. One for every letter of the alphabet, and a few that are sure to challenge you and your team's linguistic skills.

Supplies   Pencils and copies of the puzzles below are all that is needed. You can present these puzzles via an overhead projector and transparencies, computer generated images, images or papers mounted to the walls or flash cards made from index cards. You can find additional puzzles in many newspapers or create your own by using the words associated with your organization, corporation or group. Challenge Works sells two sets of laminated word puzzle cards (www.challengeworks.com).

Teachable Moments   There is often a moment of insight, sometimes referred to as a B.F.O. (that's a Blinding Flash of the Obvious), between gazing at one of the word puzzles below and the realization of what it is trying to tell you. Decoding ciphers, ancient languages, secret messages, encrypted documents or in this case, very modern versions of hieroglyphics with a few modern pictograms thrown in for good measure, can be a fun way of stimulating the portion of the brain that deals with words, language and speech. While the rules that define the word puzzles below do not follow the standard rules of grammar, they do encourage participants to look carefully at each puzzle and interpret what the writer was hoping to convey. In a similar fashion, after decoding a few of these word puzzles, present your group with a paragraph from their own organization such as a mission statement, rules of conduct, vision statement, core values, policy information, letter of praise for a job well done, or some other written commentary. Next, have the group 'decode' this document in a similar fashion to the word puzzles below. By rewriting the document in their own words and creating clarity and discussion around the content, you will have raised their level of involvement with this information and greatly increased their retention of this material.

Mike Anderson mentions that he uses this activity in his classroom to discuss perspective (looking at things in a different way). Sometimes the answers are right in front of us, we just need to adjust our vision or perspective, to see it.

The ability to 'decipher' or to 'read' people is a valuable skill for both team members and team leaders. The field of Neural Linguistic Programming (NLP) focuses on this concept. For more information on this topic, read: NLP at Work: The Difference That Makes A Difference in Business, 2002, Sue Knight, Nicholas Brealey Publishing, New York, NY USA ISBN 1-8578-8302-0.

Teambuilding Puzzles

Variations Create word puzzles that include words and topics familiar to your organization, school, summer camp or corporation. Consider incorporating international words, phrases and themes for culturally diverse organizations.

Hints and Clues Try speaking each word puzzle out loud. Sometimes the solution is in the pronunciation.

A. GESG

B. <u>Traveling</u>
   CCCCCC

C. 2 UM + 2 UM

D. EILN PU

E. HIJKLMNO

F. YOU/JUST/ME

G. RLD

H. Often, Often,
   Often, Not, Not

I. <u>T I M E</u>
   abdefgh

J. _____ it

K. LOOK KOOL CROSSING

L. bit MORE

M. ME NT

O. ISSUE x 10

P. THEHANGRE

Q. nafish nafish

R.
| more more more |
| more   more |
| more more more |

S. WOOD
   BRIAN
   OHIO

T. **SOM**

U. 2THDK

V. <u>WIRE</u>
   Just

W. BAN ANA

X. SSSSSSSSSSC

Y. SIGHT LOVE
   SIGHT
   SIGHT

Z. Wheather

28. A Quick Study
Learning is Easy Once You Know the Rules

Here is a puzzle built with twenty-six of the most familiar things in our world: the letters of the alphabet. The goal is to write these letters in the same order as presented below after viewing them for only ten seconds. Ready, Go!

Part I   AEFHIKLMNTVWXYZ / COS / BDGJPQRU

Supplies You can perform this puzzle on a flip chart or blackboard or by using wooden letters (available at many craft stores) or mailbox letters (available at most hardware stores). You'll need two complete sets of letters to present this puzzle. You could also project the above collection of letters to a large audience with an overhead transparency projector or a computer generated graphics package and projector.

In order to reproduce the arrangement of letters presented above with insufficient time to memorize their location, you'll need to understand the sorting procedure responsible for this order. Once you know, it becomes quite simple to reproduce the arrangement shown.

For effect in a training presentation, show the entire class the arrangement of letters in Part I above. Inform the class that you plan to step outside the room with one other participant and teach them how to reproduce this order of letters with only a few seconds of training. After selecting a student to join you, inform them of the sorting procedure and return to the classroom, covering up the portion of the blackboard with the letters written upon it. The student will then write a new series of letters, which will (hopefully) be exactly the same as those shown above. Next, ask other students to try producing the letters in the same order.

Teachable Moments A Quick Study is an interesting exercise in perception. Which group members can find the small details that makes each ordering meaningful?

Finding similar qualities in ourselves and others is no small task. How do we find these qualities? We need to look carefully for them, just as we do with these puzzles.

Variations A second variation to this puzzle involves the following arrangement of letters:

Part II   ABDOPQR / CEFGHIJKLMNSTUVWXYZ

Teambuilding Puzzles

A third version of this puzzle includes the following arrangement of the alphabet:

Part III   CIJOSU / DGLPQTVX / ABFHKNRYZ / EMW

Can you think of other categories of alphabetic letters? What about a similar puzzle for the order of the numbers zero through nine, as shown below?

Part I   147 / 03689 / 25

Part II   04689 / 12357

Part III   01689 / 237 / 45

As a bonus puzzle, see if you can determine the rule or pattern to the following sequence of numbers:

8 5 4 9 1 7 6 3 2 0

Hints and Clues Rather than trying to memorize each letter or number in sequence, look for similarities or patterns between each group of characters.

"Judge of a man by his questions rather than by his answers."
Voltaire

"Live your questions now, and perhaps even without knowing it,
you will live along some distant day into your answers."
Rainer Maria Rilke

**Teambuilding
Puzzles**

29. Inclusive Sentences
Pangrams and Inclusion

Here are several unusual sentences. There is something unique about each one. Can you identify what it is?

The five boxing wizards jump quickly.

Pack my box with five dozen liquor jugs.

Waltz bad nymph, for quick jigs vex.

How piqued gymnasts can level six jumping razorback frogs.

We promptly judged antique ivory buckles for the next prize.

Sixty zippers were quickly picked from the woven jute bag.

Jack explained the quiz, but Mark still thought it was very difficult.

Supplies Pencil and paper are essential. A dictionary can be helpful.

Teachable Moments The phrases above fit into the category of pangramatical sentences. That is, sentences that contain every letter of the alphabet. Such sentences are helpful when viewing every possible letter configuration in a particular writing style or computer generated printing font. You can use the 'near miss' pangrams below as a quality control examination.

Pangrams can be used to explore inclusion topics. The need for everyone to be a part of the team or to have their own chance to be heard is important.

Variations See if you can create your own pangramatical sentence. If you can complete the task using less than 40 letters and create a reasonable sounding sentence, you have achieved 'master' status.

A true pangram contains every letter of the alphabet. Here are a few 'near miss' pangrams. See if you can spot the missing letter(s) in each sentence.

The quick brown fox jumped over the lazy dog.

Cracking a few dozen boxes of very yellow maps is quite tough.

We had a multiple choice quiz on the Egyptian Sphinx just after breakfast

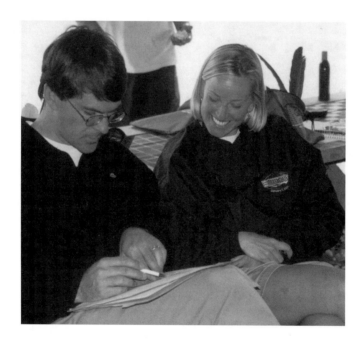

Hints and Clues To spot a true pangram, look for every letter of the alphabet. There is even a category for pangrams in the Guinness Book of World Records.

Palindromes Just For Fun

Never Odd Or Even!

 Here are a few unusual sentences that I learned during my college years from one of my favorite teaching assistants, TA Ergera Semordi Lap, or TA Lap as he signed every paper he graded. There is something unique about each one. Can you identify what it is?

Doc note, I dissent. A fast never prevents a fatness. I diet on cod.
Attributed to James Michie

A man, a plan, a canal - Panama!
Attributed to Leigh Mercer

Madam, I'm Adam.

Mr. Owl ate my metal worm.

Go deliver a dare, vile dog!

May a moody baby doom a yam?

Do geese see God?

Some men interpret nine memos.

Able was I, ere I saw Elba.

Too bad, I hid a boot.

Supplies Pencil and paper are essential. A dictionary or thesaurus may also be helpful.

Teachable Moments The sentences above fit into a category known as palindromes. Words which form the same sentence forwards AND backwards. Punctuation marks are not 'counted' as characters in this unique alphabetical modification technique. Can you design your own palindromes?

Variations In addition to sentences that are identical forwards and backwards, some individual words are also reversible (Madam, Pop, Sis). How many more can you identify? Next, can you identify words which look the same rightside up as they do when they are rotated about a line horizontally through their center. For example, in the illustration below CODE becomes CODE. Can you identify other words that also demonstrate this result when rotated?

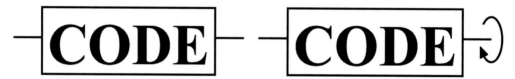

The Tide Comes In In this version of alphabet modification, we are looking for words which change into other words when they are partially submerged in water, and the reflection of their upper half becomes their new lower half. For example, the word CODE from above remains CODE when submerged to the midpoint. The word ROY however, becomes BOX. The lower portion of each word is seen as the reflection of the upper portion. In our final word rotation, the word TOMATO remains TOMATO when rotated about a line vertically through the center. How many other words, including foreign language words, can you identify that can also be rotated in this manner?

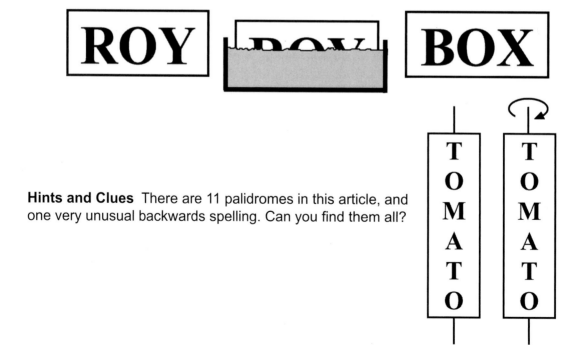

Hints and Clues There are 11 palidromes in this article, and one very unusual backwards spelling. Can you find them all?

31. Magic Carpet
Setting Goals and Working Together as a Team

What could be better than a magic carpet ride with a built-in challenge? And with this version of Magic Carpet, you can accommodate ANY size group.

Our puzzle begins by placing several plastic tarps, shower curtains or table cloths near each other, but not overlapping, on the floor. Invite teams of six to nine participants to stand on each Magic Carpet. The challenge is for each team to flip their carpet over to the other side, with the following two restrictions:

1. You cannot lift anyone up off the ground.
2. You or any part of your body cannot touch the floor.

Supplies You'll need one plastic tarp, shower curtain or table cloth for each group of six to nine participants. Select tarps that are approximately 5 feet (1.5 meters) square. For goal setting, you'll also need ball-point pens, masking tape and two flip-chart pages or large posterboards.

Teachable Moments   If you precede Magic Carpet with a competitive activity, or develop a substantial amount of team spirit for each Magic Carpet team, you'll create an interesting result. Teams often incorrectly interpret the second restriction above as: You cannot step off the Magic Carpet. In reality, you could have always collaborated with other teams, but most groups do not. This behavior, competition rather than collaboration, is in itself a teachable moment worth discussing.

Some facilitators like to call this activity 'Turning Over a New Leaf' which provides teachable moments related to identifying negative behaviors and positive ones to replace them.

When the Magic Carpet is flipped over, you could have a useful quotation, message, illustration, corporate value statement or symbol drawn on the opposite side. The discussion of this information can lead to its own teachable moment.

Variations   One outstanding variation of Magic Carpet incorporates goal setting and requires some initial work before flipping over the carpet. When your group first approaches their Magic Carpet, provide masking tape and ball-point pens so that every member of the team can write a goal they have on the tape and firmly attach this goal to the surface of the plastic tarp. Then invite everyone to read aloud the information they have written.

Next, turn over the carpet and pass out additional masking tape. On this side, invite each person to write what they perceive the barriers or obstacles might be to achieving the goal they shared on the other side. Again, invite everyone to share their views aloud.

Now ask the group to step onto the Magic Carpet. They will be on the barrier side. The challenge is for the group to make it to their goals by successfully flipping the Magic Carpet over while following the two rules given above.

When completed, draw the word 'Goals' on one flip chart page, and 'Barriers' on another. Invite participants to place their masking tape goals and barriers on the appropriate pages.

I know of one summer camp director who uses Magic Carpet during his week long staff training program every year. During the goal setting portion, he learns what each of his staff members would like to achieve to have a great summer. And the barrier portion helps his camp board identify potential areas of improvement for the camp. When finished with this activity, he captures the goals and barriers on flip charts and keeps these posted on his office door as a reminder of what his staff needs to be successful and the challenges that need to be overcome.

Hints and Clues   Flipping over a Magic Carpet with many people on it can be quite a challenge. Encourage teams to look around and identify any resources that could assist them in the process.

"Directions are rules that can be changed."

32. Pencil Pushers
Physically Challenging Puzzles

Here is a challenge that really moves. If your audience needs to use their physical abilities in a positive manner or burn off a little extra energy, this puzzle should do the trick. Don't be fooled, this puzzle can be very physically challenging.

A rope line is the starting boundary. The challenge is for teams of two to four participants to push a new, unsharpened pencil over the line and across the floor, making contact with only their hands on the floor. This challenge typically results in the group forming some type of human bridge, with the first person's feet just behind the line and other team members climbing over them as they extend the bridge. The winners are those that push the pencil the furthest distance and are still able to return behind the line without touching the floor in front of the line with anything but their hands.

Supplies You'll need a rope or some masking tape to create the starting boundary and a large, open, flat space. You'll also need one new, unsharpened pencil for each team.

Teachable Moments   Muscles alone are not enough to succeed in this challenge. Your team is going to need a good plan, endurance and teamwork.

Variations You can substitute other safe objects, such as a plastic cup of water or a stuffed toy animal. You can also reverse the challenge and place objects at a distance from the boundary line. Those teams which can recover an object can keep it. This second version explores goal setting, creative problem solving, teamwork and getting the job done.

Hints and Clues What technique would cover the maximum distance in the least amount of time?

33. Bite The Bag
Physically Challenging Puzzles from the Pub

It isn't so surprising that a number of our favorite puzzles, challenges and stunts have all made the rounds in various social gatherings. You can find puzzles showing up at corporate functions, on the jobsite, at family picnics, and occasionally even at the local pub. Here is one that we learned from some friends in the UK.

Place a clean paper sack, fully opened, onto the floor, as shown in our illustration. One member of the team at a time approaches the sack and bends over to pick up the sack with their teeth. That's right, their TEETH. The only part of their body which can touch the floor are their feet. After picking up the sack, that team member tears off the portion of the bag they contacted with their teeth, leaving a slightly smaller bag for the next player to elevate.

Supplies You will need several new paper sacks. You can use the lunchbag size, or the brown paper bags used in grocery stores. Plastic bags are not recommended.

Teachable Moments Knowing your own abilities and limitations is valuable. And while you can work on your problem solving and balancing skills with this puzzle, it is mostly for fun.

Consider placing small pieces of paper into the bag. These can be individual goals, team assets or other group reflections written by each member of the group.

As a debriefing topic, ask the group if there is a relationship between the ability and flexibility of each team member and the ability, flexibility and success of the team.

Variations If your team enjoys this type of physical challenge, you could try limbo dancing. You'll also find some other interesting tricks and stunts in the book: Bet You Can't Do This! - Impossible Tricks to Astound Your Friends, 2002, Sandy Ransford, Macmillan Children's Books, London, UK ISBN 0-330-39772-9 Fun stunts, tricks and challenges.

Hints and Clues No trick here, this challenge just requires problem solving skills, flexibility and balance.

Learning 'the rules of the game' is an important skill in life. By observing a situation, we gather knowledge and hopefully the ability to analyze the situation and understand what is happening. Here is a challenge where the opportunity is not only to learn the game, but to discover the 'key' to winning every time.

Begin by placing 15 objects in a straight line on a table or the ground. Ask for a volunteer to play against you. Consider each of these objects as the various courses of a 15 course meal. The final plate however, is not your favorite. In fact, you both know in advance that you don't want to have to eat that course. The challenge becomes making the other person choose that plate. During every turn, you can choose one, two or three plates (objects). Then the other person can choose one, two or three, and so on. The game continues until the last plate is taken.

Supplies   You'll need fifteen objects. Coins, spoons, checkers, playing cards, marbles, stones or any other convenient objects will do.

Teachable Moments   Consider the following event that happened to our friend Kirk Weisler. Kirk was invited to assist with a wilderness therapy program, in January, in a remote area of the Rocky Mountains. After a long travel by four wheel drive vehicle, snowmobile, and eventually snowshoes, Kirk and a replacement set of counselors met up with a dozen or so youth-at-risk participants of the program. While the outgoing counselors were packing up to leave, Kirk sensed the need to bond the new counselors with the young 'I'm too cool for you' program participants. He gathered 15 stones and placed them on a table in the somewhat cramped main lodge. "I've got a game," he said, "and it takes knowledge and skill. Who wants to play?" One of the young participants accepted Kirk's offer, and sat down opposite him at the table. Kirk explained the rules of the challenge (just like Version I above), and in the first round, Kirk won (no surprise there). At this point, a few of the other participants began to gather around and watch the game. Round two, Kirk wins again. But this time, there is some conversation amongst the participants. Round three, Kirk wins again. But something is definitely happening. At this point, Kirk asks the group, "so why do I win, every time?" After a brief discussion and various comments from the group, both respectful and some less than, someone offered, "you know something we don't." Bingo, thought Kirk, now is the time for a teachable moment. "Who else around here knows things that you don't right now?" Kirk asked. Eventually the counselors were identified. "The good news here," said Kirk, "is that I want you to be able to win at this game. I <u>want</u> you to beat me. I want you to be able to win, <u>every time</u>. All you need is some knowledge. Knowledge is power, and I want you to have some. Now these counselors that are here with you, they have some knowledge too, and the really great news is, they want to share it with you. They want you to win in the biggest game of all, life itself." At this point, Kirk explained that there were 'key' objects in this game, and that those who controlled those 'keys' controlled the outcome of the game. He also talked about keys to life, and how they controlled the outcome of that 'game.' Knowledge is power. Get some!

Variations In each of these versions, you can 'change the rules' by either trying to control the last object or trying not to receive it. Changing the number of objects also changes the 'key' objects needed for control. Changing the number of choices during each turn also affects the 'key' objects needed for control. You can also change the configuration of the placement of the objects (spirals, straight lines, arcs, pyramids, geometric shapes, or even a corporate logo or symbol).

Hints and Clues Like any magic or sleight of hand trick, repetition is a good technique for testing your analysis of the situation. With each repeating performance, you can gather a few more clues, test a few more hypotheses, increase your knowledge of the puzzle, and refine your guess of which objects are 'keys' to control the outcome of the game.

You can find a similar activity, entitled Knowledge is Power in the book: Executive Marbles and Other Teambuilding Activities, 1998, Sam Sikes, Learning Unlimited, Tulsa, OK USA ISBN 0-9646541-2-1

"As long as anyone believes that his ideal and purpose is outside him, that it is above the clouds, in the past or in the future, he will go outside himself and seek fulfillment where it cannot be found. He will look for solutions and answers at every point except where they can be found—in himself."
Erich Frohm

35. The Tower of Hanoi
How do your team's problem solving skills stack up?

The Tower of Hanoi is also known as The Tower of Brahma or the Tower of Burma. One puzzle, with (at least) three different names. In celebration of these three different names, we have three variations of this puzzle for you.

The challenge of the Tower of Hanoi is to move the entire stack of circular disks from one peg to another. At no time are you allowed to place a larger diameter disk on top of a smaller diameter disk.

Supplies You'll need several disks, cans, buckets or tires and three posts. See the Variation section below for other possibilities.

Teachable Moments You can use the Tower of Hanoi to illustrate that 'adding just one more' can substantially increase the effort required. As you can see from the calculations provided in the solution section of this book, each additional disk roughly doubles the number of moves required to complete the task. You can also measure the cost of errors and mistakes, by measuring the actual performance of a group compared to the theoretical number of moves calculated from the equation found in the solution section of this book.

Variations For challenge course programs, or audiences that appreciate an element of physical activity, you can create the Tower of Hanoi from telephone poles or wooden posts and various sizes of tires.

Instead of using circular disks and wooden posts, you can modify this puzzle to a new form by using several sizes of tin cans or buckets and three short wooden posts. In this version, you can either stack smaller cans on top of larger ones, or conceal smaller cans beneath larger ones. The concealment approach, shown here, creates a puzzle with a higher level of difficulty.

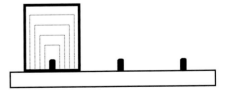

You can increase the difficulty level of this activity by increasing the number of circular disks to be transferred. As shown on the solutions page, each additional disk effectively doubles the number of moves required.

You can allow your team to freely converse during an initial planning stage, but then limit communication during the movement of the disks.

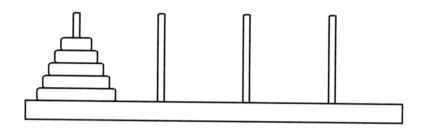

What would happen to the number of moves required if you add another post? Does this reduce or increase the number of moves required ?

Hints and Clues Begin with three disks before increasing to four, five, six or more.

The Mathematics Behind the Movement Bonus Question If you move one disk, every five seconds, how long would it take to move a stack of ten disks?

"Everyone who achieves success in a geat venture, solved each
problem as they came to it. They helped themselves. And they were
helped through powers known and unknown to them at the time
they set out on their voyage. They kept going
regardless of the obstacles they met.
Clement Stone

36. Just Passing Through
Making the most of minimal resources

This is a great activity to present first to individuals, and then to teams. Synergy, collaboration and ultimately a successful team effort are only an index card and a pair of scissors away.

The challenge of Just Passing Through is to create an opening in an index card big enough for any person to pass completely through, without further damage to the card. You can begin this puzzle as an individual challenge and then encourage participants to collaborate and work together to create the best concepts possible.

Supplies You will need an index card and a pair of school scissors for each person or team.

Teachable Moments Even small things can be made bigger, if you just know how. When the average person reads this challenge and then looks at the index card, their reaction is often "No way!" Activities that look impossible, but are not, are excellent methods for expanding our horizons. This is also a useful activity for teaching the concept of making do with what you have or making a little go a long way. Another teachable moment could be that in order to solve some challenges, we have to expand our thinking, just as the index card needed to expand.

Variations You can try this same activity with a letter size piece of paper and nothing else. Invite participants to use their hands to tear the paper as necessary. Or consider using a standard piece of writing paper and challenging the group to create an opening big enough to drive a car through!

Hints and Clues Think about geodesic spheres (Hoberman spheres) and toys that expand and contract. How could you create a similar function in a piece of paper?

Plus Est en Vous.

Which roughly translates to
"you've got more in you than you think!"

The motto of Kurt Hahn's Gordonstoun School

37. Pipe Chimes
A Musical Challenge

One of several multiple intelligences identified to date (see the reference below for more information on this subject) is the musical learning style. Another is the mathematical/logical learning style. Here is an activity that allows both of these skills to emerge from your team.

For starters, all the information you need is right here to be able to calculate and build your own set of musical pipe chimes from materials that are very inexpensive. Our puzzle begins with some mathematical calculations. Mathematical formulas are a bit like baking recipes. If you put all the right stuff in, in the right order, and follow the instructions, you end up with a final product that is just what you hoped for. The mathematical formula for calculating the length of pipes necessary to produce the middle octave of a piano is derived from free vibration beam theory and based upon what musicians refer to as the American Standard Pitch (A4 = 440 Hz).

$$\text{Pipe Length (inches)} = ((\text{Mode Factor}^2 * g * E * I)/(w * f^2))^{(1/4)}$$

The following 'ingredients' are necessary for the formula above:

Mode Factor = 3.58, for the fundamental mode, which is generally the primary and loudest mode

g = the acceleration due to gravity, which is standardly accepted as 386 inches/second^2

E = the modulus of elasticity of the pipe material. For steel, this number is 30,000,000 pounds per square inch.

I = the moment of inertia, an engineering calculation that is calculated from the shape and area of the cross section of the piping used. For a circular pipe, $I = Pi * (OD^4 - ID^4)/64$, where Pi is the mathematical quantity Pi, which equals 3.1416, OD is the outside diameter of the pipe (in inches) and ID is the inside diameter of the pipe (also in inches).

w = the weight per unit length of the material the pipe is made from. In this case, pounds per inch of length. For steel, this value is calculated by dividing the density of steel with the cross sectional area of the pipe. w(steel) = 0.0235 pounds per inch of length.

f = the frequency of pipe chime desired. This number can be found in musical and engineering texts that define pitch. In the case of the pipe chimes presented here, the A4 note, found just below Middle C on a standard piano, has a frequency of 440 cycles per second.

The results from the above equation, for the middle octave frequencies of a piano, are:

Musical Note	Length (inches)	Length (millimeters)
A4	19.60	497.8
A#	19.04	483.6
B	18.50	469.9
C	17.97	456.5
C#	17.46	443.5
D	16.96	430.9
D#	16.48	418.6
E	16.01	406.7
F	15.55	395.1
F#	15.11	383.8
G	14.68	372.9
G#	14.26	362.3
A5	13.86	352.0

Supplies Electrical conduit, which can be inexpensively purchased at most larger hardware stores or electrical supply dealers is perfect for making a set of pipe chimes. It comes in 10 foot (3 meter) lengths. Engineering values for standard 1/2" electrical steel conduit (which oddly enough has an outside diameter of 11/16" inch) has been used to calculate the pipe chime lengths provided here. You will need 2 pieces of 10 foot long 1/2" electrical steel conduit to make the pipes calculated above. We recommend cutting these pipes with a standard pipe cutting tool (found at most hardware stores). This tool cuts easily and does not leave the sharp edge that a hack saw will produce. After cutting each pipe to length, drill a hole through each pipe near the top end and pass a string through these holes. Hold each pipe by this string loop and strike with a spoon or nail to produce a tone.

Teachable Moments   Here is an opportunity to explore the skills, talents, and learning styles available from different members of your team. In many cases, different members of the team provide leadership for mathematical calculations and musical activities than might provide leadership for a physical challenge, or visual spatial puzzle, or interpersonal challenge. We recommend that you read the Thomas Armstrong book on utilizing multiple intelligences in the classroom (and also in corporate settings), shown below, to assist you in planning activities that explore the complete expanse of learning styles. This book will provide a variety of new techniques for you to present activities to your audiences.

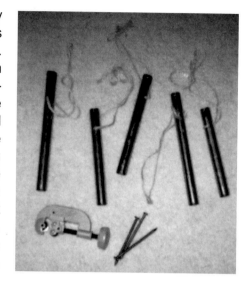

Variations Rather than calculating the lengths of pipes you'll need to complete a musical octave, you can have your team cut tubes at random lengths. Or, you can provide tubes with no musical designation or identification, and ask the group to sort out which ones the will need to perform a specific piece of music. This is another opportunity for exploring the 'Good to Great' (see below) book information mentioned in activity #8, Archimedes Puzzle, earlier in this book.

If you enjoy the musical nature of this activity, but not the complication of making the pipe chimes, you can present a slightly different challenge to your group. After a meal, provide each table with a pitcher filled with water, 8-12 glasses and the same number of spoons. Give each table group 10 minutes to 'create a symphony' using the water to tune each glass to a respectable pitch. Then ask each group to perform their musical creation for the rest of the group.

You can also tune the old fashioned glass soda pop bottles with water and a pitch pipe (available at musical instrument stores). These bottles can be played by tapping with a spoon or by blowing air over the mouth of each bottle.

Finally, you can make your own collection of tuned plastic tubes (which produce sound waves when you hit them against your palm), from the plastic golf club bag inserts available at sporting good stores or golf supply centers. For more information about tuned tubes, visit www.boomwhackers.com.

Hints and Clues The ability to 'hear' relative pitch and to create and perform music is not a universal human characteristic. But practice does improve this ability. Allow those members of the group with musical experience and ability to share their knowledge with this activity. The formula presented above is also attractive to only a minority of most groups. Again, allow those participants that have ability in this arena to share their knowledge and skill. Finally, making music should be fun. Enjoy the practice, and the performance.

A Few Words About Multiple Intelligences

The work of Howard Gardner, Thomas Armstrong and others has suggested that there are a variety of styles by which individuals come to grasp information, and in fact, learn. At present, eight styles or talents have been identified, and these include: Logical Mathematical, Bodily Kinesthetic, Visual Spatial, Linguistic, Musical, Interpersonal - Knowledge of Others, Intrapersonal - Knowledge of Self and Natural Environmental. Additional authors have proposed additional intelligences, including: Emotional Intelligence, Spiritual, Mechanical Aptitude, and Humor. For many educators and trainers, investigating these learning styles, although interesting, is difficult given a standardized curriculum, and impossible given the time available to explore such techniques. Luckily, many of the techniques explained in this book make exploring these various learning styles easy and fun. There is even a listing of various puzzles and challenges in this book that match each learning style at the end of this article. In the meantime, here are a few examples of various attributes of each learning style as they relate to the information presented in this book.

Intelligence or Talent	Teambuilding Puzzles Learning Opportunity
Logical-Mathematical	Problem solving skills, analysis, planning
Bodily-Kinesthetic	Hands-on learning, physical activities, movement
Visual-Spatial	Map reading, visualizing multiple solutions
Linguistic	Clear expression, reading instructions, debriefing
Musical	Rhythm, timing, sounds of nature
Interpersonal - Knowledge of Others	Understanding, empathy, coaching, teamwork
Intrapersonal - Knowledge of Self	Self analysis, relating, journaling, self reflection
Natural-Environmental	Connection to the outdoor setting, exploring

Teambuilding Puzzles

Intelligence	Category	Puzzles that explore this intelligence or talent
Mathematical	Quantification	Nothing Can Divide Us, Mathematical Magic, Pipe Chimes
Kinesthetic	Movement	Corks, Magic Carpet, Pencil Pushers, Bite the Bag
Visual	Artistic	2B or Knot 2B, Arrowheads, Not Knots
Linguistic	Speech	Tongue Twisters, Modern Hieroglyphics, I'm In Games
Musical	Rhythm	Pipe Chimes, Concentration
Interpersonal	Knowing Others	Sharing Connection, Circle of Connection
Intrapersonal	Knowledge of Self	Labyrinth (self reflection)
Natural World	Environmental	Adaptation or Extinction, The Bridge

Suggested Reading

Multiple Intelligences in the Classroom, 2000, Thomas Armstrong, ASCD Alexandria, Virginia USA ISBN 0-87120-376-6 This book provides examples for designing your own curriculum with multiple learning strategies.

7 Kinds of Smart - Identifying and Developing Your Multiple Intelligences, 1999, Thomas Armstrong, Plume, New York, NY USA ISBN 0-452-28137-7.

Good to Great - Why Some Companies Make the Leap...and Others Don't, 2001, Jim Collins, Harper Collins, New York, NY USA ISBN 0-06-662099-6.

"If a problem has no solution, it may not be a problem,
but a fact - not to be solved, but to be coped with over time."
Shimon Peres

"If you can solve your problem, then what is the need of worrying?
If you cannot solve it, then what is the use of worrying?"
Shantideva

Sometimes our first answer to a puzzle, riddle or challenge is good, but not necessarily the optimal or best solution. Brainstorming sessions sometimes come to an abrupt halt the moment a workable suggestion is made. Here is a puzzle that requires multiple working solutions and encourages going beyond the first workable solution.

Your team's challenge is to lift the pyramidal structure described below three times into the air, using one of the following objects for each attempt: a length of rope, a stick and a playground ball. You cannot touch the wooden pyramid with your hands or body in any way, only individually with each of the three objects. Thanks to Tim Borton for sharing this interesting puzzle.

Supplies The pyramidal structure is composed of three thin wooden boards, 1 inch by 2 inches by three feet long (25 mm by 51 mm by 1 meter long). Two of the boards have been hinged together at the top, and tipped slightly to the side. The third board is used to hold these hinged boards up, forming a pyramid as shown in the illustration. A piece of flexible rope, about 3 feet (1 meter) long is the first prop, followed by a standard dowel rod, also 3 feet (1 meter) long. Finally, for the third prop, a playground ball about the size of a volleyball or soccer ball (although a football will also work) is required.

Teachable Moments Once you have one workable solution, don't stop. Some of the most elegant solutions might be just around the corner. Consider this quotation attributed to R. Buckminster Fuller:

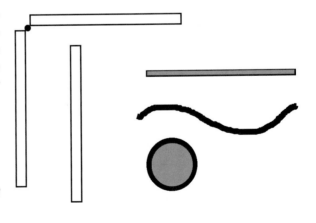

*When I'm working on a problem, I
never think about beauty.
I think only how to solve the problem.
But when I have finished, if the solution
is not beautiful,
I know it is wrong.*

Variations Consider other interesting props such as a wooden spoon, a newspaper, a glass of water, a computer diskette or a paperclip for this challenge.

Hints and Clues

If the only tool you have is a hammer, you tend to see every problem as a nail.

Abraham Maslow

Maslow's quotation has an interesting translation for this puzzle.

"If the only tools you have are a rope, a stick, and a ball, search for solutions that use each of these three props."

"The significant problems we have cannot be solved at the same level of thinking with which we created them."

Albert Einstein

Putting the Right Pieces Together

The Great Pyramids of Egypt required hundreds of years and thousands of workers to complete. Here are a few simple pyramids that your team can assemble in much less time.

The Great Golf Ball Pyramids are four levels high, contain twenty balls, are assembled in four or five pieces, and can be very challenging to assemble. Begin the challenge by presenting the group with the pyramid already assembled. We've built some wooden bases to hold and transport our whiffle ball pyramids. Next, turn the base over, and spill the pyramid into its four or five distinct pieces. Finally, invite the group to reassemble the pyramid.

Supplies You'll need 20 balls for the four level pyramids shown. We recommend using whiffle golfballs, baseballs or softballs, and joining them together with plastic cable ties (available at most hardware stores). These pyramids will be light weight, moistureproof, and durable. Join the balls together in the four shapes shown below.

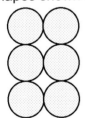
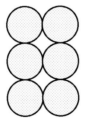
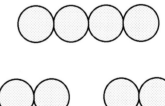

Teachable Moments You can use the balls shown above to create pyramids as a personal challenge by timing participants as they attempt to individually assemble their own pyramid. After recording the time of their first attempt, allow them additional trials and also record these times. The goal is not necessarily to have the best time, but rather to look at how much improvement is possible by practicing and learning from previous mistakes.

As a team challenge, you can enlist half of the team as mentors or coaches who must verbally instruct a partner in assembling the pyramid, but not touch any of the balls themselves.

Variations You can alter the total number of balls in a pyramid from four balls for a two level pyramid, to ten balls for three levels, to twenty balls for four levels, and even thirty-five balls for a five level pyramid. The dissection of the pyramid into various collections of ball shapes is almost limitless, so you can group two, three, four and more balls together to make your own unique pyramid puzzle. You can also vary the size of the balls used from ping pong balls to whiffle softballs and beyond. For example, you can use inflatable beach balls and fasten these together with double sided tape.

Hints and Clues See if you can identify the lines of symmetry in a pyramid. That is, where could you cut the pyramid in half and produce two identical pieces?

For a mathematical investigation of stacking balls, we invite you to read:

Kepler's Conjecture - How some of the greatest minds in history helped solve one of the oldest math problems in the world, 2003, George G. Szpiro, John Wiley & Sons, Hoboken, NJ USA ISBN 0-471-08601-0

"Indecision may or may not be my problem."
Jimmy Buffett

"Every big problem was at one time a wee disturbance."

*"Creativity can solve almost any problem. The creative act,
the defeat of habit by originality, overcomes everything."*
George Lois

Here are two templates for creating your own pyramid puzzles from paper. Two of the first pieces will form a tetrahedron (pyramid). Three of the second pyramidal pieces will form a cube. Provide these three-dimensional geometric pieces to teams and ask them to create the appropriate shape.

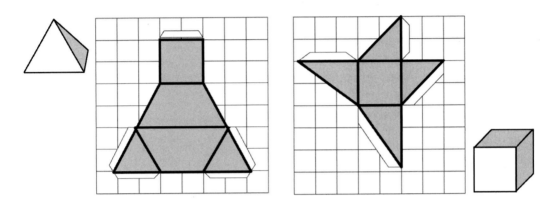

Supplies You'll need several pieces of paper, a pair of scissors or art knife, a straightedge ruler, a pencil or pen and adhesive tape or glue. You may want to make your first pyramid or cube pieces directly from graph paper. The square in each design above works well when it is exactly 2 inches (about 50 mm) square. The pyramid piece on the left uses 60 degree angles for each of the slanting sides. The white tabs can be included if you wish to glue your pyramids together. (You may copy & enlarge the graphic for use.)

Teachable Moments Dividing any big job into smaller pieces is never easy. Neither is completing a big job from pieces you aren't sure will work to begin with.

If you place key words, concepts, or appropriate quotations on each side of the pieces above, you can create teachable moments as participants attempt to place each word near another related word or phrase. You can also write clues on the exteriors of each puzzle piece to assist puzzlers in solving them.

Variations In addition to these simple three-dimensional shapes, you can try dissecting other three-dimensional paper objects. Several of the other puzzles in this book are also 'dissection' puzzles. See puzzle #14, T.H.E. Puzzle; puzzle # 7, Tangrams; puzzle #8, Archimedes Puzzle; puzzle #39, The Great Golf Ball Pyramids, and puzzle #45, Pentominoes.

Hints and Clues Look for lines of symmetry in each three-dimensional object.

41. SNAP!
Taking the Stress Out of the Job

**Teambuilding
Puzzles**

Here is a kinesthetic challenge with a quantifiable result.

With the entire group holding on with both hands to a circular band of sewing elastic, ask them to stand over a standard archery (bulls-eye) target and pull on the elastic until it is stretched to the limit. Participants are asked to keep their feet in this same position throughout each of the following attempts.

We believe that any group working as a team should have the split second timing skills to coordinate their efforts. In this case, if everyone lets go at exactly the same time, the elastic band will snap to the center of the circle and fall directly on the central ring of the bulls-eye. The actual location of the elastic band's landing is a quantifiable measurement of the team's performance. So, on the count of three, we are all going to let go. Ready? One, two, three!

Supplies A length of 3/4" (18-20 mm) sewing elastic, available at most fabric and sewing stores. Each style of elastic stretches differently, but you'll need about 6 feet (2 meters) for a group of 8-12 participants. We do not recommend using shock (bungie) cord for this activity. Sewing elastic has substantially less spring force than bungie cord and gets the job done with less energy. You may want to have a flip-chart or blackboard available for recording various stressors identified by the group during the post-activity discussion period.

Teachable Moments Never underestimate how stress can affect the productivity and effort of a group. By removing some of the tension (stress) in the elastic band, the team may be better able to focus on the task and perform at a higher rate of success. What are some of the stressors in your environment that are affecting the outcome of your work, your studies, or your life?

Hints and Clues Encourage participants to identify factors that contribute to errors. Brainstorm and try various techniques proposed by members of the group.

Is it possible to solve this challenge? Yes, but it takes a very rare group to do so. Why do it then? Offer this activity BECAUSE it is difficult to complete successfully. If your groups typically solve these puzzles quickly and easily, this is your chance to present a greater challenge. It is exactly this type of challenge that will require higher levels of team skills, patience, tolerance and the ability to handle frustration. Use this style of puzzle to break through with your group to a higher level of teamwork. You can also use this opportunity to discuss the group's feelings toward lack of success with a task.

Variations Instead of a bulls-eye target, a bucket or other container can be placed in the center of the group to serve as a destination target. For smaller groups or partners, consider using a standard rubber band for the elastic and a large paper cup as the target.

"If human beings are perceived as potentials rather than problems, as possessing strengths instead of weaknesses, as unlimited rather than dull and unresponsive, then they thrive and grow to their capabilities."
Bob Conklin

"Nothing in the world can take the place of Persistence. Talent will not;nothing is more common than unsuccessful men with talent. Genius will not;unrewarded genius is almost a proverb. Education will not; the world isfull of educated derelicts. Persistence and determination alone areomnipotent. The slogan "Press On' has solved and always will solve the problems of the human race."
Calvin Collidge

42. Blind Square
Working Together With Limited Vision

Leadership is essential, especially when your team has limited vision. Here is an activity that is simple to explain, but amazingly difficult to perform with an entire team. Thanks to Karl Rohnke for sharing this now classic team activity.

The activity begins with the facilitator inviting each member of the team to place a blindfold over their eyes. Next, they are informed that their first task is to find something in the area with which they can build a perfect square. A rope has been placed nearby.

After finding the rope, each member of the group is instructed to maintain contact with the rope at all times as they attempt to create a perfect square.

Supplies A blindfold for each member of the group. A flat, grassy area outdoors, or a flat carpeted floorspace indoors, with no obstacles. One continuous long rope, 50-100 feet long, depending upon the number of team members, and the size of the space or room.

Teachable Moments Because of the blindfolded nature of this activity, there are many teachable moments related to 'sharing the vision.' Here are a few others:

The difference between knowing the vision and actually contributing to making the vision real is easily explored in the Blind Square. Everyone knows what a square is. They can draw one. They can describe the geometrical details (four equal sides, four equal 90 degree angles). But the reality of actually communicating and creating a square, while blindfolded, is very difficult. This topic opens the door to meaningful conversations about other core values or vision statements that participants may understand, but ultimately find difficult to make a contribution towards.

The issue of who has power and how this power is used often surfaces in The Blind Square. Many times, team members standing at corner locations control more of the activity, and occasionally the conversation, than participants standing at less key positions. Discussion of empowerment, leadership styles, inclusion and buy-in are possible here.

Hints and Clues Creating four equal lengths of rope can be accomplished by folding the rope in half twice and placing a person at each of these corner locations.

If you enjoy this style of rope challenge, you might also enjoy the new collection of adventure-based and active learning equipment found in the Ropework & Ropeplay Kit, from Teamwork & Teamplay. This kit includes equipment to lead more than 400 different team activities and challenges, plus a copy of the Book on Raccoon Circles and an extensive Ropework & Ropeplay Facilitator Guide. For more infomration about the kit, visit www.training-wheels.com or call 1-888-553-0147.

You will also find a substantial collection of rope related challenges in the POSSIBLESbag, from Chris Cavert and FUNdoing. (www.fundoing.com)

For even more activities, Tom Heck created a useful collection of team activities that you can present with only a shoelace. (www.teachmeteamwork.com)

43. Shape Up
Learning the Ropes Together

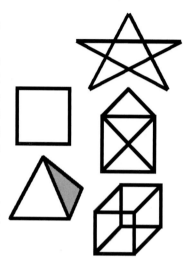

Learn how to use a 50 foot long piece of rope to explore leadership issues with your team.

Present a long rope to your team and invite everyone to connect together by holding the rope. Ask the participant standing near the ends of rope to tie these ends together with a knot. The facilitator then shows one person in the group a picture of the first geometric shape. Their duty is to lead their group in creating this shape using the rope. A discussion of their technique and leadership takes places after each shape.

After several individual leaders have assisted the group, show the group the picture (shared vision), and ask them to work together to reproduce it with the rope.

Supplies You'll need a long rope for this activity. Fifty feet (15 meters) is sufficient for group sizes up to 25 participants. It is also helpful to have large illustrations of the shapes you wish for the group to create.

Teachable Moments You can explore leadership styles, communication, empowerment and coaching using Shape Up. You can also critique each leader with the categories of 'effective' and 'efficient.'

Variations Geometric shapes can be two-dimensional (easier) or three dimensional (more difficult). You can vary the length of the rope. For example, consider using a segment of cord only 10 feet (3 meters) long. This will certainly bring the group closer together. You could also use a thin string that breaks easily if the group encounters any stress.

You can try to replicate any line art shape or pattern. A square is easy compared to a five sided star. Three dimensional shapes, like the pyramid and the cube, take even more effort.

You can also impose additional 'red tape,' rules and restrictions. For example, create the five sided star or house shape without crossing any lines. This additional level of scrutiny requires additional group problem solving beyond the first solution identified.

If you enjoyed puzzle #42 Blind Square, this puzzle requires some of the same skills and is in fact the 'unblind' version of puzzle #42, with a few additional shapes to create.

Hints and Clues Once you establish a fixed point on the geometric design, it is a bit easier for other members of the group to see where they should move.

44. Corporate Maze
Finding the Right Path as a Team

Here is the perfect puzzle for exploring issues of competition vs. collaboration. You will need two facilitators, one for each team, for this puzzling activity.

The Corporate Maze is a puzzle for two teams. Starting on opposite sides of the maze, each team attempts to identify their correct path through the maze to the other side. Participants choose a space to step into, and a facilitator informs them if this space is on the correct path or not.

Additional information and a self-directed information sheet are provided at the end of this activity description, along with an example path through the maze (for the facilitator's eyes only).

Supplies You will need an 8x8 grid for the Corporate Maze. You can build your own grid on-site, using masking tape on the floor or by drawing grid lines on a plastic tablecloth, tarp or large piece of fabric. You can also purchase the Corporate Maze Grid from Robertson Harness at 702-564-4286 or at www.robertsonharness.com.

Teachable Moments One of the most significant moments in The Corporate Maze occurs when teams realize that the correct path through the maze is <u>exactly the same for both teams</u>! They just happen to start and end at different locations.

You can also explore how a competitive environment directs the thinking of everyone on the team. Finally, consider discussing win-win, win-lose and lose-lose scenarios with this activity.

Variations One of our favorite alternative grid activities is an interesting way of demonstrating the power of teamwork. This activity is called 'Chasing Sheep.' We begin with two volunteers to be the sheep. Two additional volunteers are the farmers. The challenge begins as shown in the grid below. The farmers have the first move, followed by the sheep. Both farmers and sheep can move one step horizontally or vertically (but not diagonally) during each move. The task is for each farmer to catch their own sheep (the one nearest them at the beginning of the activity). Will they ever be able to catch their own sheep? Next, reframe the task for this puzzle, and simply request that the two farmers catch both sheep. Is this possible?

Farmer 1 □
Sheep 1 ○

Farmer 2 ■
Sheep 2 ●

As an extension of this activity, you can ask the remaining team members watching the farmers and sheep to advise the farmers where to move. This alternative will engage more members of the group in the planning and solving process.

Another grid activity that works with group sizes from 2 to 22 (and a few more too) explores the concept of change in the workplace. This can be a change in resources, environment or even corporate culture. And this puzzle requires change at a rapid pace as well.

Begin with an empty grid. Inform the group that as 'new employees' they may be asked to be flexible as the new company culture is formed. Ask about three members of the group to stand within the 8x8 grid pattern so that there are an equal number of team members on each of the four sides of the grid. We wish to have everyone on our team active, so only the outside boxes of the grid are available for occupation. It is possible to have the same number of participants on each side of the grid if some folks occupy the corner spaces (so that technically, they represent both sides from this position).

After this initial number of team members, quickly ask for additional team members to join the group and for previous team members to change position to 're-equalize' the number on each side. You can begin with three people and grow to 5, 9, 10, 13, 17, 18, 19, 20 and 25. The illustration shows one solution for placing 17 team members onto the grid with a total of 5 team members on each side.

The teachable moment explored in this style of rapid corporate growth is the need for all members, including existing team members and even those who have already gone through previous changes, to be flexible and willing to relocate if necessary for the team to succeed.

As a final alternative activity, you could make a king size set of pentominoes (see puzzle #45) and use the Corporate Maze as a building grid. The twelve different pentominoes will cover 60 spaces, leaving the four central spaces unoccupied. Or, you can make a king size set of checkers, or play 'human checkers' with your team.

Hints and Clues The Corporate Maze fits into the category of activities that provide more impact when the group discovers the similar path for both teams rather than looking for it from the very beginning.

You can find additional explanations of similar grid activities in the books:

Feeding the Zircon Gorilla and Othe rTeam Building Activities, 1995, Sam Sikes, Learning Unlimited, Tulsa, OK USA ISBN 0-9646541-0-5 'The Grid'

Teamwork & Teamplay, 1998, Jim Cain and Barry Jolliff, Kendall Hunt Publishers, Dubuque, IA USA ISBN 0-7872-4532-1 'Gridlock'

**Teambuilding
Puzzles**

The Corporate Maze

Team A

Team B

☐   For your team, there is only one correct path through the corporate maze.

☐   Once a person has placed both feet in a square, the facilitator will provide feed back on whether this location is on the correct path or not.

☐   Only one person from your team may be in the maze at any time.

☐   Your team must plan the order in which members will go through the maze.

☐   The correct path requires only moves to adjacent squares (forward, sideways, backwards, diagonally), but does not include any jumps or skipping over any squares.

☐   When a person steps on an incorrect square, the facilitator will provide feedback indicating that this location is not on the path. This person must then exit the maze via the **same route** they took. Exiting errors cost your team $500.

☐   There is NO PENALTY for the first time a team member steps on an incorrect square. A repeat of this mistake, which is avoidable, costs the team $500.

☐   The remaining team members cannot verbally communicate to their team member when they are inside the maze.

☐   A 5 minute planning session begins this activity. Additional planning time can be purchased for $500 per minute. Your team must also come up with a team name (identity) and a slogan or cheer for your team.

☐   Once the planning time is up, verbal communication is also up (i.e. no talking).

☐   When all team members have gone, the sequence repeats as necessary.

☐   Each team starts with $5000.

From Teambuilding Puzzles, *by Anderson, Cain, Cavert and Heck, 2009*

**Teambuilding
Puzzles**

Facilitator Information Sheet

The Corporate Maze
The Correct Path

					X	X	X	
				X			X	
				X	X		X	X
					X			
	X	X			X			
			X	X				

Team A →   ← Team B

☐ Once a person has placed both feet in a square, the facilitator will indicate whether or not it is on the correct path. The facilitator may wish to mark the above grid with a pencil to keep track of the spaces used by a team.

☐ Only one person from each team may be in the maze at the same time.

☐ When a person steps on an incorrect square, the facilitator tells them so. This person must then exit the maze via the **same route** they took. Exiting errors cost a team $500.

☐ There is NO PENALTY for the first time a team member steps on an incorrect square. A repeat of this mistake, which is avoidable, costs the team $500.

☐ The remaining team members cannot verbally communicate to their team member when they are inside the maze.

☐ A 7 minute planning session begins this activity. Additional planning time can be purchased for $500 per minute. Each team must also come up with a team name (identity) and a slogan or cheer for the team.

☐ Once the planning time is up, verbal communication is also up (i.e. no talking).

☐ When all team members have gone, the sequence repeats as necessary.

☐ Each team starts with $5000.

From Teambuilding Puzzles, *by Anderson, Cain, Cavert and Heck, 2005*

45. Pentominoes
Pulling Even a Diverse Team Together

Pentominoes represent all of the two-dimensional variations of joining five cubes together. You'll find complete diversity in the pieces, but unity in the shapes they are able to create. If you make large scale versions, you can even use the Corporate Maze, puzzle #44 in this book, as a grid for building several versions of a square like the ones shown here. The four spaces filled in each grid below represent spaces left intentionally empty. See if your team can fill the following areas using all twelve pieces. Each team member should be responsible for at least one piece. If it is placed, or needs to be moved, the person responsible for that piece should perform this task.

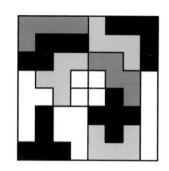

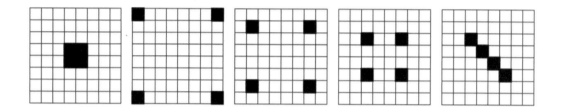

Supplies You'll need a set of pentominoes. You can make these from a chessboard pattern by slicing each of the 12 profiles shown. You can also create a set from any 8x8 grid or by gluing five 1 inch (25 mm) wood blocks together. If you plan to use the Corporate Maze shown in puzzle #44, each grid is approximately 12 inches (30 cm) square. If you make pentominoes from large pieces of plywood, you can attach foot straps and invite teams to walk around to form the various patterns and shapes requested. Finally, if you create a grid pattern using the draw feature of your word processor, you can create pentomino shapes that can be manipulated, rotated and placed using your computer mouse. Students can then print their answers to various shapes and patterns.

Teachable Moments The complete diversity of the various pieces (no two look alike) and the unity required to complete each shape provide a strong message about cooperation, collaboration, unity, community and connection. Some creative problem solving skills are also required to place each pentomino correctly.

Variations There are a variety of shapes that pentominoes can be used to make. Some require all twelve pieces, others only a few. Choose pieces wisely. Not all pieces will work in each of the following shapes and patterns. From a Human Resources perspective, you can partially fill in a shape with two or three pentominoes, and then choose the remaining shapes that work best with the shapes (team members) already in place.

Here are a few other shapes to create. 1. A 3x5 rectangle with three pentominoes. 2. A 4x5 rectangle with four pentominoes. 3. A 5x5 square with five pentominoes. 4. A 3x10 rectangle with six pentominoes. 5. A 5x7 rectangle with seven pentominoes. 6. A 4x10 rectangle with eight pentominoes. 7. A 3x15 rectangle with nine pentominoes. 8. Use all twelve pentominoes to form: a 6x10 rectangle, a 5x12 rectangle, and a 4x15 rectangle. As a bonus, if you have pentominoes made from 1 inch wood cubes, try to create the three dimensional shape shown here.

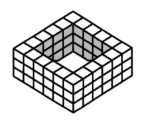

Hints and Clues Try various pieces and see which ones work the best in each of the shapes and patterns suggested.

For additional information, try reading the definitive book on pentominoes and other polyominoes, entitled: Polyominoes - The Fascinating New Recreation in Mathematics, 1965, Solomon W. Golomb, Charles Scribner, New York, NY USA. Updated copies of this book are available from Kaydon Enterprises in Pasadena, Maryland USA www.gamepuzzles.com or kadon@gamepuzzles.com. Think Fun sells a variety of pentominoe games. www.thinkfun.com

*"Some people think only intellect counts: Knowing how to solve problems,
knowing how to get by, knowing how to identify an advantage and seize it.
But the functions of intellect are insufficient without courage,
love, friendship, compassion and empathy."*
Dean Koontz

46. Five Rooms and One Extension Cord
A Lesson in Topology

Teambuilding Puzzles

Believe it or not, when I was growing up, our house had only one extension cord. Luckily, it was a very, very long extension cord. You could pretty much plug it into any electrical outlet in the house, and it would reach just about any other place you might have an electrical appliance. Little did I know that my childhood experiences with extension cords would turn into some advanced puzzle solving skills, at least until I discovered the following puzzle.

You have a floorplan of a house with five rooms and one very, very long extension cord. You must confirm that the cord reaches every wall in the house, but passes through each wall only once. There are a total of sixteen wall segments in our house, as shown below. Your challenge is to stretch a single cord through each wall segment of the house exactly once, without passing through any wall twice. The third illustration below gives an example of one potential starting pattern. There are many, many others. Good Luck!

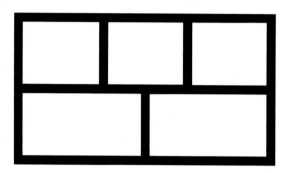

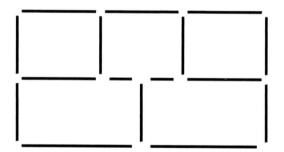

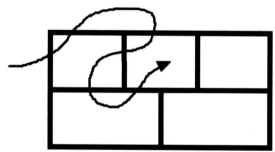

Supplies You can present this activity as a paper and pencil challenge or by projecting the floor plan onto a whiteboard (where the extension cord line can be drawn), or by creating this floorplan on the floor using wide masking or duct tape and using a rope or actual extension cord.

Teachable Moments Knowing where to begin and, more importantly, how to finish, is key to successfully solving this puzzle. Identifying opportunities along the way is helpful. So is identifying and discussing problems, barriers or challenges which exceed your present capabilities to manage them.

At some point, random guessing must be replaced by critical thinking to reason out a solution. This is true in real life situations as well.

Variations You could begin this puzzle using a single room floor plan and adding more rooms, one at a time, to increase the level of challenge.

Hints and Clues If you always do what you've always done, then you'll always get what you've always gotten before. What do you need to do differently here, so that you can be successful?

"If knowledge can create problems,
it is not through ignorance that we can solve them."
Isaac Asimov

"Each problem that I solved became a rule
which served afterwards to solve other problems."
Rene Descartes

"When life seems chaotic, you don't need people giving you easy
answers or cheap promises. There might not be any answers to your problems.
What you need is a safe place where you can bounce with people
who have taken some bad hops of their own."
Real Live Preacher,
RealLivePreacher.com
Weblog, August 12, 2003

47. True North
Moving Forward in the Same Direction

Part of the 'vision' of a corporation is knowing in which direction they are moving forward. Here is a simple activity to see if your team is moving in the right direction.

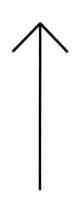

The facilitator gathers the team into a circle and stands at the center to explain the challenge. "We need to adjust our personal compass for the journey ahead. I would like this team to create an arrow, with one long central shaft, and two shorter tip lines, pointing exactly north.

Supplies An accurate compass, map, or GPS unit are valuable props for the facilitator to check the group's direction. No supplies for participants. They are left to find True North without instrumentation.

Teachable Moments Achieving consensus and agreement is only the first step in True North. Beyond agreement comes the action necessary to actually make the arrow point in the direction chosen by the group. Motivating some team members to change position requires negotiation skills and tact. This is also an excellent activity to use before an orienteering or geocaching event.

For additional consensus building activities, see puzzles #1 and #50 in this book.

Variations Rather than creating a large arrow, you can ask individual members to each point in the direction they believe is True North (or towards the company headquarters, or the college union, or the Eiffel Tower, or some other prominent landmark or location).

Hints and Clues It is interesting to try this activity in a location without significant geographical clues, such as streets or signs. An interior conference room is ideal, as is a sloping hillside in an area without man-made elements.

Thanks to Erick Erickson for permission to share this activity. You can read this and other experiential learning activities in the book, Dancing Naked with Pine Trees, by Erick Erickson. www.ericksoninternational.net or Erickson@acninc.net

We also recommend that you read: The Compass in Your Nose - And Other Astonishing Facts About Humans, 1989, Marc McCutcheon and Rosanne Litzinger, Jeremy P. Tarcher Publishers, ISBN 0-8747-7544-2

"Good questions outrank easy answers."
Paul A. Samuelson

*"What is important is to keep learning, to enjoy challenge,
and to tolerate ambiguity. In the end there are no certain answers."*
Martina Horner, President of Radcliffe College

48. Human Knot
Solving Problems in Close Quarters

**Teambuilding
Puzzles**

Ever feel like your team is tied up in knots? Now you can find out what to do about it.

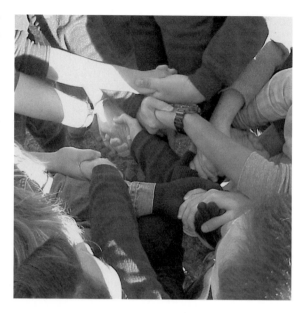

Human Knot is perhaps the first 'teambuilding' activity many of us experienced. For some, it is a completely new experience. Start with your team standing closely in a circle. Invite everyone to reach across the circle and hold right hands with another person. While maintaining contact with the right hand, hold left hands with a different person. Once the entire group is 'connected' in this manner, the challenge is to untangle this mess without letting go, and ending up in one circle.

Supplies None. However, if flexibility or mobility is an issue, you can use short segments of rope, about 3 feet (1 meter) in length to lengthen the distance connecting participants. Or, how about using sections of foam noodles (see picture on the next page)?

Teachable Moments Was there a leader in the group? How did they assist the completion of the challenge? If you were asked to perform this task again, what would you do differently the next time to guarantee success? Explore the concept of order and chaos. What order can be achieved here?

You can also explore classical knot theory with this activity. A circle is in fact called an 'unknot.' See the following book for more information:

The Knot Book: An Elementary Introduction to the Mathematical Theory of Knots, 1994, Colin Adams, W. H. Freeman, New York, NY USA ISBN 0-7167-2393-X.

**Teambuilding
Puzzles**

Variations From a mathematical view, there are at least three potential outcomes of the Human Knot. Your team can form one complete circle, although some members may be facing inward and other members outward. Your team could also form two linked circles or, in the third configuration, your team could form two or more unlinked circles. To verify that your team has created a single circle, you can use the following technique:

After joining hands, but before untangling your Human Knot, invite one person to pulse (squeeze) their right hand. When each person in turn feels one hand squeezed, they squeeze the other, and the pulse travels around the group. If it returns to the original person, without touching some team members, you'll need to reform the knot to include these other folks.

You can also find several other variations of knot activities in The Book on Raccoon Circles, including: Believe It or Knot, A Long Line of Knots, 2B or Knot 2B, Not Knots, Tree of Knots, Knot Right Now, Knot on the Phone, Knot by Myself, and It's Knot Our Problem - is it? This book is available from Kendall Hunt Publishers, Training Wheels, Inc., and your local bookstore. ISBN 0-7575-3265-9.

Hints and Clues Your team members may find it helpful to occasionally allow their hands to rotate with their partners, but not let go. This movement prevents excessively twisting anyone's hand or arm. In the event of an extremely difficult knot, you may benefit from a visit to the Knot Doctor. The Knot Doctor can temporarily disconnect any two hands, rejoin them in another location, and then allow the activity to continue.

49. Line Up
Making Order Out of Chaos

"EILNPU"

From the time we were school children, we have learned how to line up. This continues into our adulthood as we learn how to place information in order, sort data and addresses, arrange books on a bookshelf and organize the CDs in our music collection. The following challenges will provide many different ways for your team to line up in style.

Given the following information, sort the members of your team and line up in the following order:

By your birthdate, from January to December, without talking.

By your height, from shortest to tallest, with your eyes closed.

By the first letter of your middle name, from A to Z, without talking.

By the last digit of your telephone number, from zero to nine, without talking, and with your hands in your pockets.

Supplies You can perform this puzzle with no props at all, although it is helpful to have a rope line to guide the group. Some of the variations below require a few props. Most are easy to find.

Teachable Moments Some of the variations suggested below include real information content, such as chronological dates of events in history, environmental education, language skills, mathematics, science, measurements, and other valuable knowledge and life skills.

Variations No matter what the line up criteria is, you can modify the communication techniques available to the team members. You can limit verbal talking, hand motions, vision, dominant language in favor of a foreign language, and facial gestures.

**Teambuilding
Puzzles**

In addition to the themes mentioned above, you can use the following props and invite your group to line up by several different sets of rules.

Prop	Line Up Procedure
Playing Cards	Alphabetically - Ace of Diamonds comes BEFORE the Three of Hearts
Dominoes	Total numeric value
Presidential Photos	Chronologically, by term of office
Baseball Cards	Batting Average
Atomic Weight	Cut a large periodic table of the elements into individual element pieces
Semaphore Flags	Alphabetically, using cards with the semaphore (flag) alphabet
Morse Code Cards	Alphabetically, using cards with individual Morse code letters
Braille Cards	Alphabetically, using cards with the Braille Alphabet
Sign Language	Alphabetically, using cards with sign language hand gestures
Events in History	Chronologically by the month, day and year the event occurred.
Measurement Cards	By unit of measurement, from shortest (Angstrom) to longest (Nautical Mile)
Roman Numerals	Numerically, using cards with Roman Numbers
Wind Character Cards	Increasing Beaufort wind strength scale numbers, from 1 to 12
Photos of Planets	In order of appearance, from the sun outwards
Items of Trash	Chronologically by the amount of time each item requires to decompose

Hints and Clues While talking easily conveys each person's information, see what non-verbal techniques you can use to share information with other members of the group.

Note, when using index cards with Roman numbers, cards can be turned over to create other numerical possibilities. XI can become IX with a quick rotation of the card.

50. Paint Stick Shuffle
A Visual Dilemma

Next time you visit your local hardware or paint store, ask for two dozen paint stirring sticks, and you'll have all the props you need for this next puzzle.

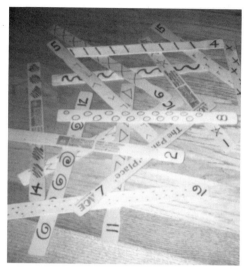

The Paint Stick Shuffle is a visual puzzle that requires problem solving skills, teamwork, consensus building, and the ability to see things from someone else's point of view. A pile of paint stirring sticks is placed on a floor or table, like pick-up sticks, well before the group arrives. Each stick will need some form of identification (letters, numbers, symbols or colors).

The challenge of this visual puzzle is for team members to reach agreement on which sticks match the following criteria:

A. Which stick would be the last one picked up?
B. Which two sticks are on the same level?
C. Which stick identification is missing from view?

At this point, ask the group to carefully study the pile of sticks for one minute. Then step away to discuss the following questions:

D. Does stick number 2 touch stick number 5?
E. Are all the sticks the same length?
F. How many sticks were there?
G. Which stick was on top?

Supplies You'll need about 24 paint stirring sticks (which are available, sometimes for free, from hardware and paint supply stores) and something to identify each stick (paint, markers, wood burning stencils, stickers or hand written letters, numbers or symbols).

Teachable Moments Some participants can look at this type of puzzle and intuitively know the answers. These are the same people that straighten pictures on your walls when they visit your house. But knowing the answer and being able to communicate that vision to other members of the group, are two different things. The second, and some feel most important part of this challenge, is to reach consensus with other team members before moving on. This often requires developing a sense of empathy for our leaders. It also requires many of us to consider another person's point of view.

Variations You can create a pile of almost anything as a variation to this problem. For a king size version, use 2x4's that have been thrown into a random pile. You could also use handtools, kitchen gadgets, technical hardware, office supplies or sport equipment. If you choose to use long hardwood dowel rods, about 1 inch (25mm) in diameter and 4 feet (1.3 meters) long (available at most hardware stores), you can also play a king size version of pick up sticks as part of the challenge.

The questions asked about each of the items in the pile can be varied from simple to complex. You can also require some folks to join the group after viewing time has expired and make their decision based upon second-hand information, not personal experience.

Hints and Clues Two dozen pieces of information is a substantial amount for any single person to remember. Group memory is often superior to individual memory. Encourage team members to view the entire puzzle, but to really focus on one specific area that they will be able to speak about with superior knowledge.

If you enjoy making things from paint stirring sticks, you can build your own boomerang with directions found on page 307 of the book: Teamwork & Teamplay, 1998, Jim Cain and Barry Jolliff, Kendall Hunt Publishers, Dubuque, IA USA ISBN 0-7872-4532-1.

Also, visit the FUNdoing website for information about Chris Cavert's long awaited sequel to the Affordable Portables book. The Mondrian, a challenging puzzle made from paint stirring sticks, will be featured in this book. www.fundoing.com

*"An undefined problem
has an infinite number of solutions."*
Robert A. Humphrey

51. Seven Boxes of Bolts
Working Smarter, not Harder

Farmer Bob is back again. Let's see what he is up to now.

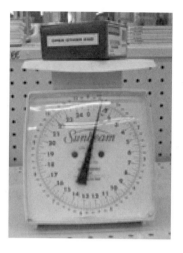

Every spring, Farmer Bob visits the hardware store and buys seven boxes of large bolts to use on his farm equipment, fences, livestock gates and some of his other inventions. When he gets back to the farm, he opens each of the boxes and over the course of the year, takes some bolts from each one. In August, he discovers that some of the bolts have broken, but has no idea which box they came from. He takes one of the broken bolts back to the hardware store, and discovers that it weighs 0.90 pounds, which is 0.10 pounds less than the regular bolts he typically buys.

The store owner tells Farmer Bob that he can return the out-of-specification bolts, but Bob isn't sure which box they came from, since they all look exactly alike and he doesn't have an accurate scale to weigh them

"If you'll bring in all seven boxes of bolts, I can think of a technique for finding the bad box of bolts with my weighing scale, and I'll only have to use it once," say the store owner. How does the hardware store owner plan to identify the bad bolts, using his scale only once?

#1 $4.95 BOX OF BOLTS	#2 $4.95 BOX OF BOLTS	#3 $4.95 BOX OF BOLTS	#4 $4.95 BOX OF BOLTS	#5 $4.95 BOX OF BOLTS	#6 $4.95 BOX OF BOLTS	#7 $4.95 BOX OF BOLTS

Supplies You can present this puzzle as a pencil and paper or thought challenge or you can bring in seven bags of bolts and an accurate scale, and prove that it can be done with just one scale weighing.

Teachable Moments   There are two techniques for solving Farmer Bob's bolt problem: brainpower and horsepower. Both work just fine, but with a little ingenuity you can reduce the total time spent solving the problem. What other tasks are part of your job that could be made easier by a bit of analysis? How can team members work together to find a convenient solution to this puzzle?

Variations You can alter the total number of bags. Five bags are fine, so are twenty. You can also suggest other objects instead of bolts.

Hints and Clues The goal is to identify which bag holds the out-of-specification (lighter weight) bolts with only a single use of the scale.

What other uses can you find for this box of bolts?

52. A Problem of Weight
Discovering What is Essential

Teambuilding Puzzles

We begin this puzzle with a small dilemma. You have eight small containers each filled with a rare and precious material. One of the containers is marginally lighter than the others. Although you cannot tell simply by holding these containers, it is possible to measure the difference in weight using a simple balance scale. A local business owner happens to own just such a balance scale, but must charge you $5.00 for every time you use the scale. How many times will you need to use the scale to be sure you have found the lighter container? How much money will this cost you?

Supplies You can perform this puzzle as a simple thought experiment, as a paper and pencil activity, or using real containers and a balance scale to prove the point.

Teachable Moments Trial and error methods may eventually lead to a solution for this puzzle, but it is possible to reduce the total number of weighings if you know how. Obviously you can confirm the balance of each individual container against the others. This technique will require seven tries. Next, you could weigh several containers at the same time, always eliminating the heavier containers on the balance. This method will require at least three tries. Is it possible to perform this task with less than three tries? How can you assist a group in finding the minimum number of tries?

Variations If you find a technique to minimize the number of weighings for eight containers, see what you can do with nine containers.

Hints and Clues A scale balance does not directly measure weight. It only compares the weight of objects placed on each side of the balance.

Is there any method by which you can eliminate some of the containers without ever weighing them?

For more information about creating your own inexpensive PVC two pan balance scales, pendulums, catapults and other simple devices for exploring science and physics, see the publication "Slip Fits - An Introduction to Physcial Science" 1990, Darell Speer and Lyla Dixon, DaLy Enterprises, 363 West Drake Road, Suite 7 Fort Collins, CO 80526 Phone (970) 419-7574

53. Count Six
Kinesthetic Team Work

Our goal in writing this book was to find as many different techniques for challenging teams as we could. Some puzzles are cerebral, others are visual, mathematical or even musical. The following team puzzle will challenge your whole brain capacity, your rhythm, your creative problem solving capabilities and your teamwork. Thanks to Sam Sikes and John Irvin for helping us exercise both sides of our brain.

Welcome to 'Count Six.' An innocent enough challenge with just the right amount of movement, that is difficult to perform flawlessly. Begin by assembling your team, all facing in the same direction towards the front of the room. With the facilitator standing in front of the group, and also facing forward, demonstrate with the **right hand** the following motions as you count to six. The illustration here shows a rear view of the stick person facilitator.

| One | Two | Three | Four | Five | Six |

Next, demonstrate the **left hand** movements, as you again count to six.

| One | Two | Three | Four | Five | Six |

Finally, inform the group that everyone is going to perform Count Six with **both hands**. Like this:

| One | Two | Three | Four | Five | Six |

At this point, some laughter and general confusion occurs. Inform the group that their job is going to be to help each other be successful in this task. Working together in groups of six people, they have exactly four minutes to practice and demonstrate their proficiency in performing Count Six.

Supplies None.

Teachable Moments You can use Count Six as a quick stretching exercise during a long training program, even in a fixed seated auditorium. The greatest value however, comes when small groups try to work together to demonstrate their proficiency. Notice that the challenge is not to 'individually' demonstrate proficiency, but rather as a team. This opportunity for teamwork should encourage several possibilities for creative solutions, including dividing the various motions up between members of the group, partnering, and standing in various formations.

Variations Count Six is a bit like the childhood task of patting your head while rubbing your stomach, and rubbing your head while patting your stomach. It requires both sides of your brain to perform the task, something that most humans find challenging. The good news is that you can improve by practicing. You can find other whole brain and body kinesthetic references by searching the Internet with phrases such as whole brain learning. You can also read:

A Celebration of Neurons - an Educator's Guide to the Human Brain, 1995, Robert Sylwester, American Society of Curriculum Development, Alexandria, VA USA ISBN 0-87120-243-3.

Smart Moves - Why learning is not all in your head, Carla Hannaford, 1995, Great Oceans Publishers, Arlington, VA USA ISBN 0-915556-27-8.

Hints and Clues This is a great activity for any audience that just needs to move a bit. After an hour or more sitting and listening, it is exactly this type of activity that invigorates and recharges the brain and the body.

Movement is the door to learning.
Dr. Paul Dennison, Author of Brain Gym

You can find Count Six, and other teambuilding activities that require no props at all, in the books:

Executive Marbles and Other Team Building Activities, 1998,
Sam Sikes, Learning Unlimited, Tulsa, OK USA ISBN 0-9646541-2-1

The Empty Bag, 2003, Dick Hammond & Chris Cavert,
FUNdoing Publications. www.fundoing.com

54. The Coiled Rope
Working Out Difficulties

**Teambuilding
Puzzles**

For those times when life becomes a tangled mess, here is a team puzzle to help you work through it. This is an alternate form of the Human Knot, presented in puzzle #48.

Start by loosely coiling a rope on the ground, as shown in the illustration. Team members are asked to grasp one location along the rope. When all members have connected with the rope, the challenge for the team is to untangle this mess, and eventually stand in a circle, with every member facing inwards.

Supplies A long rope for the group. Fifty feet (15 meters) is about right for a group of up to 20 people.

Teachable Moments Invite the group to analyze the puzzle and set a goal or estimate of a completion time before grasping the rope. Discussions related to estimating and goal setting are appropriate here. You can also discuss how some team members had easy assignments, compared to other members that encountered difficulties in their portion of the rope.

Variations In addition to simply coiling and dropping a rope, you can add several knots, weave several ropes together or connect different ropes with rock climbing hardware.

The rope illustrated here is untied at each end. You can create a higher level of challenge for the team if you tie the ends of a rope together first, and then coil this on the ground.

Hints and Clues Encourage the group to untangle the rope slowly at first to avoid placing additional and unwanted knots into the rope.

Thanks to Mike Spiller for sharing this activity. Mike is an exceptional games resource. Visit Mike's website at: www.physiciansofphun.com

Here is a puzzle that you can use as an icebreaker or a debriefing tool. We begin by discussing the team's contributions, but you can use any appropriate subject or topic.

After a short discussion related to the contributions each member makes to the team, distribute the puzzle pieces to the group. Ask each person to list some of their strengths (skills they have to contribute) using one color marker and the skills they wish to improve in the coming months with a different color marker. Remind them to write comments that they would be willing to share with the other members of the group.

When the group is finished writing, ask them to assemble the puzzle and then read the comments written on each piece.

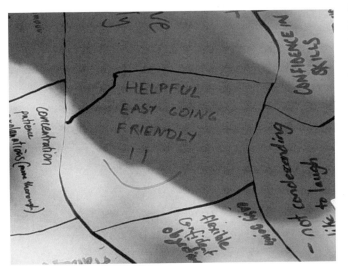

Supplies You can make this puzzle from the same whiteboard material with which dry erase markers are used. You can typically find this at some of the larger hardware stores. You can also use chalkboard (blackboard) material or corrugated cardboard for your puzzle. A suitable collection of dry erase markers, chalk, crayons or colorful markers, depending on the medium, will also be helpful. You can find two sizes of this puzzle, called the Adventure Puzzle, from Grip-It Adventures, (www.grip101.com)

Teachable Moments Did you notice any consistency from the group's comments? Are there skills that many people possess or skills that several people all wish to improve? Were there any skills that some team members possess that could benefit others that are trying to improve in this same area? Do you notice that even though we all share different talents, that we are connected in this puzzle, and in our team? And finally, the most important question of all. How do we fit together as a group?

Variations You can certainly vary the theme used on each puzzle piece. This particular example used contributions, strengths and opportunities. You could also consider using:

personal talents, abilities, favorite (foods, sports, TV shows, music, movies, books), personal history, or any other appropriate theme. Instead of using words, you can ask each person to draw pictures of their strengths.

If you enjoy this jigsaw puzzle activity, you might also try The Giant Jigsaw Puzzle #56, An Unusual Jigsaw Puzzle #57, and the Placemat Puzzle #65. For an icebreaker with a significant message about inclusion, try puzzle #85, Finding Your People.

Hints and Clues As the facilitator, you might begin this activity with a puzzle piece already completed with your own strengths and skills needing improvement. You can use this as an example for the members of the team to follow.

We recently discovered an interesting book on the history of the jigsaw puzzle:

The Jigsaw Puzzle - Piecing Together a History, 2004, Anne D. Williams, Berkley Books, New York, NY USA ISBN 0-425-19820-0 Who knew the story of the jigsaw puzzle has so many pieces?

"A problem is a chance for you to do your best."
Duke Ellington

"The road to wisdom?
Well it's plain and simple to express:
Err and err and err again, but less, and less, and less. "
Piet Hein

56. A Giant Jigsaw Puzzle
High-Torque Communication

If you thought putting together a jigsaw puzzle was a piece of cake, wait till you see this version!

Invite the team to have a seat, either at a large round table or on a carpeted floor. Tell them that you are going to give them some equipment, and their job will be to put this equipment together. Ask for one volunteer to be an observer, and pass out blindfolds for the remaining team members. Inform them that this activity will require clear communication, just as telephone conversations and email messages do.

Place most of the pieces of the large wooden jigsaw puzzle in the middle of the group, but save about three for the exterior of the circle, and one to hold in your own hand. Let the group know that each of the items they will need are within arms reach of where they are right now. There is no need to stand or walk around to find them, they are all within arms reach, including one that you are holding slightly above their heads.

The role of the observer is to be a quiet surveillance camera: observing but not interacting with the group. This role will be important during the debriefing event after the completion of the activity.

Finally, instruct the group that they can ask any three questions during the course of their construction project and that you will answer them. Ready, begin!

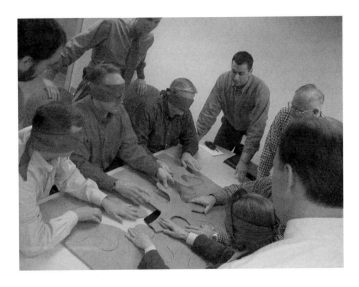

Supplies A king size wooden jigsaw puzzle with approximately one piece for every member of the group. One blindfold for each member of the group.

Teachable Moments Without our vision, our ability to receive and provide information is greatly reduced. Our comments are less effective and easily misinterpreted without body language, hand gestures, facial expressions, and a variety of other non-verbal components to our communication patterns. No wonder that sometimes our telephone conversations and emails are misinterpreted.

Even though information is provided at the beginning of the activity as to where the pieces are, teams frequently misinterpret this information. They think, *only in the middle,* or *only on the ground,* when in reality the pieces are positioned in the three-dimensional world around them. How can we work better as a team and avoid making these kinds of mistakes in the future?

You might wish for the observer to address the group before debriefing this activity. Many times information, especially related to a team's performance, comes better from a member of the team than an outsider.

Finally, there are teachable moments surrounding the use of the three questions. Some groups use them early, some groups not at all. If the group is struggling, the facilitator can remind the group by saying, "perhaps you would like to use one of your questions now." These questions are resources for the group. Were they used appropriately and successfully, or not?

Variations You can vary the number of pieces for this style of jigsaw puzzle. You can also create a puzzle with an irregular shaped outline, rather than a regular shape (such as a square or rectangle).

There are several other jigsaw puzzles in this book, including The Whiteboard Puzzle #55, An Unusual Jigsaw Puzzle #57 and Placemat Puzzle #65. If you like this style of limited vision puzzle, you might enjoy puzzle #85, Finding Your People, in this book.

Hints and Clues Blindfolded participants often want to know how many pieces there are, what shape the puzzle makes, and if they have all the pieces. Encourage teams to ask questions that provide more information than simply a yes or no answer.

57. An Unusual Jigsaw Puzzle
Challenging Assumptions and Shifting Paradigms

It looks like an ordinary large scale version of a jigsaw puzzle. But is it?

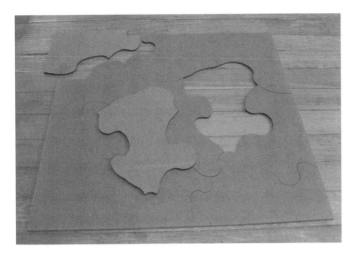

Here is a large scale wooden jigsaw puzzle for your team to assemble on a table or smooth floor. And this version requires no blindfolds. Good Luck!

Supplies This particular jigsaw puzzle has a unique feature. Two of the pieces are reversed. This means that rather than having each piece same side up, two will display the 'bottom side' rather than their 'top sides' when correctly placed in the puzzle. This puzzle was created by cutting two puzzles at the same time, using a bandsaw. Two boards were joined together in multiple places with masking tape and then cut into the puzzle pieces shown. When sawing was complete, two of the pieces from each puzzle were traded, creating the one shown in the above illustration and a second mirror image puzzle as well.

See the solution in the next chapter of this book, along with an explanation of how to obtain this type of puzzle.

Teachable Moments In almost every case, teams assembling a jigsaw puzzle will turn over all the pieces so that the 'same side' is facing upwards. This assumption or paradigm has certainly worked in the past, and seems likely to work here again. The fact that the puzzle illustrated in this particular activity is different brings about the very first teachable moment. What assumptions did your team make when first attempting to solve this puzzle? In some cases, we are unaware that we are even making assumptions. Once we realize that we have made certain assumptions (gravity is constant, darkness comes at night, jigsaw puzzles need to be assembled with the same surface facing upwards), we can begin to challenge these assumptions. Allowing for alternative possibilities or new paradigms to emerge is part of the creative growth process. By identifying the barriers to this creative growth, we can plot a new course to avoid dead-ends in our creative thinking patterns.

Variations You can alter a jigsaw puzzle in many ways. For example, you can paint illustrations, patterns and textures on each piece rather than the whole puzzle thereby creating a collage or patchwork quilt rather than a single scene. You can vary the size and number of pieces in each puzzle. You can use materials of different thickness, or different materials (different species of wood, for example) for each piece of the puzzle.

There are two more possibilities for assembling large jigsaw puzzles in unusual ways. First, you can use large plywood puzzle pieces with an added foot strap, so players can walk around looking for the other team members they need to connect with (thanks to Scott Trent for this innovative design feature).

For a totally different paradigm, Sam Sikes suggests building a puzzle on the ceiling using foamboard, posterboard or flip chart paper. You could also use this principle to assemble puzzles on a wall, or as part of a display. You can find the ceiling puzzle, and several others, in the book: Raptor and Other Team Building Activities, 2003, Sam Sikes, Learning Unlimited, Tulsa, OK USA ISBN 0-9646541-7-2.

For more information about paradigms, read: Paradigms - The Business of Discovering the Future, Joel Barker, Harper Collins, New York, NY USA ISBN 0-88730-647-0. One of the first and certainly one of the definitive books on paradigms. Chapter Eight provides some puzzling questions.

Hints and Clues While most of the pieces of this puzzle are fairly simple to piece together, several pieces seem not to fit at first. This is a perfect time to ask the group, "what are your assumptions about how a puzzle should go together?" Then ask the group to revisit these assumptions and challenge the validity of each one.

58. The Whole Story
Putting Things in Order

Sometimes you hear all the right information, but not necessarily in the correct order. Here is a chance to *get your story straight*!

Take any appropriate story for your team, from a children's book with a positive message to a segment of a recent corporate book on leadership, and place each sentence, phrase or word of the story on a separate slip of paper. Pass out each piece of paper, and ask the group to form a coherent message from these scrambled phrases.

Supplies You'll need copies of a brief story that has meaning and relevance for your team. You can search the Internet or your local library for some possibilities. Then print or copy these stories on paper with plenty of space between each sentence.

Teachable Moments Life provides us with clues about the order and significance of things, just as these phrases and words do. Sometimes we need to share the small pieces of our own lives with others in order to make sense of them, and to see how we all fit together.

You may have only a single, small, seemingly insignificant word (or voice),
but it may make all the difference in the world to those of us that are looking for it!

This puzzling activity is useful for exploring the relevance of syntax in regards to working with a team. Syntax refers to the systematic and orderly arrangement of words and ideas. To illustrate the impact that syntax provides, consider the following sentences:

Terry ate the vegetables.

The vegetables ate Terry.

Both sentences contain the exact same four words, but the syntax is very different. The success of a team is often determined by their ability to create meaning from messages that may be less than clear. Ask your team to discuss how they decipher messages from management or other teams. How do we make sure that everyone on the team knows 'the message?'

Variations You could present your story on identical puzzle pieces and then ask the group to assemble the puzzle in what they believe is the correct order. You could also use

Teambuilding
Puzzles

a school motto, appropriate quotation, corporate value statement, code of ethics, mission statement, personal credo, or some other significant information for this activity. An example for a quotation is given below.

As another form of communication, you could whisper a key word or phrase to each member of the group, and ask them to form a coherent message from the whole while remembering their own specific contribution. This technique requires a bit more focus and memorization, and may lead to some interesting paraphrasing of the original message.

A third form of this activity involves pictures rather than words. Using picture books, comic books, or newspaper comic strips that have been cut into individual frames, ask your team to reassemble each picture sequence in the correct order. We recommend the two books listed here as picture book possibilities for this activity. If you remove the binding from either of these two books, you'll have a story-telling sequence with pictures that makes for an interesting 'put-the-puzzle-back-in-order' activity.

Zoom, 1995, Istvan Banyai, Puffin Books, New York, NY USA ISBN 0-14-055774-1

Re- Zoom, 1995, Istvan Banyai, Puffin Books, NY, NY USA ISBN 0-14-055694-X

Hints and Clues In addition to the words printed on each slip of paper, you can attempt to align the edges of the paper since adjoining phrases were probably cut from the same piece of paper.

Example The following words and phrases make up an appropriate quotation for the team. See if you can assemble these to form a coherent message. The answer can be found in the solutions section of this book.

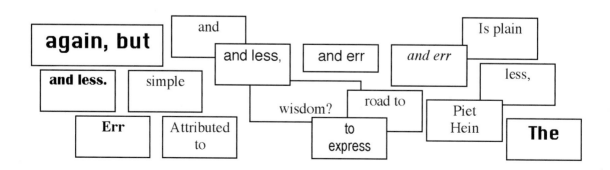

59. Tongue Twisters
Linguistic Puzzles

Here are a few linguistic challenges that are sure to test your team's verbal skills. You can attempt to speak the following phrases by yourself or in unison with the other members of your team. Tongue Twisters are a sequence of often alliterative words which are difficult to quickly articulate. Try saying the following words or phrases three times quickly:

A critical cricket critic	Does the wristwatch shop shut soon
A regal rural ruler	Fast Frank fries frankfurters and French fries
Unique New York	I thought I thought of thinking of thanking you
Cheap ship trips	Eleven benevolent elephants
Six selfish shellfish	The sixth sheik's sixth sheep's sick
Six thin thistle sticks	Rubber baby buggy bumpers
Toy boat	Blame the big bleak black book
Truly rural	Old oily Ollie oils oily autos
She sees cheese	He threw three free throws
Real rock wall	Red leather, yellow leather
Aluminum - Linoleum	Singing Sally Sat on the Sidelines

Nettie knitted nightly knitting knotted nighties for the navy

A proper cup of coffee from a proper copper coffee pot

Danny diggers dirty dog drinks diet drinks on the doorstep

Supplies You can search for tongue twisters on the internet, using the phrase "tongue twister." You can even find tongue twisters in foreign languages at:

www.uebersetzung.at/twister

This is an amazing collection of almost 3000 tongue twisters in 105 different languages, making it one of the largest collections in the world.

Teachable Moments It may seem odd to some participants that they can demonstrate proficiency with other puzzles in this book and yet have so much difficulty when it comes to just talking. The good news is that verbal ability is a bit like physical ability, it improves when you exercise. Some keynote speakers, actors and professional TV and radio personalities use tongue twisters to warm up before a broadcast or performance. They are also a favorite of speech therapists.

Variations Try the foreign language tongue twisters with your foreign language class. Or create your own tongue twisters based upon your company's technology, mission statement, or other prominent writings.

Chris Cavert proposes this unique technique for using Tongue Twisters with groups:

> *An interesting way to use Tongue Twisters with groups of ten participants is to pass out ten cards with a different Tongue Twister on each. The group's challenge is to go for the best TTTT (Tongue Twister Total Time). Each Tongue Twister must be said three times, quickly in a row, without mistakes, for time. The best time for each Tongue Twister is recorded, and all times are added up for the team's TTTT. It will be up to the group how they present each twister to the audience. Each person can be responsible for one, or it can be a group effort. It is possible to break down each phrase into different words that different people in the group pronounce. Good Luck!*

Hints and Clues Try saying some of these phrases backwards. You can also work on your articulation and diction by pronouncing each word carefully and pausing before saying the next word.

60. The Shape of the Future
Finding Where the Pieces Go in a Changing Environment

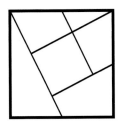

Flexibility, cross-training, multi-tasking and competency in a variety of challenges can all be useful skills. Here is a simple puzzle to test your team's ability to produce different results with the same six resources.

Using the six puzzle pieces shown in the square above, create each of the following profiles.

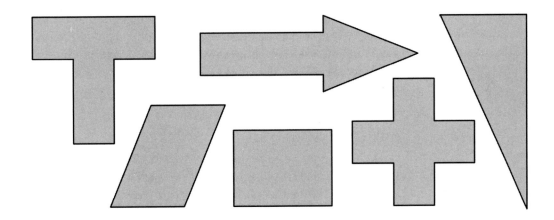

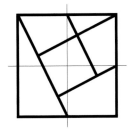

Supplies You can create your own version of The Shape of the Future puzzle using paper, cardboard, posterboard or plywood. Create a template for your puzzle from a large square piece of graph paper. Begin by drawing four light lines from each corner to the mid-point of the opposite side. Next, you can erase a portion of three of the lines to match the illustration shown.

Teachable Moments While specific skills and talents are assets, sometimes it is necessary even for specialists to perform in new arenas. The championship punter on a football team may need to pass the ball. The co-pilot on a trans-Atlantic flight might need to assist the pilot in ways unforeseen at take-off. Learning how to assist the team in getting the job done is part of what teamwork really means. You can also use this puzzle during a new employee orientation program to discuss rotations to various departments and the need for flexibility and contributing in different ways for different groups.

Variations The puzzle shown here is just one of the possible variations that can be made by dissecting standard geometric shapes. You can also dissect letters of the alphabet, numbers, symbols, corporate logos, parking lot configurations, and any other geometric shape that has relevance or meaning to the team that is using it. The Tangrams Puzzle #7 and Archimedes Puzzle #8 in this book are classic examples of wooden shapes that can be used to form hundreds of different profiles.

Try some of these puzzles with blindfolded team members, or limit talking to the planning portion of this activity and maintain quiet during the actual building process.

Hints and Clues Provide outlines that are to scale for the various configurations you wish your team to produce with the above pieces. After some practice, you can ask them to demonstrate each of the outlines shown here and record the amount of time necessary to perform this task.

You may need to turn over individual puzzle pieces in order to complete some of the above profiles.

If you like this style of team puzzle, you can also try the activity Real Estate, found on page 153 of: Teamwork & Teamplay, 1998, Jim Cain and Barry Jolliff, Kendall Hunt Publishers, Dubuque, IA USA ISBN 0-7872-4532-1. One of the most extensive collections of teambuilding activities, and teambuilding references ever assembled, including building plans, sequencing information and much, much more.

"Problems are only opportunities in work clothes."
Henry J. Kaiser

Here are the perfect puzzles for those long school bus rides, evenings sitting around the campfire, rainy days indoors, or before everyone has arrived for the staff meeting.

A. A tornado reportedly passed through a small town in Oklahoma. Of the 345 residents, it was reported that all survived the twister. After the local rescue squad surveyed the damage they ended up with three Dead residents on their list. How can this be?

B. Dr. Billings is one of the best surgeons in his home town. His patients never complain, even though he does not use anesthesia before operating. How is this possible?

C. Tom was observed from time-to-time looking into the windows of his neighborhood houses. No one ever reported him, and even when the police noticed his habit, they ignored him. Why?

D. The newly chosen queen was brought to the country estate and did not leave for five years. Why?

E. Sandy and her brother stayed away from the nearby school even though everyone there was really sharp. Why?

F. Taylor's cut hurt badly. No size bandage or medical assistance would help. However, healing came quickly after Taylor was picked up. Why?

G. Baxter Knox preferred the leather couch over the cotton fabric recliner. Mr. and Mrs. Knox were very upset. Why?

H. The pool had no water in it but Don, Betty and Larry used it almost every day. Why?

I. If a chicken and a half can lay an egg and a half in a day and a half, how long will it take 12.5 chickens to lay 37.5 eggs?

Supplies None, although you may want to write down a few of these mysteries on index cards for quick review.

Teachable Moments   How we explore incomplete information and look for reasonable outcomes is a process which we can learn and improve by practicing. Solving Lateral Puzzles as a group provides the opportunity for each member of the team to benefit from other participants' questions and answers, in a sense pushing everyone forward towards the correct answer. While Lateral Puzzles can be difficult for any one individual, groups are often successful. This is just another example of the power of teamwork.

Lateral Puzzles can be used to develop group interaction skills like many other teambuilding activities. They can be presented just about anywhere without equipment or space restrictions. Answers to Lateral Thinking Puzzles are most often found through a series of questions and answers. The reader shares the story and the participants ask questions that can be answered by the reader with a Yes, No, or Does Not Matter response. Through this inquiry process participants build on the questions asked by other participants and the answers given.

Lateral Puzzles allows groups to experience frustration, redundancy, support, encouragement and ultimately success. This process also provides opportunities to practice community building skills such as listening, deductive reasoning, sharing ideas, participating, leadership, persistence, problem-solving and critical thinking.

Variations   Create a lateral thinking puzzle for your own team, including personalities, places and activities that your team would enjoy.

You can find additional Lateral Thinking Puzzles on the Internet by searching the phrase 'lateral puzzles.' Visit www.lateralpuzzles.com and for additional puzzles visit Paul Sloan's homepage at http://dspace.dial.pipex.com/sloane/

Hints and Clues Lateral thinking puzzles, although of few words, generally provide some hints within the actual puzzle itself. Many of the puzzles presented above have words which may have multiple interpretations.

**Teambuilding
Puzzles**

62. A Strange Day
Our thanks to Douglas Adams' appreciation of the quirky.

The concept for this page of the Teambuilding Puzzle book came midway through what I can only describe as a very, very strange day. At some point in the morning, I managed to endure the latest round of airport security checks and found myself in transit to Cincinnati, Ohio. While onboard, I had been reading the completely strange and yet interesting book, A Salmon of Doubt (see reference below), which pulls together some interesting tidbits from the life and stories of Douglas Adams. If you understand Adams' wit, you will no doubt appreciate the conundrums that follow. And, if you can figure out ALL the answers to this lot, drop us an email. We will be glad to tell you if you have succeeded, and we'll email along some additional puzzles in return. (jimcain@teamworkandteamplay.com)

Anyway, back to my story. Somewhere during our descent to Cincinnati, I experienced a brief moment of panic when I was informed of our actual destination. The moment passed quickly, but remains a bit unsettling to this day. And so, this initial brush with the unexplainable and unusual becomes our first question...

1. When you land at the Cincinnati airport, what state are you in?

2. What did David Bradley create that is an essential part of our modern lives?

3. To whom is the following quote attributed, and on what date in history did it occur?

Eppur si muovo

4. Three adventurers (one from New York City, one from St. Louis, and a third from Los Angeles) independently depart from their home cities and walk a straight line to the north pole and down to civilization on the other side. When they return home, they discover that only one of them can actually claim to have been at the North Pole. Why?

5. What is the name of the closest star (other than our own sun) to earth?

6. A businessman flies west for an important business meeting the following day with a client. When he arrives, he checks into a hotel. After he arranges his clothes for the next day, he decides to turn in. He notices that the only light switch in the room is near the door, and that the bed is on the opposite

side of the room. He manages, however, to turn off the light switch and make it comfortably into bed before the room gets dark. How is this possible?

7. Which side of a house gets the most direct sunlight?

8. What is the difference between a typhoon, a monsoon, a hurricane and a cyclone?

9. You pack up your gear and head out to the mountains for a weekend camping trip. Although you didn't bring a thermometer, one of your friends says they can tell the temperature by listening to the crickets. If this is true, how do they find the temperature?

10. Why are 1996 U.S. dimes worth almost $200.00 U.S. Dollars?

11. What gets wetter the more that it dries?

Teachable Moments What unusual facts can you discover about your organization, team, school or corporation that would make for a positive and interesting quiz?

Variations If you enjoy this unusual collection of even more unusual questions, you might enjoy some of the following books:

Puzzles and Essays from "The Exchange" - Tricky Reference Questions, 2003, Charles R. Anderson, Haworth Information Press, New York, NY USA ISBN 0-7890-1761-X 35 years of librarian reference questions, and their sometimes surprising answers.

Schott's Original Miscellany, 2002, Ben Schott, Bloomsbury, New York, NY USA ISBN 1-58234-349-7 A unique collection of facts, some trivial, some essential, all quite interesting.

The Uncyclopedia, 2004, Gideon Haigh, Hyperion, New York, NY USA ISBN 1-4013-0153-3 Everything you never knew you wanted to know.

That Book...of Perfectly Useless Information, 2004, Mitchell Symons, William Morrow, New York, NY USA ISBN 0-06-073149-4

Hints and Clues Do not be surprised if you cannot find all of the answers on the Internet. Try visiting your local library, and make friends with a book or two.

If you enjoy the sometimes bizarre humor of Douglas Adams, we invite you to read: A Salmon of Doubt - Hitchhiking the Galaxy One Last Time, 2002, Douglas Adams, Harmony Books, New York, NY USA ISBN 1-4000-4508-8 With content pulled from Adams' four computers, after his death in May of 2001, you'll gain a special insight into his strange and wonderful way of viewing the world.

Don't Panic - Douglas Adams and the Hitchhiker's Guide to the Galaxy, 2003, Neil Gaiman, Titan Books, London, UK ISBN 1-84023-742-2.

Hitchhiker - A Biography of Douglas Adams, 2003, M. J. Simpson, Hodder & Stoughton, London, UK ISBN 0-340-82766-1.

"It is a mistake to think you can solve any major problems just with potatoes."
Douglas Adams

63. Changing Sides
Solving Puzzles on a Grand Scale

You can take this classic bead and string puzzle and make it ten times larger. The basic components of the puzzle are shown in the illustration: a piece of wood with three holes, two wooden beads, and a piece of string.

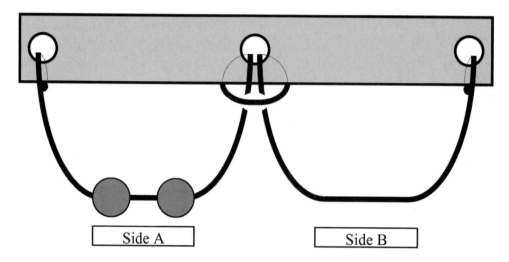

Side A   Side B

Instructions are provided below to make a king size version of this puzzle with team members instead of wooden beads. The goal for these team members is the same as it is for the wooden beads - to find a path to the other side of the puzzle (i.e. from Side A to Side B).

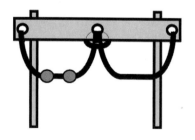

Supplies To make a king size version of the puzzle, use a 2x6 board that is 10 feet (3 meters) long with three 3 inch (75mm) diameter holes, and a 40-50 foot (12-15 meter) long piece of climbing rope. Instead of the wooden beads found in the traditional puzzle, use carabiners to attach ten participants by their climbing harness, belt or belt loops to one side of the puzzle. Knot each end of the climbing rope to the wooden beam. You can mount the 2x6 board like the top rail of a fence, about 3 feet (1 meter) off the ground, as shown.

Teachable Moments Some things that look impossible in the beginning just need a little effort to make everything turn out fine. This puzzle not only requires one person to solve the puzzle, but for every member of the team to learn how to do it for themselves.

You can also conduct this puzzle as a consensus building activity by initially placing half of the team members on each side, and asking them to come together as a team, and reside on only one side.

Variations There are a variety of tavern puzzles, ring and string puzzles, and small manipulative puzzles which can be enlarged. You can also try puzzle #2, Handcuffs and Shackles, and puzzle #48, Human Knot, for similar team challenges.

Hints and Clues There are two possible directions that your team can proceed on the rope. Which seems to hold the most promise?

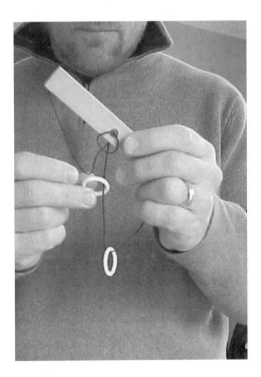

*"A positive attitude may not solve all your problems,
but it will annoy enough people to make it worth the effort."*
Herm Albright

64. Classical Knot Theory
Tying Knots Just for Fun

Here is a classic puzzle that has been around for generations. We have found two different solutions. Can your team find more?

Begin by placing a 6 foot (2 meter) length of rope in a straight line on a table. The challenge is to pick up this rope, and without letting go, tie an overhand knot in the rope.

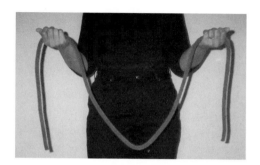 

Supplies A 6 foot (2 meter) long section of soft, flexible rope. It is a bit easier to present the rope when it is placed upon a table or other flat surface than when placed on the ground.

Teachable Moments Sometimes we can find solutions from trial and error attempts. At other times it takes additional skills of logic and reasoning. Which method of discovery do you think is necessary here?

'Planning' is equally important to 'doing' in this task. You may find that having a plan before picking up the rope is a valuable asset.

Variations You can 'reverse' this challenge by presenting a rope with an overhand knot already in place. Then ask participants to take hold of the rope, and without letting go, remove the overhand knot from the rope.

For a different challenge, ask your team to form a long line, and place one segment of rope between each two people. You will need one less rope than you have participants in your group. Next ask them to form an overhand knot in each section of rope without anyone in the group letting go during the process. You can also 'reverse' this challenge, and ask the group to remove each of the overhand knots present in each segment of rope. Be prepared - in this activity the participants located at each end of the group's line will be more active than those nearest the center.

You'll find this and many more knot activities in The Book on Raccoon Circles. See the reference section of this book for information.

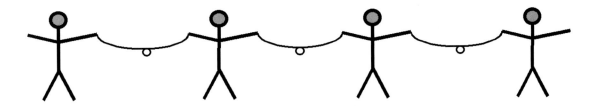

Hints and Clues Try working as individuals first, then as partners, small groups and finally as a whole team. Think about what you might do to prepare for picking up the rope before you actually pick it up.

*"You know that children are growing up when
they start asking questions that have answers."*
John J. Plomp

*"Sometimes we do a thing in order to find out the reason for it.
Sometimes our actions are questions not answers."*
John Le Carre,
Magnus Pym in "A Perfect Spy"

*"The scientist is not a person who gives the right answers,
he is one who asks the right questions."*
Claude Levi-Strauss

65. The Placemat Puzzle
Getting to Know Each Other

Here is a colorful and fun puzzle technique for forming groups and jump starting the introduction process.

One piece of a puzzle is presented to each member of the group. The challenge is for each person to find other participants with similar pieces and assemble their puzzle as a group.

Tom Heck used this activity as part of his YMCA Adventure Day programs for the Asheville, NC public schools. "I always used this activity to divide the class into two teams. I would work with the class as a whole for a short time until I was able to determine how I wanted to split the class. Rather than counting off by twos, I would use this activity. I became familiar enough handing out each puzzle piece that I could determine the make-up of the two teams. All this without the awareness of the students, who thought the process was completely random."

Supplies You'll need some colorful placemats available at discount or kitchenware stores. Cut each placemat into a number of pieces equal to the group size you would like to have. If you happen to have more puzzle pieces than participants, you can give multiple pieces to some group members (just make sure these pieces are from the same puzzle).

Teachable Moments Here is a simple and almost random technique for forming smaller groups from large audiences. Tom Heck also provides the following two commentaries:

"After the group has formed into two teams, I ask everyone to sit down and discuss the lessons presented through this activity. One lesson I often share is that we all bring something totally unique and useful to the team. We are just like pieces of the puzzle. A puzzle is made up of many unique but related pieces. When a piece is missing we know it and the whole is diminished. There is a wonderful paradox presented by this activity - the fact that we are all unique and yet are all part of the whole. Our greatest achievements as a society happen when we realize this fact."

"To drive home the value of diversity, consider this version of the Placemat Puzzle for a group of 20 participants. Divide one place mat into ten pieces (just as you did previously) for the first group of ten participants. For the next group of ten, purchase 10 identical placemats, and cut the same size and shape piece from each lower left corner of these place mats. Pass out these identical ten pieces to the group. The team that receives these puzzle pieces will soon realize that they are unable to complete the challenge. A discussion of the value of diversity is perfect at this time."

Variations Here are several additional ideas for forming groups with puzzles and other simple props. We begin with a wooden bone puzzle. The bone puzzle is a collection of wooden strips cut from a single block of wood. We used a bandsaw to make the one shown in the photograph. By using different colors of wood, you can create puzzles that participants can use to 'find their team.' Cut the same number of pieces from each block of wood that you would like in each group. Twelve wooden pieces for twelve people per group. Mix all the various blocks of wood together in a large bowl or bucket. As participants enter your event, ask them to take a piece and to find the other members of their group.

You can also use nuts and bolts in a similar fashion. Present different styles and sizes of bolts to several team leaders. Next, place one threaded nut in a bowl or bucket for each participant in the group. There should be the same number of each style nut for the desired size of each group. When each team has all of their members, your next activities can start.

You can also randomly distribute playing cards, dominos, pasta shapes, or any additional objects you can find in sufficient numbers to form smaller groups. With playing cards, you can form groups by suit, color, number and poker hand. With dominos, after finding a new partner, invite each person to share a number of things about themselves that is equal to the number on their domino.

Hints and Clues Some folks may feel initially uncomfortable in a group with members they do not know. Encourage them to meet these new folks and make some new friends today.

66. Making Contact
Techniques for Coming Together

Teambuilding Puzzles

Here are a few close contact puzzles that requires some mathematical and geometrical analyses, or a really good guess and a whole lot of luck. The goal is to see how many different ways you can make 'contact' between the objects mentioned below.

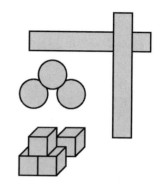

Tennis Balls - How many tennis balls can be in contact with one tennis ball? How many tennis balls can be in contact with each other?

Building Blocks or Cubes - How many wooden blocks or cubes can be placed in contact with one wooden cube? How many can be placed in contact with each other?

Sticks or Dowel Rods - How many sticks can be placed in contact with each other? Show solutions for 2, 3, 4, 5, 6, 7, and 8. What if the dowel rods used in this activity were replaced with 3 feet (1 meter) long foam noodle segments?

Coins - How many coins can be placed in contact with each other? Does it matter if size of each coin varies?

People - How many people can you connect with in the next 30 seconds? How many people can be in contact with each other at the same time? Can you find a way to connect your whole team together?

Supplies You will need enough tennis balls and wooden blocks or cubes for each group to have 15. You'll also need about 10 new pencils, dowel rods or PVC tubes (available at most hardware stores), or foam pool noodles for each group. Eight to ten coins per group will also be sufficient.

Teachable Moments It takes some effort to 'make contact' with each of these shapes, just as it takes an extra effort to connect with different people. The same techniques do not work for every shape, nor for every person, community or culture. For more information about connection, read the book, Connect - 12 vital ties that open your heart, lengthen your life, and deepen your soul, 1999, Edward M. Hallowell, Pantheon Books, New York, NY USA ISBN 0-375-40357-4 Connection improves the quality and length of your life, and here is the information that proves it! Soon authors Jim Cain and

Kirk Weisler will unveil their latest book, entitled: The Value of Connection - In the Workplace. Watch the Teamwork & Teamplay website for more information about this book.

Variations If you like these versions of close contact activities, try the Human Knot, puzzle #48 in this book. Also try, Commonalities, which is found on page 88 of The Book on Raccoon Circles (see reference below). For a mathematical discussion of the tennis ball contact, read: Kepler's Conjecture - How some of the greatest minds in history helped solve one of the oldest math problems in the world, 2003, George G. Szpiro, John Wiley & Sons, Hoboken, NJ USA ISBN 0-471-08601-0

What other geometrical shapes can you use to explore contact? Tin cans, metal rings, rope, pieces of paper, Tangrams, plastic soda pop bottles, flexible materials such as clay or inflatable toys and rubber bands all have different abilities to connect with each other.

Hints and Clues You can make more contact in a three-dimensional space than a two-dimensional space for most of these objects.

The Revised and Expanded Book of Raccoon Circles, 2007, Jim Cain and Tom Smith, Kendall Hunt Publishers, Dubuque, IA USA www.kendallhunt.com (1-800-228-0810) ISBN 0-75-75-3265-9. Hundreds of activities (including some puzzles) using only a single, simple prop.

50 Ways to Use Your Noodle, 1997, Chris Cavert and Sam Sikes, Learning Unlimited, Tulsa, OK USA ISBN 0-9646541-1-3 Great teambuilding games and activities using those foam pool noodles.

50 More Ways to Use Your Noodle, 2002, Chris Cavert and Sam Sikes, Learning Unlimited, Tulsa, OK USA ISBN 0-9646541-5-6 Even more teambuilding games and activities using foam pool noodles.

67. Nothing Can Divide Us
A Challenge for the Mathematically Inclined

While some of us can hold our own when it comes to puzzles, there are a few mathematical wizards out there that really know their stuff. Here is an opportunity for those with such mathematical skills.

A prime number is a whole number (an integer) larger than 1 and divisible only by 1 and itself.

How many prime numbers are there between one and one hundred? List them.

Supplies You can perform this puzzle with no props at all, although pencils and a few index cards will make each team's answers a bit easier to check.

Teachable Moments The title of this activity is actually our first opportunity for a teachable moment related to prime numbers. Prime numbers are those integers (whole numbers, not fractions) that cannot be divided by any other whole number. What attributes of your team are so strong that they 'cannot be divided?'

Variations Instead of prime numbers you can invite participants to count in Fibonacci sequential numbers, exponents or other mathematical formulas.

Hints and Clues A mathematical learning style is just one of the multiple intelligences proposed by authors such as Howard Gardner and Thomas Armstrong. For more information, read:

Multiple Intelligences in the Classroom, 2000, Thomas Armstrong, ASCD, Alexandria, VA USA ISBN 0-87120-376-6

Seven Kinds of Smart - Identifying and Developing Your Multiple Intelligences, 1999, Thomas Armstrong, Plume, New York, NY USA ISBN 0-452-28137-7

68. Where Do You Stand?
Quick Moves and Quick Thinking

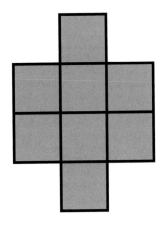

Here is a human-sized puzzle that explores mathematical skills, creative problem solving and movement. The puzzles shown are designed for teams of eight. You can modify any of these puzzles for smaller or larger groups by adding or removing squares.

Begin by assigning team members numbers from one to eight. Participants can either remember their number or wear a button, badge or sticker showing this number. After a very brief (1 minute) planning period, teams are asked to locate each member in one of the squares on the grid. The only restriction is that no two sequential numbers can be placed on squares that adjoin horizontally, vertically or diagonally.

After accomplishing the first grid pattern and another brief planning session, move quickly to the next grid pattern.

Supplies You can make a floor grid using masking tape for each puzzle or draw these grids on a large tarp or shower curtain. You can also use carpet squares, gym spots or large pieces of paper to represent each square in the grid.

Teachable Moments Part of any reorganization is the theme or underlying purpose for such a reorganization in the first place. The need to move quickly and occasionally to be able to trade places with another team member that is not located in the right position (or not needed in that capacity) is an important team skill. Reorganization is not only the physical movement of people within an organization, but also the language and communication that occurs between those team members in motion. Practice using inclusive language rather than commands.

Variations Here are several variations of the Where Do You Stand puzzle. Not all of these have a solution.

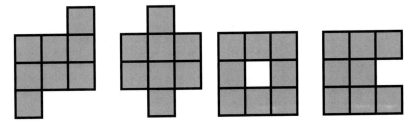

Hints and Clues Identifying opportunities for various team members is important, but how this information is communicated to them is even more important. Be kind and work together as a team.

69. Adaptation or Extinction
A Changing Environment

If your team's work, school or personal environment is going through some rapid changes, try this kinesthetic team puzzle.

Invite your team to spend a day in the Thousand Islands region of New York state. You are welcome to swim in the crystal clear waters, but when a lifeguard yells 'buddy check,' you need to have your feet inside the perimeter of one of the islands to be safe.

Start the activity with all islands in place. You'll need about a dozen islands for a group of twenty people. After each buddy check, when participants have gone back in the metaphoric water, remove one of the islands so that participants see this happening. Continue until each island becomes very crowded.

At this point, you can ask the group what is happening. Is there a trend? Do you think the trend will continue? How will you adapt to this changing environment? OK, back in the water for the next round....

Supplies You'll need several round circles for islands. You can cut these from a shower curtain, tarp, carpeting or fabric. You can also use rope for creating circles, or tubular nylon climbing webbing (known as a Raccoon Circle - see reference books). Each island should hold 2-6 people comfortably.

Teachable Moments Adapting our behavior to a new and changing environment sometimes comes too late. We retain our outdated methods and are slow to embrace new techniques and technologies. Just ask your team how many people still have their favorite music on vinyl record albums. Change is difficult. But, if we know it is inevitable, and we have the capability, then we can be at the cutting edge, rather than the trailing edge or the left behind.

In each round, previous situations no longer apply, creating new behaviors and the problems that come with them. This is a great activity to reinforce the concepts found in the book Who Moved My Cheese, by Spencer Johnson (1998, Penguin Putnam, New York, NY USA ISBN 0-399-14446-3)

Variations You can modify the number and size of islands available. You can write key corporate concepts or values on each island and see which ones are missed when they are taken away. You can provide character concepts, like trust and responsibility, on islands and discuss how the world would be if these concepts were not a part of our society.

A somewhat different concept that encourages collaboration and inclusion is to begin the activity with rope circles that are not tied together at each end. These circles can later be combined with other islands to form new, larger islands for more people.

When one group was asked what the minimum number of circles necessary to support their group was, they responded with "none! The rules say you are safe when your feet are in the perimeter of the circle." So they made a circle with their feet inside the perimeter. And you know what? They were safe!

Hints and Clues Keep reinforcing the rules with this phrase: "you are safe when? That's right, when your feet are within the perimeter of the island."

*"The greatest challenge to any thinker
is stating the problem in a way that will allow a solution."*
Bertrand Russell

*"Ignorance more frequently begets confidence than does knowledge:
it is those who know little, not those who know much, who so positively
assert that this or that problem will never be solved by science."*
Charles Darwin

70. The Fence
Working Smarter, Not Harder

Farmer Bob has returned again. This time, he wants to reduce the size of one of his grazing pastures. The four corner fenceposts are very heavy and difficult to move, and Farmer Bob just doesn't have the time during planting season. Can you help him create a new square pasture design that is half the area of his present square pasture and requires the least number of corner fenceposts to be moved? An aerial view of his pasture is shown below. How would you relocate the existing corner posts? Draw a sketch of your new grazing pasture design.

Supplies This puzzle works well as a pencil and paper challenge. You can also provide sub-teams with a 5-10 minute long planning period and then an opportunity to share their group's design with the entire audience.

Farmer Bob's Present Grazing Pasture

Fence ———
Corner Posts ●
Other Posts ○

Teachable Moments Learning is not only about discovering new information, but occasionally 'unlearning' some techniques and replacing them with better choices. While it is obviously possible to reduce the size of the present pasture by 50% moving three corner fenceposts, is it possible to perform this same task moving fewer corner fenceposts? And, if it is theoretically possible, then it becomes our job to show how it is physically possible as well.

Define the 'pathway' from your original thoughts to your final recommendation for Farmer Bob's pasture. How did you choose some designs and dismiss others? What criteria did you use to evaluate a good design and a poor one? What additional information would have been helpful before beginning this problem?

Variations What if the new grazing pasture did not need to be in the shape of a square? How many corner fenceposts would you need to relocate to produce a pasture with half the area of the present pasture? What about a design with 25% percent of the present pasture's area? How many corner fenceposts would you have to move then? It is possible to produce a new pasture with 25% of the existing pasture's area without moving ANY corner fenceposts. Can you show how?

Hints and Clues How many different ways can you draw a square?

71. Land of Lakes
Expansion With Limitations

Learning how to expand your horizons and still remain within necessary limitations is an essential life skill. Here are a few puzzles to test your team's abilities to do just that.

The township park has a beautiful pond as the centerpiece. The township officials have decided to expand the area of this pond by a factor of 2. There are two small constraints however:

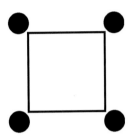

1. The new pond configuration must also be a square.

2. The four trees surrounding the pond cannot be moved and must remain where they are, on dry land.

How would your team propose to design the new pond?

Supplies You can present this puzzle with pencil and paper, or create a real scenario with a 100 foot (30 meter) rope and several props to represent trees.

Teachable Moments Identifying and learning how to work within limitations is a valuable life skill. Think of some horizon expanding experiences you have had and the limitations placed on you during such times. Share your experiences.

Variations Here are a few additional geometrical configurations with which you can challenge your teams. Follow the instructions, and save the trees!

Increase the size of the star-shaped lake, by at least a factor of 4, while the lake remains star-shaped.

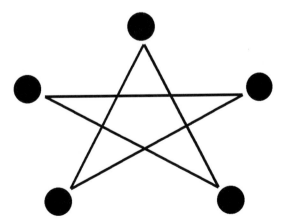

Increase the area of the triangular lake by 300% but keep an equilateral triangular shape.

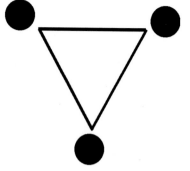

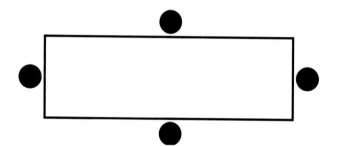

Increase the area of the rectangular lake by a factor of 2. The new lake configuration must also be a rectangle.

Now that your team has experience in expanding with limitations, develop a plan so that the circular lake holds twice as much water.

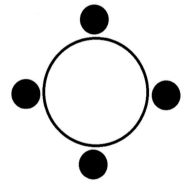

Hints and Clues It might help to forget the original configuration of each lake and only work on creating the new lake configuration within the boundaries or limitations presented. The circular configuration may require a different technique.

**Teambuilding
Puzzles**

72. Sharing Connections
Lines of Communication and Connection

One essential element of a successful teambuilding program is creating a sense of connection, community and unity within the team. Here is a fun activity to tie your team together.

With the group seated or standing in a circle, one person (who happens to be holding a ball of yarn) begins by mentioning various things they enjoy. For example, they might offer, "I like to ride my mountain bike. I enjoy cooking. I like to read." When one of these statements rings true for another participant in the group, they hold up both hands, and the person holding the ball of yarn rolls this ball over to them while keeping hold of the very end of the yarn. The second person (now holding the ball of yarn) begins sharing some of the activities they enjoy until another participant holds up their hands. And so the ball is passed around the group with each participant becoming connected to the other members of their group by the things they have in common.

In most cases, group members only catch and roll the ball once. Each person catching the ball holds onto the string as the ball continues along its path to every other member of the group. After everyone has caught the ball, the final person must keep sharing information until the starting participant can agree with one of their comments.

At this point, you can reverse the process by discussing personal goals for the day, challenges you are looking forward to, resources needed or other suitable topics. The ball is passed from person to person along the string connecting them. Each person, when they receive the ball, carefully winds the yarn back into place before passing the ball on to the next person in the connection line.

Supplies You will need a ball of twine, yarn or string at least 10 feet (3 meters) in length for every person in the group. 10 people = 100 feet (30 meters). For groups larger than 20, you should increase the length of yarn to 25 feet (8 meters) per person.

Teachable Moments   Unity, community, and connection are an essential part of any teambuilding program. Read the commentary below for additional insight.

Variations This is a great activity for large groups, especially those attempting to find commonalties. If you would like to make this a true puzzle, limit each person to only a single comment. Then see how many people you can connect together before the group 'stalls.' If you reach a point where no one shares the topic or activity mentioned, rewind the ball and begin again at another position.

Hints and Clues Sharing Connections is a bit more of an activity than a true puzzle. In order to reach every person in the group however, participants must be flexible, creative and willing to speak up - all talents and skills useful in solving problems and working together as a team. For the true puzzle version of this activity (the one limited to only a single comment), success is more likely with general comments, but more interesting, and often outrageous, with more personal disclosures.

Building Unity, Community and Connection
by Jim Cain, Ph.D.

For 36 years now, I've been active in the field of adventure-based learning (and along with it the many other names that this style of education includes, such as: experiential learning, experience-based training, teambuilding, leadership development, ropes and challenge courses, and most recently, active learning). During this time, there has been a flow of ideas, grass root programs, curriculum development, research and general discussion that has allowed this field to mature and proliferate. Adventure-based learning now spans the extremes from collaborative and cooperative games played by children on the school playground and at summer camps, to experiences that test the leadership principles and alter the culture of international corporations in their boardrooms.

With such a rich history, and a strong presence in our modern society, the obvious question is "What's Next?" I believe that in order to answer this question for the future, you must first look at the past.

Ten years ago, a consultant or a challenge course operator could approach local corporations and mention the word 'teambuilding' and easily attract business. More recently, the focus has changed from teambuilding to exploring leadership issues. Corporations want to take existing employees and help them achieve the skills they need to become leaders within the organization. To this end, many of the activities used for adventure-based teambuilding have been reformatted to focus not only on the team completion of a task, but also on the leadership talents utilized during the project. Even more important in this transition is the change from simply accepting what a challenge course standardly offered, to corporations requesting facilitators to frame activities and initiatives around specific themes or goals. In many cases, the actual activities used in each of these cases is the same, but the organization, preparation, and facilitation of these activities has dramatically changed.

With this in mind, it is now time to revisit our initial question from above, "What's Next?" While the following opinions and comments are certainly my own, there are an enormous number of authors who agree with me. The reference and resource listings in my upcoming book on this subject contain more than 200 books, publications, journal articles and websites. Many of these references did not exist just a decade ago and are the result of expanding interest and perceived value in this arena.

I believe, as we go forward, that the next wave in adventure-based programming, teambuilding and active learning will be shaped by the word 'connection.'

The National Longitudinal Study of Adolescent Health (the study funded after the Columbine High School tragedy a few years ago) had two not-so-surprising results. Students that felt a connection to their families, and students that felt a connection to their schools, were incredibly well insulated from nearly all of the traditional risky behaviors associated with adolescence. Corporations have discovered that employee retention improves as an employee feels a sense of connection in the workplace. Even our current conventional wisdom on organizational effectiveness shows that there are three things required for highly effective teams:

1. A clearly identified, articulated and worthy task.
2. The opportunity for growth, advancement and building new skills
3. The opportunity to create connection and maintain relationships with other members of the group. Sometimes referred to as the 'social capital' of the organization.

The third item mentioned above clearly demonstrates the need for connection in our corporate world. The NLSAH results show similar needs in the world of our children. And additional studies, such as the Alameda County Study (1979) by Dr. Lisa Berkman of Harvard University, show that for even the elderly in our communities, personal health and the quality of their lives improve with the amount of connection they have to the other members of their community. For more information about these subjects, see the references listed at the end of this article.

It is time for us to do what we have always done well - build unity, community and connection through activities that utilize a wide variety of life skills and that open the door to meaningful conversations about subjects that matter.

I would encourage each of you that read this article to find the following information at your local library, on-line or at your local bookstore, and learn how to apply it in your pursuit of the next wave in adventure-based, teambuilding, and active learning. And, if you would like a publication that is a bit more specific to the corporate adventure-based learning field, visit the Teamwork and Teamplay website at: www.teamworkandteamplay. com, for information about "The Value of Connection - In the Workplace" by Jim Cain and Kirk Weisler.

Reference Articles

Connect - 12 vital ties that open your heart, lengthen your life, and deepen your soul, 1999, Edward M. Hallowell, Pantheon Books, New York, NY USA ISBN 0-375-40357-4 Connection improves the quality and length of your life, and here is the information that proves it!

The Value of Connection in the Workplace - <u>You</u> can become the catalyst for building community and creating a positive work environment in your corporation, Jim Cain and Kirk Weisler "A new classic in creating the kind of unity, community and connection in the workplace that you always knew was possible, in an active, fun and productive manner. This book contains the philosophy, research and easy-to-follow activities for anyone to have a positive impact on their own organization."

Exploring the Stages of Group Formation Using Adventure-Based Activities, Jim Cain, Teamwork & Teamplay website www.teamworkandteamplay.com, 2003.

Peer Harassment, School Connectedness, and Academic Achievement, Marla Eisenberg, Diane Neumark-Sztainer and Cheryl Perry, *The Journal of School Health*, Volume 73, Number 8, October 2003, pages 311-316.

Protecting Adolescents From Harm: Findings From the National Longitudinal Study on Adolescent Health, Michael Resnick, Peter Bearman, Robert Blum, et.al., *Journal of the American Medical Association (JAMA)*, Volume 278, Number 10, September 10, 1997, pages 823-832.

Social Ties and Susceptibility to the Common Cold, Sheldon Cohen, William Doyle, David Skoner, Bruce Rabin and Jack Gwaltney, *Journal of the American Medical Association (JAMA)*, Volume 277, Number 24, June 25, 1997, pages 1940-1944.

The National Longitudinal Study on Adolescent Health - Preliminary Results: Great Expectations, Jonathan Klein, *Journal of the American Medical Association (JAMA)*, Volume 278, Number 10, September 10, 1997, pages 864-865.

*"We are continually faced with a series of
great opportunities brilliantly disguised as insoluble problems."*
John W. Gardner

73. The Bridge
Exploring History, Invention and Structural Engineering

While the paintings, inventions, sculptures and illustrations of Leonardo Da Vinci are often viewed as classical artwork, a few actually lend themselves to the world of puzzles. Da Vinci's design of a transportable bridge provided one concept to the challenging problem that military troops faced when trying to safely cross a river or chasm. It is not only a unique design, but one that enchants puzzlers as well.

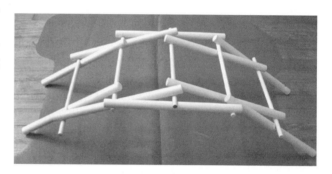

The puzzle here is to assemble a freestanding bridge or arch using only the components provided. The materials provided come in two distinct shapes and the final bridge requires no additional fasteners or connectors. When complete, the bridge will be able to support the weight provided and will not touch the water.

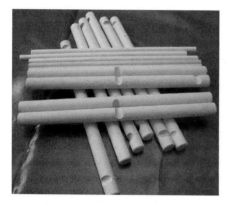

Supplies Two styles of wooden dowel rods (or PVC tubes) are needed for this puzzle. The photograph illustrates a collection of ten 1 inch (25.4 mm) dowels 15 inches (38 cm) long with notches and five 1/2 inch (12.7 mm) dowels, also 15 inches (38 cm) long without notches. An illustration of the 1 inch diameter dowels is shown below. Notice the three circular notches cut, drilled or sanded into each of these pieces.

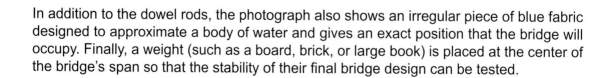

In addition to the dowel rods, the photograph also shows an irregular piece of blue fabric designed to approximate a body of water and gives an exact position that the bridge will occupy. Finally, a weight (such as a board, brick, or large book) is placed at the center of the bridge's span so that the stability of their final bridge design can be tested.

Teachable Moments   What is the practicality of this bridge design? Is it possible to construct this bridge from just one side of the water? What could you modify in this design to improve the performance of this bridge? How many people would it take to assemble such a bridge? How much time would be required to build this bridge? What component is most likely to fail during usage? Is it a simple task to manufacture this bridge design, or could you suggest improvements for greater manufacturability? How could you use this concept to create a bridge that would span a greater distance? Is it possible to build this bridge with components that are all identical? This bridge design, from Leonardo di Vinci, is hundreds of years old. Can you think of alternative portable bridge designs that use modern materials and techniques?

Variations   The bridge shown in the above illustration uses wooden dowel rods. PVC tubing can also be used. Consider other bridge designs made from cardboard, popsicle (craft) sticks, foam noodles, pipe cleaners, a single sheet of paper, or other building materials. As an alternative to the blue fabric, two tables (foundations) can be spaced 30 inches apart and the bridge assembled upon them.

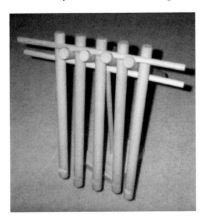

The nail puzzle (Plenty of Room at the Top, #11) can also be performed using these same pieces. By inserting one of the 1/2 inch dowel rods into a wooden base, the remaining pieces can be used just like the nails in puzzle #11. We call this version, **The Balance**.

Hints and Clues   The larger dowel rods are used as the side structure to the bridge. The smaller diameter dowel rods simulate the climbing rungs.

For more information about bridge construction, read:

Bridges! Amazing Structures to Design, Build & Test, 1999, Carol Johmann and Elizabeth Rieth, Williamson Publishing, Charlotte, Vermont USA ISBN 1-885593-30-9 Some interesting information and bridges you can make from household items.

The Creation of Bridges, 1999, David Bennett, Fitzhenry & Whiteside, Toronto, Ontario Canada ISBN 1-55041-552-2 Stunning photographs of bridges from around the world.

74. Three Kinds of Memory
A Mental Marathon

Enjoy this collection of three similar puzzles that explore kinesthetic, auditory and visual learning styles and memory, along with all that stuff you've been keeping in your junk drawer at home

This activity begins by sharing a tray filled with one or two dozen unusual objects. In round one, the objects are shared by passing them around, hand to hand, but without looking at them. Participants can feel each item, but are not allowed to look at it. After round one, ask everyone to write down what they touched.

In round two, drop each item a short distance onto a metal tray that has been placed outside the sight range of the team. Participants are asked to remember the sound make by each item. After the last object is dropped, participants are asked to write down what objects they have heard.

Finally, in round three, the tray is slowly passed around the room so that each participant can view it for about 15 seconds at the most. This time, participants write down what they have seen.

Supplies You will need an unusual collection of 'stuff.' The kinds of things you find in kitchen or workshop junk drawers are perfect. Sets of keys, balls, rolls of tape, new unsharpened pencils, coins, jewelry, sewing thimbles, a cassette tape, a plastic spoon, a spool of thread, nuts & bolts, marbles, a paperback book, paperclips and buttons are a good start. You'll also need a metal tray, cookie baking sheet or serving plate and a sack to store these items.

Teachable Moments   During which round of this activity did you remember the most items correctly? Which style of memory is your dominant or most efficient style? What other things do you remember in this way? For example, the way food smells during the holidays, the sound of your doorbell ringing, the texture of grass on your feet or the smile on the face of a friend.

How can differences in learning styles benefit our group? How have learning style differences affected your life in the past?

Variations You can choose objects with a particular theme such as office supplies, tools from the toolbox, kitchen gadgets, computer gear, antique junk or toys from the toybox. Do not include any objects with sharp edges or points.

Teambuilding Puzzles

Hints and Clues If your dominant memory style is visual, try to picture what your are feeling or hearing. If it is auditory, imagine what sound the object you are looking at makes. If it is tactile or kinesthetic, imagine what it would feel like.

*"The building of a perfect body crowned by a perfect brain,
is at once the greatest earthly problem and grandest hope of the race."*
Dio Lewis

*"Man is not born to solve the problem of the universe,
but to find out what he has to do; and to restrain himself
within the limits of his comprehension."*
Johann Wolfgang von Goethe

*"I know that most men, including those at ease with problems
of the greatest complexity, can seldom accept even the simplest and most
obvious truth if it be such as would oblige them to admit the falsity of conclusions
which they have delighted in explaining to colleagues, which they have
proudly taught to others, and which they have woven,
thread by thread, into the fabric of their lives."*
Leo Tolstoy

75. Matchmaking
A Memory Puzzle for Teams

Who knew that turning over a new leaf could be so much fun. Here is a kinesthetic, visual and auditory activity that should keep most parts of your brain working overtime.

A collection of twenty plywood squares are placed as shown and surrounded by a rope. These squares have pictures on the bottom side and are identically blank on the top. One team member at a time enters the rope enclosure and is allowed to turn over two of the squares. If a match occurs, these squares remain turned over (so that the pictures are visible). If no match is found, both squares are replaced face down, and the search continues until all squares have been turned over. Team members are encouraged to use their group memory capabilities and assist each team member as they enter the rope enclosure.

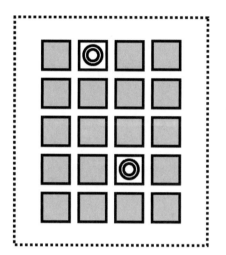

Supplies You'll need several plywood or cardboard squares decorated on one side with images, photographs or symbols, and identically blank on the reverse side. Each image will appear twice.

Teachable Moments There are plenty of opportunities here to work on your management 'hunches.' But more importantly, can you learn from your mistakes? Also, can your team define a systematic method for finding all the matches with the least number of moves possible? Is there a way to improve on your memory skills as well?

Variations You can use as many or as few squares as necessary, but always an even number for matches of two. You could use three matches, or even four, instead of two. For a greater mental challenge, when two unmatched squares are turned over, trade places before turning them back. You can also use images that are similar but not exactly the same as other images on different squares.

Rather than using plywood squares, you can conceal various three-dimensional objects with opaque drinking cups, cans or small buckets. Instead of turning over the wooden squares, participants lift two containers at a time. This three-dimensional version is a bit more visually stimulating.

For an acoustic version of this activity, create a 4x5 grid of small containers (35 mm film canisters work well) filled with various objects. Each team member gets to shake the containers and look for an acoustic match. If a match occurs, these two containers are removed from the playing grid. The match continues until all containers have been removed. Contents can include, coins, small bells, beads, dried beans, nuts & bolts, wood blocks, rice or sand.

Hints and Clues Start in one corner, and follow a path agreed upon by the group. Use everyone's memory to identify matches. Coach and assist your teammates throughout the activity.

For a large format double-deck of character cards printed in full color (including character quotations) contact Creative Concepts at: www. GivaGeta.com or (860) 657-0770. With this deck of 58 cards, you can facilitate 12 different icebreakers, teambuilding challenges and character building activities, plus play all your favorite card games, including the Matchmaking activity presented here. Instructions are included. You can also purchase these Teamwork & Teamplay Character Cards from Training Wheels, Inc. at 1-888-553-0147 or www.training-wheels.com.

76. Changing Directions
Change is Easier Than You Think

True or false? Changing the direction of a team, a workforce, an organization, or a community only requires changing the minds of a few key players. Let's find out if this is true using the imaginary story below:

Your team of firefighters has been battling a forest fire for almost a week. Just when the wind should be dying down at the end of the day, a weather pattern shift has caused a change in the direction of the wind and the advancing direction of the fire. You are part of a team of 12 firefighters, and it is up to you to turn this team around to avoid the fire that is now moving directly towards you. Your team is standing in the standard 'arrow' formation you were trained in, as shown by the sketch on the right. What is the most efficient method to produce an identical arrow that points in the opposite direction?

Supplies You can perform this puzzle with no props at all using people to form the arrow formation. You can also use coins, poker chips, checkers, drinking glasses, rocks, foam noodle chips (from foam pool noodle toys) as shown in the pictures, or any other convenient twelve items at your disposal.

Teachable Moments Surprisingly, this simple puzzle proposes some significant leadership principles. First, that you can disrupt the entire organization, have everyone reorganize and relocate to meet the new corporate model, or you can minimize disruption to the entire corporation and only relocate those individuals in key positions necessary to change directions. Secondly, that even though the organization is pointing in one direction, some individuals might still be facing or moving in a totally different direction. And finally, whichever way the organization is moving, it is a pretty good idea for those in key positions to communicate this vision (and direction) to everyone.

This is also an interesting time to discuss if the original statement above is true or false. In order to help our organization move forward 'in the other direction,' is it only necessary to change the minds of a few key players?

Variations

You can utilize this puzzle with 10 participants, moving only 3 people.

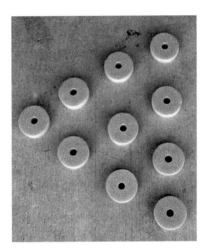

Or, with 6 participants, moving only 2 people.

Hints and Clues Create a 'vision' of what 'the opposite direction' looks like, and minimize the number of people that need to move to create this new image.

For more activities with foam noodle chips (and the whole noodles too) see:

50 Ways to Use Your Noodle: Loads of Land Games with Foam Noodle Toys, by Chris Cavert and Sam Sikes. Learning Unlimited Publications. ISBN: 0-9646541-1-3

50 More Ways to Use Your Noodle: Loads of Land and Water Games with Foam Noodle Toys, by Chris Cavert and Sam Sikes. Learning Unlimited Publication.
ISBN: 0-9646541-5-6 (Both books are also available at www.fundoing.com)

77. Island Hopping
Efficiency and Effectiveness

The bridge puzzle of mathematician Leonhard Euler, known as the Seven Bridges of Königsberg, remains a classic to this day. We have created two variations of this style of puzzle, with one important opportunity - a chance to fix the problem in each puzzle! We call these variations Island Hopping and Closing All the Doors.

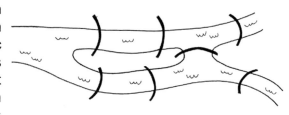

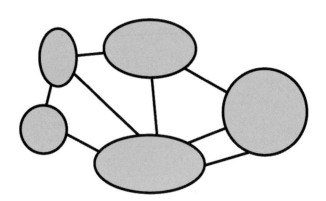

Island Hopping For the island geography shown here, is there an island where your team can begin and walk to all the other islands, crossing each bridge exactly once, and returning to the same starting island?

As a variation, from which islands can you cross the most bridges just once, and still return to the same starting location?

Closing All the Doors At the FUNdoing world headquarters, Joe the night watchman is a vision of efficiency. His last task before leaving each night is to close and lock each of the various office and supply room doors. Being a bit of a stickler for efficiency, Joe was wondering if there was a room from which he could begin locking up for the night where he would pass through each door on the way out only once, locking them all behind him as he leaves, and ending up on the outside of the building. Joe likes to double check each door after closing it. For the floor plan shown (on the next page), can you find a route that will help Joe meet his goal?

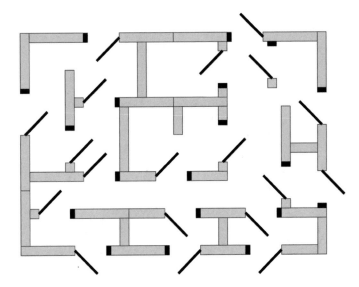

Supplies You can present this puzzle as a pencil and paper exercise, but we encourage you to use masking tape to produce an outline of the river and islands, and 2x4's for the bridges. You can also create the floor plan model for Closing All the Doors with masking tape indoors, or flagging tape (used by surveyors and available at most larger hardware stores) for outdoor puzzle sessions.

Teachable Moments Creative problem solving relies on one essential assumption, that there is in fact a solution. Each of the puzzles above requires an important next step, deciding what to do when your first assumptions prove to be wrong. For the Island Hopping puzzle, where would your team suggest building or removing a bridge? For the Closing All the Doors puzzle, how would your team recommend the office be reconfigured to meet Joe's goal?

Variations If you would like to try your hand at this style of puzzle making, try beginning with an aerial view of the streets of a major metropolitan city. Now write in your own one-way road signs, and ask your team to navigate from Point A to Point B, following all of the road signs. For an additional challenge, ask your team to complete this task and only turn right the entire trip.

If you enjoy this style of puzzle, try number #46.

Hints and Clues How can we be absolutely sure that there is no solution unless we add another bridge or install another door?

78. Line Up the Glasses
One Chance, and One Chance Only

It seems like quite a few of the puzzles we enjoy today are recreations often shared and enjoyed in the local pub. Tavern puzzles, those wrought iron tangled contraptions, even carry the identity of their origin in their name. Well, in keeping with this classic tradition, here is a quick puzzle that you can share at the dinner table or your next happy hour celebration.

Begin with six glasses, alternatively filled and empty, as shown here.

Moving only a single glass, produce the new pattern of all filled glasses on the left side and all empty glasses on the right.

Supplies Six regular drinking glasses or cups. Transparent glasses are preferable. Fill three glasses with a colorful liquid.

Teachable Moments Like many puzzles, the solution lies within our interpretation of the rules explaining the challenge. Which of the 'rules' involved in completing this task can be interpreted in a unique manner that makes success assured? Why is it that we have difficulty in seeing such solutions the first time and often do not find them a tall?

Variations You can attempt a similar challenge with eight glasses and allow any two glasses to be moved. As a physical challenge, present this problem using 5 gallon buckets filled with water, or even 55 gallon barrels partially filled with water.

Hints and Clues Invite the group to begin this puzzle using the least amount of moves to achieve the final configuration. Further challenge them to move only a single glass. Ask the question, "what does it mean to 'move' a glass?"

79. Mathematical Magic
One Simple Operation

Even if numbers and math are not your favorite things, you should be able to perform one simple operation that will make the following equations work out.

Perform one operation on the following equation so that the result equals 825.

$$1 + 6 + 806 + 101 - 8$$

Perform one operation on the following equation so that the equation becomes true.

$$IX = X + I$$

Supplies Write the two above equations in bold letters on a piece of cardboard or plywood. Have a few markers available. You can also present this puzzle on a small piece of whiteboard, using dry erase markers.

Teachable Moments Serendipity is the process of looking for one thing, and finding quite another. What is it about 'the operation' that needs performing which causes us to forget to look for the obvious.

"If the only tool you have is a hammer, you tend to see every problem as a nail."
Abraham Maslow

We are sometimes so prepared to use our favorite tool or skill that we can miss all the information that says we should be using a different tool or skill altogether. Before we begin working on the answer to a puzzle or problem, we should be sure to listen completely to the question first.

Variations How many other equations can you create that would benefit from these same operations?

Hints and Clues How many different kinds of 'operations' are there?

80. Parking Cars
Possible or Impossible?

Teambuilding
Puzzles

There is a big difference between things which are theoretically possible and those you can actually demonstrate at the drop of a hat. Here is a puzzle which is simple to explain, but incredibly difficult to prove. Good Luck!

Figure A

Figure B

Figure C

Figure D

We begin with a standard chess or checkerboard pattern - an 8x8 grid of alternating color squares (See Figure A). Imagine this surface as our 'parking lot.' A standard vehicle, represented by a domino in this case, fills exactly two squares of the checkerboard (as illustrated in Figure B). The 8x8 grid parking lot contains 64 squares and can hold 32 vehicles.

If two corners of the checkerboard are removed (as shown in Figure C), only 62 squares are left. Can you find an arrangement for 31 vehicles to fill this space?

Finally (and here is the tricky bit), if two corners are removed (as shown in Figure D), again only 62 squares are left. Can you find an arrangement for 31 vehicles to fill this space? If not, why not?

Supplies A standard checkerboard and 32 dominoes are needed for this puzzle. Conversely, you can make your own computer generated checkerboard pattern of any size. You will just need your 'vehicles' to be exactly two squares long and one square wide for the parking lot portion of this puzzle.

Teachable Moments Most researchers and inventors will tell you that while looking for a new discovery, technique or innovation, they encountered moments of frustration and even defeat when they realized that the path they had chosen did not in fact arrive at the destination they had in mind. Some had to start over on a new path. Some wondered, "how did I get here?" But in the end, they decided that no matter how much time they put into the task, the result they searched for was not going to happen. In short, they pulled the plug on the whole operation. The question here then, is to determine why it is not possible to park 31 vehicles in the parking lot shown in Figure D. Answer this question, and you will understand why no amount of effort will produce a successful configuration.

Variations Although the 8x8 checkerboard is a familiar standard, you can alter this design in many ways. A rectangular shape, a checkerboard pattern made from your company's logo, letters of the alphabet, and even a checkerboard mobius strip can be created for this puzzle. The only constant necessary is that initially the checkerboard pattern is made up of an even number of squares, and that any 'vehicle' takes up exactly two adjacent squares.

Other variations for Figures C and D above include removing any two squares along the perimeter or interior of these checkerboards.

Hints and Clues What is different about the checkerboards in Figure C and in Figure D.

If you enjoy this style of mathematical recreation, we invite you to read:

Math Hysteria - Fun and Games with Mathematics, 2004, Ian Stewart, Oxford University Press, Oxford UK ISBN 0-19-861336-9. Stewart states that "No matter how many times you try something and fail, that doesn't prove it's impossible. It just shows that you don't know how to do it. To prove something is impossible, you have to rule out all attempts at a solution..." See Chapter Two, Domino Theories.

Q.E.D. Beauty in Mathematical Proof, 2004, Burkard Polster, Walker & Company, New York, NY USA ISBN 0-8027-1431-5. See "Treacherous Truth - What Proofs are all About" on pages 2&3.

"All progress is precarious, and the solution of one problem brings us face to face with another problem."
Martin Luther King

81. The Tower
Creativity in Small Spaces

Here is a challenge to see how your team's creativity stacks up.

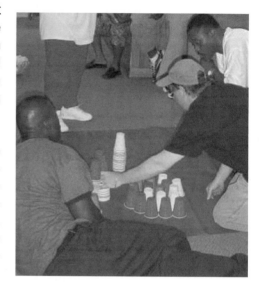

The Tower is a team challenge that requires the collaboration of every member of the group. We begin in the 'planning zone' where team members are given 150 small plastic cups and allowed a few minutes to plan their construction project - to build the tallest tower possible using only these 150 paper cups.

After the planning time has expired, one team member at a time leaves the planning zone and goes to the nearby 'construction site' where they begin to build the tower designed by the team, one cup at a time. We recommend using a table with a 24 inch (60 cm) masking tape square clearly visible for the construction site. Here are a few instructions for the building process:

1. Each team will have a maximum of 5 minutes to build a tower.

2. One person, carrying one cup at a time, is allowed at the construction site.

3. A cup that is dropped or that falls off the tower cannot be picked up or reused.

4. The rotation of team members and cup placements continues until all cups are placed, or until time has expired.

Supplies You will need 150 plastic cups for each team. Discount and grocery stores sell inexpensive cups like these.

Teachable Moments   This is a great activity for exploring limited resources, time constraints, inclusion of all team members, creative problem solving and communication.

Hints and Clues The larger the base, the more stable the tower, especially at heights approaching 10 cups. Experiment with different geometries for the base layer. Which foundation is more stable, a straight or curved profile?

Teambuilding Puzzles

Variations Try using larger cups and containers. Plastic 5 gallon buckets or paper popcorn buckets are interesting choices. You can also implement time limits for both the planning portion of the activity and the construction portion.

For a higher level of challenge, fill each cup with water. Expect teams to spill plenty of water in this version, and have a sponge or mop ready.

"Man is the only animal for whom his own existence is a problem which he has to solve."
Erich Fromm

"A human being should be able to change a diaper, plan an invasion, butcher a hog, conn a ship, design a building, write a sonnet, balance accounts, build a wall, set a bone, comfort the dying, take orders, give orders, cooperate, act alone, solve equations, analyze a new problem, pitch manure, program a computer, cook a tasty meal, fight efficiently, die gallantly. Specialization is for insects."
Excerpt from the notebooks of Lazarus Long,
from Robert Heinlein's "Time Enough for Love"

82. A Single Drop of Water
We can do more than we imagine if we stick together

**Teambuilding
Puzzles**

Here is an terrific challenge that explores the fact that we can probably all do more than we think we can.

The challenge is to place as many drops of water on the head of a penny (coin) as possible. Before starting, let each member of the group estimate the total number of drops they believe will fit. Write down these values and keep track of the actual number of drops used.

Supplies You will need a penny, an eye dropper (available at drug stores), a glass of water, and a napkin to clean up.

Teachable Moments We sometimes underestimate our own capacity. Just as this penny can hold many more drops than is often estimated, so can we accomplish more than we believe. Tom Heck says it this way: "This is an awesome activity to show the effect of setting goals. The first time I did this, I completely underestimated the number of drops I could fit on the head of my penny. I learned a great lesson - or should I say, I EXPERIENCED a great lesson: I must be careful when setting goals because I may be greatly underestimating my real potential."

If you are wondering about the difference between the last drop that fits on the penny and the next drop that doesn't, we invite you to read: The Tipping Point - How Little Things Can Make a Big Difference, 2003, Malcolm Gladwell, Wheeler Publishing for Little, Brown, Boston, MA USA ISBN 1-58724-393-8. Read and understand how some of the smallest things can make some of the biggest differences, then apply these to your work and life.

Variations Try other international coins, or a different liquid, such as soda or orange juice. Mix ingredients with the water that will alter the surface tension, such as laundry detergent.

Hints and Clues The water stays on the penny as a result of surface tension. Apply each drop slowly and you will be able to place 30-40 drops before the water cascades over the side.

Ultimate Teamwork
Thoughts About Teamwork and Sticking Together

Have you ever considered what was the most impressive team of all times? You might suggest a classic sport team from the past, or a medical research team that found a cure for a life-threatening disease, or engineers that perfected a new technology, or volunteers that came to the rescue of accident victims. You can even make this question into an activity for your next team. Ask them to list the characteristics of a high performing team.

As you think a bit farther, you can extend the scope of this question beyond the human world. Sled dogs and drivers race the Iditarod each year. The Kentucky Derby winner celebrates the accomplishments of both horse and rider. Honey bees, ants and many other animals and insects cooperate and work together for the good of the entire colony.

I would like to propose that the true ultimate team, at least in our world, is water. That's right, H20, water. Now hear me out. I'm not saying that water can replace the '64 Mets or the New York Yankees. I'm saying that by any metric, water illustrates the best of what a team can be.

Let's begin with a single drop of water. Here is our first teammate. An individual member of a much larger team. All by themselves, there is not much they can do. One drop of rain does not ruin a picnic or help a tree to grow. But just look what can be accomplished when a few drops of rain stick together. Fog so thick you can't see through it. Rain so heavy that it moves anything in it's path. And just look what can happen with a tidal wave or hurricane. Water is essential to life, it helps things grow, it covers seven tenths of our planet, and fills the majority of our bodies.

Next, it adapts. Consider what happens when the temperature drops below freezing. Water becomes something new. Snow or ice or sleet or hail, or dozens of other names for transformed water.

A single snowflake can't do much, but look what can happen when they stick together.

Water renews itself. It evaporates. It condenses. It rains. It flows. It is consumed and yet recovers. It is frozen for millennia and then thaws again. It adapts to changes in environment and temperature. You wish your team members were as adaptable as water.

So the next time you wonder just how good your team is, hand them each a bottle of water and talk about it.

Jim Cain

83. Extreme Origami
How many times can you fold a piece of paper?

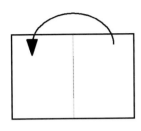

Take a standard sized piece of writing paper (8 1/2 x 11 inches or A4) and fold it in half. That's one. Now fold it in half again. That's two. And again. And again. Until you have made seven folds. Can you do it?

Supplies Any standard size paper, approximately 8 1/2 x 11 inches, or A4 format. Newspaper is not recommended as it tends to tear easily.

Teachable Moments If practice makes perfect, why doesn't folding paper get easier with each fold rather than more difficult? What happens between the fifth, sixth and seventh folds that is different than between the second, third and fourth folds? The starting point (in this case, the initial size of the paper) directly affects the outcome of this challenge. What other events in life mimic this same behavior? For example, does the amount of education (the starting point) directly affect the contributions (the outcome) a person makes in their job or their life?

Just as we underestimated the number of drops of water we could fit on a coin (puzzle #82), so might we overestimate the number of folds we can produce with a piece of paper. Our own experiences are our guide to goal setting. Without experience, our estimates are little more than random guesses.

Variations How large of a piece of paper would you need to be able to easily perform this task? Try this task with several sizes of the same paper. Then with the same size of several different papers. Next try different shapes of paper (circular, square, rectangular, triangular).

Before presenting this activity to a group, demonstrate folding a piece of paper successively in half three or four times. Then ask each member of the group to estimate how many times they could fold a piece of paper in half. Write their estimates on a flip-chart or blackboard, calculate the numerical average and range, and ask them to agree on a group goal. Then pass out paper (just like the piece you used in the demonstration), and begin.

As a final option, for just the right audience, hand out one dollar bills for the paper. Tell audience members that if they can fold the bill in half seven times, they can keep it.

Hints and Clues Do you think that the thickness of the paper has anything to do with this challenge? What is it about the size of the original paper that contributes to the difficulty in performing the task of folding the paper in half seven times? Would it be possible to fold the paper in half a different way, to make this task easier?

84. Arm Wrestling
Competition or Collaboration?

The next time you need an active method for showing the potential of a win-win solution, try this challenge with your team.

Sitting across a table or desk from each other (or lying on the ground), two partners are presented with this challenge. With your right elbows on the table, arms raised upwards, grasp the hand of your partner. Each time you can make their hand touch the table, you receive one piece of candy. Each time they make your hand touch the table, they receive a piece of candy. You'll have 30 seconds to win as much candy as you both can. Ready, GO!

Supplies Comfortable seating and sturdy tables or desks. You might want to have some candy on hand as well.

Teachable Moments Although the initial puzzle definition above never mentions the words 'arm wrestling,' most participants automatically assume that they will be competing for rewards. Most struggle to pin their partner's hand. If both partners work together, they can earn quite a bit of candy by cooperating rather than competing.

Variations In the following activity Tom Heck shares his version of an activity often referred to as Cross the Line. This is an excellent technique for exploring win-win, win-lose and lose-lose negotiation scenarios.

This activity requires a single rope stretched into a straight line, or a long masking tape line on the floor. With half of the group on one side of the line and standing about 6 feet (2 meters) behind the line, and the other half of the team on the other side, the scene is set for a moment of conflict (of "us" vs. "them"). Make no mistake, this activity is a bit higher level than most, but it is excellent for setting the stage to talk about conflict, negotiation and win/win, win/lose, and lose/lose scenarios.

Tom Heck calls this activity, "Their Ain't No Flies On Me!", and begins this activity by having one side say, "There ain't no flies on me, there ain't no flies on me, there might be flies on you (point to folks on the other side), but there ain't no flies on me!", and then boldly take a step towards the line (with just the right amount of attitude). The other side now replies, "there ain't no flies on me, there ain't no flies on me, there might be flies on you, but there ain't no flies on me!", and takes a step towards the line. The first side now repeats, and moves to the line, followed by the second side repeating their lines, and stepping face to face with the other side.

Now the facilitator says, "you have 5 seconds to get the person across the line from you onto your side of the line!"

Typically, this phrasing results in a rather quick tug of war between partners, and usually a physical solution (for one person at least) to the challenge. Leaving open a major opportunity to discuss conflict, challenge, attitude, negotiation, and how to resolve differences between people.

Hints and Clues Listen carefully and look for a win-win solution.

85. Finding Your People
Inclusion and Active Learning

Teambuilding Puzzles

While working on a book project related to the value of connection in the workplace, Jim was searching for an activity that would celebrate inclusion and acceptance. He developed one, then shared it with his friend, co-author and sometimes co-facilitator, Kirk Weisler, who suggested including the story mentioned here. The result was magical. We hope you enjoy sharing this activity with your group.

Begin with a collection of different color wood craft shapes (houses, trees, fish, animals). There should be several of each style. Also include just one star shaped piece of wood. Place enough of these shapes into a bag for the exact number of participants in your group. Invite each person to take one piece of wood from the bag, but not to look at it. They are allowed to touch the outline of their shape, and to talk about it, but cannot look at it or show it to anyone else. The challenge is simple... 'Find Your People.' Participants are encouraged to find the other shapes that are like themselves, but only by talking about them. This is very much an auditory puzzle, not a visual one.

After a minute or two, encourage any team members that haven't yet located the rest of their 'people' that they have one minute left. When that minute expires, ask the group to lock their feet in their present location, look at their piece of wood, and listen carefully.

Ask each group to identify their shape. The house group is here. The pine tree group is over there. But what about our Star? You can ask the person holding the star to share their experiences in trying to find 'their people.' What was it like trying to fit in?

Next ask participants to look at the color of their wood shapes. Who has red? Look around you, aren't these some of 'your people?' What about green? Look around, these are some of 'your people.'

At this point mention to the group that you would like to share a story about another person that wanted to fit in. We absolutely recommend 'The Mermaid' story, found in the Robert Fulghum book All I Really Need to Know I Learned in Kindergarten (see reference below), to follow this activity. It works well with youth, teenager and adult audiences, in schools, camps and corporations. There are many other readings in this book worth sharing with your group as well.

Teambuilding Puzzles

Supplies You'll need a collection of wood shapes. You can find these at many craft stores, and occasionally even at hardware stores, or you can purchase a set from Training Wheels, Inc., www.training-wheels.com or call 1-888-553-0147. You could also substitute animal cracker cookies, and after the activity, pass around the milk and read the suggested story. Milk and cookies and a story, what a great combination!

Teachable Moments   The concept of 'different' vs. 'similar' is very important here. For those participants left without a group, there is definite anxiety. This in itself is an excellent discussion topic.

   Those participants with wood shapes that are the same color typically did not know this when they were trying to find 'their people.' Mostly because they were not able to look at the pieces. They did not know that these other folks were 'their people.' This is true in life too. At the start of the school year, the first day of summer camp or the first week on a new job, we don't yet know who 'our people' are.

Variations You can invite participants to share their own stories of inclusion and group unity. You can also follow up this activity with Sharing Connections (#72) or A Circle of Connection (#93).

Hints and Clues Don't worry if members of your audience cannot find 'their people.' The suggested story will create an excellent opportunity for discussing inclusion and acceptance in a group.

The original edition of Robert Fulghum's book, All I Really Need to Know I Learned in Kindergarten, was released in 1986 and followed by paperback versions shortly thereafter. The 15th Anniversary Edition was recently released, reconsidered, revised and expanded with twenty-five new essays. 'The Mermaid' story can be found in all of these editions. We highly recommend this book.

All I Really Need to Know I Learned in Kindergarten - 15th Anniversary Edition, 2003, Robert Fulghum, Random House, New York, NY USA ISBN 0-345-46617-9

86. I'm In Riddles
Listen Carefully and Act Accordingly

Teambuilding Puzzles

The following collection of puzzles falls into the 'I'm In' category. One or two presenters share the following riddles, and then ask audience members to re-create their same presentation, or solve the mystery of how the task was successfully accomplished. The goal is to learn what is going on and then be able to add to the presentation, or simply reply, "I'm in!" Think of these as cultural linguistic puzzles and consider the following story.

This past year I found myself in Paris, France. During the late afternoon, I paid a visit to a sidewalk cafe and for several minutes tried to get the attention of a waiter so that I could place my order. Now Paris is a long way away for an Ohio farmboy and, as you can imagine, my grasp of the local language and customs was limited. Suffice to say that I was less than successful in my attempts, even as other customers around me were placing their orders, eating their food, and leaving. During this time, I noticed a new customer approaching, and watched carefully as they placed their order. When they were finished, I performed the exact ritual that I had seen them perform, and voila!, mission accomplished.

Jim Cain, Travels in France

Observation and imitation are excellent techniques for gaining understanding, learning new skills, and exploring cultural awareness and sensitivity. The following riddles employ this same skill. By carefully observing the presenter, the audience soon picks up some of the more subtle hints and behaviors they demonstrate. The ultimate test is to see if they can correctly imitate this same behavior.

Silly Tilly Williams - The solution to this verbal riddle is to find out what Silly Tilly Williams likes and dislikes. Begin by introducing Tilly, saying, "Silly Tilly Williams is a bit odd, but not unusual. She likes doors, but not windows. She doesn't like the ceiling, but likes the floor. She likes football, but not rugby. She likes skiing, but not ice skating. She reads books, but not magazines. She likes parallelograms, but not circles."

When a member of the audience thinks they have Tilly figured out, they tell the other members of the team something that Tilly likes and also does not like, such as "Silly Tilly Williams likes apples, but not pears."

Johnny Whoops - This verbal and visual puzzle begins with a facilitator holding their left hand open, so that the audience can see the back side of their hand, including all four fingers and thumb. With the right index finger, they begin touching each of the fingers on the left hand, starting with the smallest finger, saying, "Johnny (pinkey finger), Johnny (ring finger), Johnny (middle finger), Johnny (index finger), Whoops, Johnny (thumb), Whoops, Johnny (index finger), Johnny (middle finger), Johnny (ring finger), Johnny (pinkey finger)." The 'whoops' portion of their speech comes when the right index finger slides down the curve between the left hand index finger and thumb, and again on the return trip, in the opposite direction. After finishing the facilitator informally folds the fingers of their right and left hands together in front of them.

The Moon Is Round - A leader stands before the group and says the following phrase (while drawing the shapes shown at the right, with their left hand): The moon is round (draw a circle around your face), it has two eyes (point your index and middle fingers towards your eyes), a nose (point your index finger towards the tip of your nose), and a mouth (draw a simple smile curve over your mouth with your index finger). Audience members stand and attempt to replicate these same motions and words.

Crossed or Uncrossed? Of all the 'I'm In' games around, this one can keep folks guessing for hours. This is a true lesson in understanding the culture of an organization. Begin in a circle with everyone seated in chairs. The leader, holding a large pair of ordinary scissors says, "I pass these _____," and hands the scissors to the person on either side of them. The blank line here represents either the word, CROSSED or UNCROSSED. From this point on, the person receiving the scissors says, "I receive them _____, and pass them _____." The goal is to determine when a person is correct and when they have made a mistake. If incorrect, that person is given back the scissors, and asked

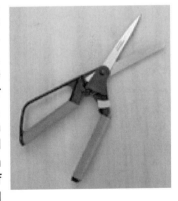

to perform the task again. The challenge is to understand exactly what crossed and uncrossed refers to. Those audience members that have figured out the challenge can add some confusion to the task by opening or closing the scissors, handing them left or right handed, turning them over, or other imaginative strategies to hide the true meaning of crossed and uncrossed.

Magic Writing - A leader that is well versed in 'magic writing' uses a long stick to create a word on the floor. Using a series of taps, spoken words, turning around, and stick movements, they create each word. Audience members that have discovered the secret of this style of writing are asked to share their own word with the rest of the group.

Polar Bears and Ice Holes - You will need several dice (two to five) for this activity. The leader shakes several dice in their hands, and then opens them, palms up, to reveal all the dice. There can be an ice hole without a polar bear, but there cannot be a polar bear without an ice hole. Now, how many polar bears and how many ice holes are there?

Card Tricks - You will need a partner and an audience for this one. Arrange six cards on a table as shown. You can hold the remaining cards from the deck in your hand. Next you ask your assistant to leave the room. A member of the audience then chooses one of the six cards on the table, and your assistant is asked to return. After a bit of misleading conversation between your assistant, yourself, and the audience, your assistant correctly identifies the card chosen by the audience. How?

Another variation of this activity is to place nine newspapers, books, or magazines on the floor. An assistant leaves the room, and a member of the audience chooses one of the publications. When the assistant returns, the leader, using a long stick, points to each of the objects and says, "is this it?" The assistant replies, "no," until the correct object is identified. How?

Supplies Most of the above puzzles require only a few simple props or none at all.

Teachable Moments Observation of foreign behaviors provides insight. Imitation requires understanding and mastery. The above puzzles require both for success.

Hints and Clues For each of the above riddles, repetition is important. Additional clues can be given by emphasizing the key portion of each riddle during presentation.

87. 63/64/65
The Search for the Truth

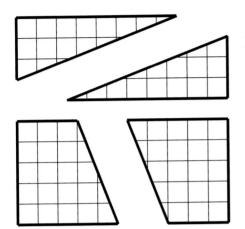

Here are four geometric shapes cut from an 8x8 checkerboard pattern of linoleum flooring. The assistant that is working with you on your home renovation tells you that he can use these same four pieces, without cutting any of them, to completely cover the floor in any of three separate rooms, even though each room has a different area. He even produces the following sketches to prove his point. Is this possible?

Figure A

Figure C, 65 Square Units

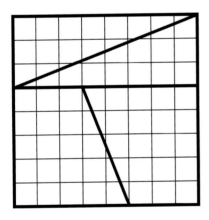

Figure B, 64 Square Units

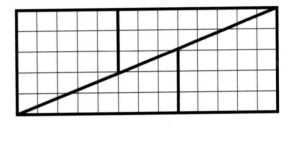

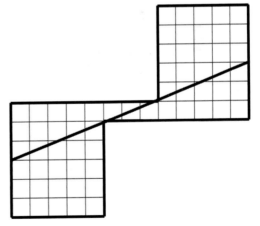

Figure D,
63 Square Units

Supplies You can make your own set of 63 / 64 / 65 geometric shapes, like those shown in Figure A, by creating an 8x8 grid pattern, like Figure B above (a larger printable copy can be found on next page), and cutting out the four patterns shown. Rearranging these four shapes will produce the patterns shown in Figures C and D.

Teachable Moments   It appears as though the same shapes can produce three different areas. Is such a thing possible? Discovering how to identify a hoax can be a valuable life skill. Having the mathematical skills to prove it is even better.

Variations   This can be an interesting puzzle to present to a group as an overhead transparency projected onto a large viewing screen at the front of the room.

Hints and Clues   Check the slope of each diagonal cut when creating the four geometric shapes. The two triangles shown at the top of the checkerboard pattern have a slope of 3 to 8, while the two trapezoids shown at the bottom of the checkerboard pattern have a slanting side with a slope of 2 to 5. If you calculate the area of each individual piece, you will find which total area is correct.

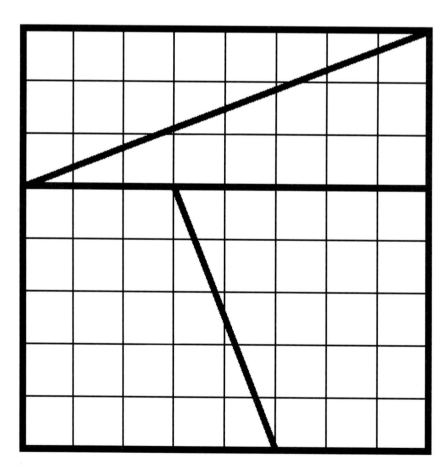

88. The Parade
A Kinesthetic Puzzle of Changing Proportions

Enjoy this kinesthetic challenge that requires some physical contact between the members of your group as they adapt to changing requirements.

Your team has been asked to prepare a unique parade float, made up of only the members of the team themselves, and to transport this float, intact, from starting location A to ending position B (a distance of about 20 feet (6 meters)). Because of local customs and the location of the parade, only X number of feet can be touching the ground (for any group, start with the number of participants as a reasonable starting number. 10 people = 10 feet can touch the ground). Musical content is strongly encouraged (singing, chanting, whistling, humming, percussion or other musical skills) as part of the parade presentation.

After completing the first parade trek, your team has been invited to bring their float to another festival, but this time in a country with substantially narrower streets necessitating that even fewer feet be touching the ground this time (for any size group, try the number of participants divided by 2. 10 people = 5 feet can touch the ground).

If requested, a third parade route with greater restrictions can be introduced (the number of participants divided by 3, for example, yields only 3 feet touching the ground).

Supplies None, although a long rope or masking tape line to identify the start and finish line of each parade route is helpful.

Teachable Moments Ask the group to consider what the minimum number of feet possible would be for their parade float. How were individual participants selected for their various roles? Were choices possible, or were roles assigned?

Variations You can vary the location, group size, distance traveled and content of the parade float as you like, especially to reinforce holiday celebrations, corporate themes, school holidays, or summer camp special events. Parade participants can create costumes or be asked to transport specific objects as part of their float (foam noodles, cardboard signs or slogans, candy for spectators, etc.).

Hints and Clues Some contact between participants is essential in the successful completion of this activity. Remember, the challenge is to create the float with a minimum number of FEET touching the ground. No other body part restrictions are required.

89. First Flight
100 Years after the invention of flying

On December 17, 1903, at 10:35 am, Orville and Wilbur Wright demonstrated heavier-than-air flight was possible as they flew their airplane for 12 seconds, covering a distance of 120 feet.

Now, more than 100 years later, your team has been asked to perform a similar task. Your assignment is to keep a single piece of paper from touching the floor for 12 seconds. You can use your brainpower, but cannot physically come in contact with your paper once the countdown has begun. You can fold this paper into a shape that will fly for 12 seconds. You can collectively blow this paper into the air (like a feather on the wind). You can place this paper against a wall and keep it there with your collective breaths. You can fold it, shape it, bend it, crumple it.... but you cannot add anything to it (such as adhesives, additional weights, etc.), nor can you use anything other than yourselves to keep this paper off the ground.

Supplies You will need a sheet of paper for each 'team.' Lighter papers, such as tissue paper, are a bit easier to control.

Teachable Moments It is amazing just how much air it takes to 'control' a piece of paper. And 12 seconds can seem like an eternity when you are using every ounce of air in your lungs! How does the word 'teamwork' affect your success with this challenge? What other tasks can you think of that require a team effort? How can you make sure that every member of the team knows their assignment, and how their contributions affect the overall success of the project?

Variations You can alter the duration of the flight. You can also skip the time element and instead go for distance, height, or precision in landing in a predetermined target zone.

Hints and Clues A flat piece of paper flies or floats in an unpredictable manner when dropped from any height. You'll need to have a bit more control over the paper than that to be successful. How can you modify the shape of the paper, or its location, to improve your technique?

If you enjoyed this introduction to flight, we recommend:

The Wright Way - 7 Problem-Solving Principles from the Wright Brothers That Can Make Your Business Soar, 2004, Mark Eppler, AMACOM, New York, NY USA ISBN 0-8144-0797-8.

To Conquer the Air - The Wright Brothers and The Great Race for Flight, 2003, James Tobin, Free Press, New York, NY USA ISBN 0-7432-5536-4.

*"Every generation thinks it has the answers,
and every generation is humbled by nature."*
Phillip Lubin

*"Our problems are man-made,
therefore they may be solved by man.
And man can be as big as he wants.
No problem of human destiny is beyond human beings."*
John F. Kennedy

90. Your Move
Competition and Collaboration

Here is a team challenge for two teams at once. Let's see which team comes out the winner.

Your Move is played with 24 tennis balls and a soda bottle case. Pretty simple props for a team puzzle that is sure to create some positive discussion about competition vs. collaboration. The object of the game is to score the most points possible in the time allowed. Each team is given 10 tennis balls of different colors (yellow or orange) and 2 additional 'wild card' balls (blue). The following rules apply:

1. Ten points are scored for each alignment of four similar colored balls (four-in-a-row). A ball may be counted multiple times in any horizontal, vertical or diagonal arrangement of four-in-a-row, but not counted twice in the same line or plane.

2. Wild card balls, which are a different color than either team's regular tennis balls, may be counted by either team. At the end of each round, the same wild card ball may benefit neither, either or both teams.

3. Each team places one ball at a time, alternating turns. Wild card balls may be played in place of a regular ball at any time. Once a ball has been played, it cannot be moved.

4. Play continues until all balls have been played, time elapses or there are no available spaces left that would benefit either team.

5. During the game, no communication is allowed between members of the two teams.

6. The facilitator sets the time limit for the game.

Supplies You will need 10 balls of one color, 10 more of a different color and four additional 'wild card' balls of a third color. An old-fashioned soda bottle case works well for the game frame. You'll need the kind that holds four six-packs (24 bottles).

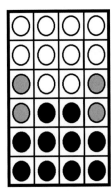

Teachable Moments It should quickly become obvious for both teams that they are using valuable resources any time they attempt to block the other team. Resources that they could be using to score more points. Even though the challenge is clearly stated at the very beginning, *"the object is to score as many points as possible,"* few teams look for the win-win scenario and instead settle for the win-lose, or even worse, the lose-lose result. A discussion of competition and collaboration are appropriate at this time. The illustration shown here is an example of a configuration that produces a high score. In this case, each team would score 70 points, for a grand total of 140.

Variations If you cannot find a soda bottle case, try making your own flat surface board and use colorful stones, checkers, poker chips or coins for playing pieces. What about creating a three-way board for three teams at once?

You are welcome to modify the above rules a bit, but we suggest that you try out these different rules before using them with two teams. For example, you could count only horizontal and vertical rows of four, not diagonals.

Hints and Clues What resources are present that could increase your score? Did your team 'waste' any resources, thereby lowering your score?

A special thanks to Anthony Curtis, for sharing this team puzzle with us. Anthony is the founder and owner of Adventure Designs in central Tennessee, and the creator of this team puzzle which he calls 'Your Move.' Visit the Adventure Designs website at: www. adventure-designs.com.

"All the problems of the world could be settled
if people were only willing to think. The trouble is
that people very often resort to all sorts of devices
in order not to think, because thinking is such hard work."
Thomas J. Watson

91. Inuksuit
Standing Together Brings Balance

Here is a puzzle activity that celebrates both cultural awareness and balance. You can learn even more from the reference books listed below.

A few years ago, at the COEO conference in Ontario, Canada, a workshop presented the idea of 'making a 10,000 year old friend.' It turned out that the 10,000 year olds were in fact glacial rocks. I was thoroughly intrigued, and learned a bit about balancing rocks in the process.

While many inuksuit are created by individuals, some of the larger pieces certainly require more than one person to erect. How many of the things your team has created will last as long as an inuksuk?

You will find three different activities related to balancing stones in the paragraphs that follow. As a starting point, you are invited to read some of the reference books listed at the end of this activity. You can also find information about inuksuit on the Internet. Not surprisingly, most of the information originates in various Canadian provinces and territories, although there are inuksuit-like stone structures in other portions of the world such as Lapland (seites), Nepal (chortens), and the Andes (apashektas).

INUKSUK

These are powerful symbols of the Canadian arctic region, and most recently found on the flag of Canada's newest territory, Nunavut, which was established in 1999. One of these stone structures is called inuksuk or inukshuk. Two are called inuksuuk. Three or more are called inuksuit. A collection of many small inuksuit is called inuksukkat.

Inuksuk roughly translates, 'to act in the capacity of a human.'

Stone Balancing 101 - As a first activity, begin by gathering several stones from your local area. Polished stones from a river are beautiful and can be quite challenging to balance. Shale, limestone, and other rocks that demonstrate a straight profile are a bit easier to work with. Your first assignment is to see how many stones you can balance on top of each other (with no additional adhesives). Start with three and continue up to five stones. There is something elegant about a structure of balanced rocks with no mortar. If you still are not convinced that your little stone structure qualifies as 'art,' we invite you to view the artwork of Andy Goldsworthy, in his book: Stone, 1994, Andy Goldsworthy, Harry Abrams Publishers, New York, NY USA ISBN 0-8109-3847-2.

**Teambuilding
Puzzles**

Team Balancing - A Community of Unity - Using the circular wooden balance board shown here, your next assignment is to have your entire team collaborate to create a circle of small inuksuit-like structures. For this version, we will replace the stones with wooden

blocks or dominoes. The challenge is for your entire team to simultaneously build three to six structures on the balance board without tipping it over. Each member of the team can place only one piece per turn, and then must rotate to allow every member of the group a chance to contribute. A good plan, timing, balance and communication are necessary to be successful at this synchronized building event. Too much weight on any side of the balance board, and it falls over.

Inuksuit Morphology One traditional purpose of inuksuit is to imitate the human form during caribou hunting events. The challenge was to create the maximum size human form using only the stones available. This is a perfect example of how great things can be accomplished with limited resources.

   The word 'morphology' comes into this challenge because we will be analyzing the size and shape of the next inuksuit-like structure your team creates. Each group of 3 to 4 participants will have exactly the same number and size of blocks or stones. The challenge will be to use these materials to create the largest enclosed region, and still produce a stable structure that will stand for a long, long time.

   We will use a morphological parameter, the convex perimeter, to evaluate each inuksuk. The convex perimeter is simply the length of a rubber band that has been stretched around your inuksuk. You can use an actual rubber band, string or fabric measuring tape to measure this distance.

   So as your group begins to build, remember the goal is to produce the largest convex perimeter given the fixed number of blocks or stones available.

   As an alternative, you could make the significant parameter the maximum height or total armspan of the inuksuk.

Supplies When possible, and safe, use local stones. Wood blocks or dominoes can be substituted as necessary. The circular wooden balance board, shown in the Community of Unity activity, can be a plywood circle or wooden plate, with a 2 inch (51 mm) diameter wooden cylinder or candle stick holder attached.

Teachable Moments   There are plenty of opportunities for cultural assignments related to inuksuit, including Internet searches, reading assignments, book reports, sketches, drawings and photographs of these and other stone structures, writing assignments, stone structures from other cultures, art projects, and engineering evaluations (like the inuksuit morphology activity).

Aside from the cultural opportunities, there are also teachable moments related to the team skills required in each of the above activities. Stone Balancing 101 takes some internal calmness, composure, aesthetic evaluation, and balance. Team Balancing requires advanced planning, organization, timing, balance and communication. Inuksuit Morphology requires creativity and understanding of the materials to produce a structure with superior characteristics given exactly the same materials as every other group.

Variations   Stone structures exist in a variety of other cultures. In the northern hemisphere, these include Celtic, Roman, Pict and Druidic structures in Great Britain, and seites in Lapland. In the southern hemisphere, stone statues in Polynesia including Easter Island, small monuments called chortens that are filled with mani stones in Nepal, and the apashektas of the Andes region.

In addition to the cultural awareness surrounding such indigenous structures, there are also the aesthetic and artistic contributions of such objects, religious symbolism, historic interpretations, and of course structural and scientific evaluations (such as the shapes formed by different types of stones taken from different geographic regions.

Hints and Clues   Balance requires internal calm. Don't be surprised if it doesn't happen immediately. An Internet search of 'inuksuk' will return several websites with photographs, illustrations and commentary about these unique structures. Use this information as a guide for building your own inuksuk.

Some Information About Inuksuit

Inuksuit are a symbol of reassurance for those who travel in the sometimes remote regions of the Arctic. For centuries, these stone structures have provided direction, messages, and guidance. Sometimes used to assist driving herds of caribou, and at other times, personal expressions from those wishing to commemorate an event of great joy or loss. They also identify high points on land, good hunting areas, and safe passageways.

It is not uncommon to find small pieces of stone or other offerings placed into the spaces between the stones of inuksuit. These offerings are often left by adventurers, and as such, reflect their respect for the inuksuit, and a small piece of themselves as well.

In the Eastern Arctic, along the South Baffin coastline, is Inuksuk Point, the site of over one hundred Inuksuit. Inuksuk Point 'inukaugasait' means the place of many, many Inuksuit.

If you are as intrigued about Inuksuit as we are, we invite you to read:

Inuksuit - Silent Messengers of the Arctic, 2000, Norman Hallendy, Douglas & McIntyre, Vancouver, British Columbia, Canada ISBN 1-55054-778-X. Beautiful photographs and stories of Inuksuit. "Because of the importance placed on inuksuit, their construction was rarely taken lightly. Like a three-dimensional puzzle, the pieces fit together with such a precision as to be held in place by gravity. Inuksuit are not only a pleasure to behold but are so well balanced and constructed that they can withstand the ravages of time and countless storms." Quote by Normal Hallendy.

High Latitudes, 2002, Farley Mowat, Key Porter Books, Toronto, Ontario, Canada ISBN 1-55263-473-6.

The Inuksuk Book, 1999, Mary Wallace, Maple Tree Press, Toronto, Ontario, Canada ISBN 1-895688-91-4.

Make Your Own Inuksuk, 2001, Mary Wallace, Maple Tree Press, Toronto, Ontario, Canada ISBN 1-894379-10-1. Instructions for creating a variety of inuksuk styles.

And, for those of you that ponder at one of the greatest stone 'puzzles' of all, Stonehenge, we invite you to read the following book. Stonehenge, by the way, looks amazingly like a circle of inuksuit waiting to be completed. Imagine the image of 6 to 8 inuksuit, standing tall against the ages. Well, it is just a theory of course.

Stonehenge Complete - Revised Edition, 1994, Christopher Chippindale, Thames and Hudson, New York, NY USA ISBN 0-500-27750-8.

*"It's so much easier to suggest solutions
when you don't know too much about the problem."*
Malcolm Forbes

92. The Big Coverup
A simple puzzle that covers a very large space

The Big Coverup is exactly that. Using a very big space to cover up some puzzle silhouettes.

The activity begins with all team members standing in the 'planning zone.' This zone is a rope enclosed region, sufficient in size to hold the entire team and a collection of geometric puzzle pieces. The geometric pieces can be Tangrams, Archimedes puzzle pieces, shapes, king-sized jigsaw puzzles, circles, squares, triangles, corporate logos, letters of the alphabet or any other shape that has meaning for the team.

Arranged at quite a distance from the planning zone are several platforms (tables, benches, or plywood laid upon the ground) which contain a silhouette or puzzle outline, like those shown below. This distance can easily be 50 feet (15 meters) to 50 yards (46 meters).

During the planning stage, a different team member is asked to visit each of the platforms and return with information about the silhouette. Next, the entire team reviews the geometric puzzle pieces they have and decides which piece should be placed on which platform. The challenge is to completely cover each silhouette with these pieces.

One team member at a time may take one puzzle piece to any silhouette and then return to the planning zone. If any piece that is already placed at a silhouette is later decided not to fit, it must be placed in the 'scrap yard.' This location is near the planning zone, but not too close. Pieces placed in the scrap yard can be returned to the planning zone if three team members run with this piece around the perimeter of ALL the platforms.

The activity continues until all silhouettes have been successfully covered up.

Supplies You will need a collection of geometric puzzle shapes that, when assembled, will completely cover the silhouettes you have chosen. You can make these from cardboard or plywood. Silhouettes can be copied from the illustrations on the next page, created with computer graphics or drawn with a bold marker.

Teachable Moments This activity involves some kinesthetic energy, group problem solving, communication skills and visual perception. It is a great way to keep a group moving and thinking at the same time.

Variations As a possible 'hint,' the various silhouettes can be covered using shapes that are similar. For example, the triangular silhouette can be covered using only triangular shapes.

Hints and Clues Use only the puzzle pieces that just cover each silhouette. If you have too much extra coverage, you may be holding a piece intended for a different silhouette.

**Teambuilding
Puzzles**

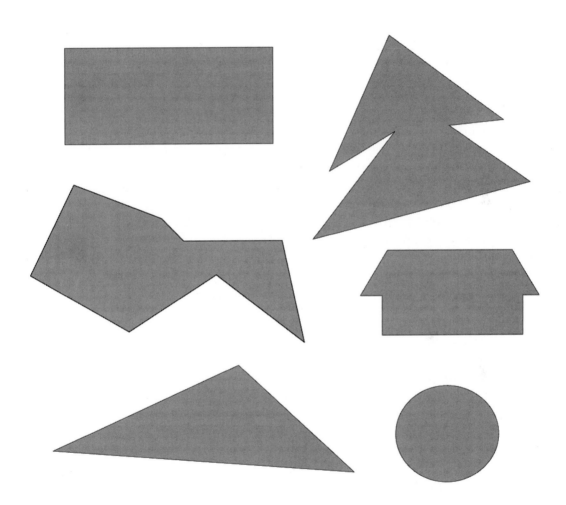

93. A Circle of Connection
That which links us together, brings us closer

Teambuilding Puzzles

Here is a simple activity that is half puzzle, half conversation. It is filled with discovery and finding out those elements of life which forever link us together with our fellow inhabitants on this planet. A special thanks to Dick Hammond for sharing this wonderful activity.

A leader begins by introducing themselves and sharing some information such as, "I enjoy crossword puzzles. I like to work in my garden. I enjoy old movies, and I like to travel." At some point, one of these recreations is sure to also be shared by at least one other member of the group. When this happens, one new person links elbows with the previous person, introduces themselves, and begins to share some of their interesting hobbies. The activity continues until all members of the group have 'linked together.' The final task is for the last person to continue sharing until the first person can link with them. At this point, there is an opportunity to say, "...and by the way. Those things which link us together, bring us a bit closer together as well!"

Supplies None.

Teachable Moments Here is an opportunity to find out just how much alike the members of your group are, rather than how different everyone is. Finding out that we have something in common with another member of our group, builds a bridge between us. Chris Cavert once mentioned, in reference to his middle school students, that "the more they know about each other, the less likely they were to hurt each other." Simply stated, those things we have in common with others help us develop a sense of empathy and connection to them.

Variations You can choose a specific theme for conversation before beginning this activity. Such topics as family vacations, sports, music, movies, collections, hobbies or talents are easy to discuss.

Hints and Clues As this activity continues, it becomes a bit more challenging for participants to link together as the number of unlinked members and the diversity of their interests diminishes. Encourage these folks by providing suggestions of various objects and topics, such as those mentioned above.

Teambuilding Puzzles

You can find this and other teambuilding activities without props in the book:

The Empty Bag - Non-Stop, No-Prop Adventure-Based Activities for Community Building, 2003, Chris Cavert and Dick Hammond, FUNdoing Publications www.fundoing.com ISBN 0-9746442-1-8

"You can do only one thing at a time. I simply tackle one problem and concentrate all efforts on what I am doing at the moment."
Dr. Maxwell Maltz

94. The Square
Working Together

Try this kinesthetic 'thinking on your feet' challenge. The goal here is not only to solve the puzzle, but to enlist the cooperation and assistance of the entire team and communicate the vision and solution method so that any member of the group could lead the completion of this task.

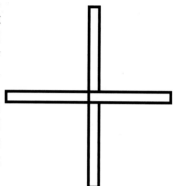

Four equal size boards are placed exactly as shown in the illustration. Members of the team are invited to stand on top of these boards, spreading out to provide some space between each person. The challenge is to create a perfect square moving the least number of boards possible.

Supplies You will need four 2x6's or 2x8's, each about 4 feet (1.2 meters) long for groups of 12 participants, or 6 feet (2 meters) long for groups of 15-20.

Teachable Moments You will find that even adults have a hard time staying on the boards while discussing the merits of this technique or that one. This puzzle is a classic example of how a vision can be shared by every member of the group, and yet still be difficult to produce in the real world. Moving two boards can certainly produce a square, but Company B (your competitors) think they can do it by moving only one board. Can your team improve on their technique and finish the job moving less than two boards?

Variations In the 'life raft' version of this activity, the board sizes are kept small (only slightly larger than necessary for the size of your group). The challenge is the same, but the decreased size of the working space requires additional teamwork to accomplish the task without anyone falling overboard. This version makes for both a physical and cerebral challenge.

Hints and Clues Ask the group to define what a perfect square is. For a serious hint, ask the group how big a perfect square would have to be.

"It is wise to direct your anger towards problems
— not people;
to focus your energies on answers
— not excuses."
William Arthur Ward

95. Team Labyrinth
Pulling Together as a Team

I first learned of a teambuilding activity using a giant labyrinth from Chris Cavert. His version was created from two 4x8 foot sheets of plywood and required both skill and strength to maneuver.

After several years of searching for a suitable, lightweight, portable team labyrinth, I met Marcus Ingold of Switzerland and was introduced to his rather unique, and very portable, team labyrinth, shown here. Ingold's labyrinth is not only outstanding, it is also double-sided with a beginning challenge on one side and a significantly harder challenge on the reverse side. You can also view this unique labyrinth at the Stucki Internet website: www.stucki.ch

Next came the creative minds of Joe Stryjewski and Andy Carrigan, both of YMCA Camp Weona. A photograph of their version of a labyrinth challenge is also shown here.

The challenge of the team labyrinth is to maneuver a ball or marble (or multiple balls or marbles) through the maze, avoiding obstacles, to a destination pre-determined by the team or facilitator. Team members are asked to take hold of one of the strings surrounding the labyrinth, and not let go for the duration of the activity. Once the wooden labyrinth is lifted from the floor or ground, it must not touch the floor or ground again until the task has been completed.

As a variation of this simple challenge, some or all of those team members holding strings can be blindfolded and verbally, but not physically, assisted by the remaining sighted team members.

Supplies You will need one of the portable labyrinths shown here, or make your own simplified version as mentioned in the 'variations' section below. Visit the Teamwork & Teamplay website at: www.teamworkandteamplay.com for more information about these useful and unique teambuilding props. Also visit www.teachme-teamwork.com or www.gophersport.com for information about the flexible and adjustable fabric maze shown here.

Teachable Moments Maneuvering one marble within the team labyrinth is challenging. Adding additional marbles quickly increases the opportunity for mistakes, chaos and stress. This complexity can be related to a manager handling simultaneous assignments in a corporation, a lifeguard watching multiple swimmers in a pool or a camp counselor keeping a careful watch over their campers.

Blindfolded participants require verbal coaching to complete the labyrinth task. This can be the principle of a corporate mentoring relationship, a 360 degree feedback session or a high school peer counseling program.

Variations You can make a very simple variation of this activity by attaching a number of strings to a flat board or panel, and transporting a ball, glass of water, or other delicately balanced object. This same labyrinth could be made to look like the Teambuilding Puzzle labyrinth logo shown at the top of this page.

For a different teambuilding activity, you can create a 'Bull Ring,' which is a metal ring with 10 strings attached that is used to transport a ball from Point A to Point B. You can find a description of the Bull Ring, along with several variations, in the teambuilding text Teamwork & Teamplay (see the reference on the following page). As an additional challenge to the team labyrinth, you can use a series of PVC tubes to transport the marbles needed for the labyrinth challenge from a starting location. You can find a description of 'Marble Tubes' in the book Teamwork & Teamplay.

For a small and highly portable team labyrinth, provide your team with a simple toy labyrinth (available inexpensively at many toy stores) and a bandanna. Place the labyrinth in the center of the bandanna and instruct each member of the team to hold onto the edge of the bandanna to control the movement of the ball.

Hints and Clues The team labyrinth requires balance, timing and understanding how your own contribution compliments the contribution of other members of the team. These skills improve with practice.

Teamwork & Teamplay, 1998, Jim Cain and Barry Jolliff, Kendall Hunt Publishers, Dubuque, IA USA ISBN 0-7872-4532-1 More than 415 pages of teambuilding activities, helpful planning tips, references and resources, and instructions for building your own portable teambuilding equipment.

96. The Puzzle Cube
A Geometrical Puzzle and a Physical Challenge

The Puzzle Cube provides both a mathematical challenge and a physical team challenge. We thank Earl LeBlanc for inspiring this intriguing activity.

The first goal of the Puzzle Cube is to assemble a perfect three-dimensional cube from the various PVC tubes and connectors provided. It is possible to build five different cubes from the materials in the Puzzle Cube kit ranging in size from 30 to 42 inches per side. After assembly, the cube is carefully balanced in a circular base, as shown in the illustration. Next, the team attempts to pass through the cube without tipping it over. At all times, the person passing through the cube must be in contact with at least one other person.

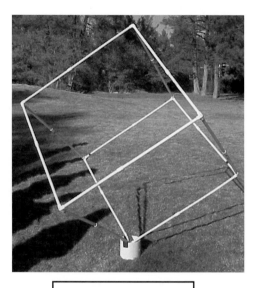

Supplies The Puzzle Cube is available from Training Wheels, Inc., at 1-888-553-0147 or www.training-wheels.com. Chris Cavert also sells the 'do it yourself' Expandable Cube kit (CD-Rom) which contains the difficult to find corner connectors, building instructions and an PDF guide with video clips for over 15 Cube teambuilding activities (www.fundoing.com).

> The Puzzle Cube is the simplest, lightest and most versatile portable spider web design on the market.

Teachable Moments   Your team will need balance, teamwork, and problem solving skills to pass through the Puzzle Cube without tipping it over. Calculating the maximum cube size, with the components available requires some mathematical, geometric and engineering skills. Balancing the cube, especially blindfolded requires tactile feedback, patience, and excellent team communication.

Variations   In addition to calculating and constructing the maximum size cube possible and passing through the cube as a team challenge, here are a few other challenges that can be performed with the 60 components found in a Puzzle Cube kit.

Once a cube has been constructed, challenge a group of 3-5 participants to balance the cube in the plastic base while blindfolded. You can encourage additional information and support from sighted team members, or not. Next, as a 3-D version of 'All Aboard,' place the cube flat on the floor or ground and see how many members of the team can fit inside the perimeter of the cube. We call this activity 'All Inboard.'

You can also use the components in the Puzzle Cube kit to build the tallest tower, and for the teambuilding activities 'The Helium Stick,' (shown left) and from Sam Sikes, 'Photo Finish,' which can be found in his book, Feeding the Zircon Gorilla, from Learning Unlimited at 1-888-622-4203 or www.learningunlimited.com.

Hints and Clues One of the techniques available for estimating the maximum cube size possible is to measure the lengths of all available PVC tubes and divide this number by 12 (the number of sides in a cube).

The Puzzle Cube is a collection of 60 different PVC components (31 tubes, 28 connectors, and a support base) from which you can build 5 different size cubes (30, 34, 36, 40 and 42 inches) for one of the most lightweight, versatile and simple portable spider web designs ever. You can use these same pieces to present ten additional challenge activities.

If you like the concept of The Puzzle Cube and you would like to debrief or review this activity in a unique manner, read the book: Secrets of The Cube - The Ancient Visualization Game That Reveals Your True Self, 1998, Annie Bottlieb and Slobodan Pesic, Hyperion, New York, NY USA ISBN 0-7868-8257-3.

You can find more information about cube challenges in the books:

Affordable Portables, 1996, Chris Cavert, Wood N Barnes Publishing, Oklahoma City, OK USA ISBN 1-885473-40-0 Teambuilding activity and building plans for dozens of activities, including a cube.

Affordable Portables 2, 2010, Chris Cavert, Wood N Barnes Publishing, Oklahoma City, OK USA.

Another innovative cube design, the Geo-Diamond, created by Tom Heck, is available from Gopher Sports (www.gophersport.com).

97. Jumping George
See if you can do this!

**Teambuilding
Puzzles**

This activity is a bit more of a stunt than a puzzle, but very challenging even so. Begin by placing a dollar bill flat on the ground. Inform your group that you are looking for someone who can jump over the dollar bill, and if they can do it successfully, they can keep it. Demonstrate the jumping position for the group. Participants are to stand with their toes together at one end of the dollar bill, and then bend over and grab the toe of each shoe with their hands, see photo. The challenge is to jump completely over the length of the dollar bill from this stance without letting go.

Here are a few rules. Participants must wear shoes at all times. The jumper must completely clear the length of the dollar bill. The dollar bill cannot be altered (it must remain flat on the floor). Participants must hold their right shoe tip with the fingers of their right hand and the left shoe tip with the fingers of their left hand. Jumpers must hold onto their toes throughout the jumping and landing sequence of this activity.

Supplies A dollar bill, or you can substitute an index card.

Teachable Moments Tom Heck mentioned that he has used this activity for years and never once has he had to pay out the dollar bill. Dave Moriah once gave up a five dollar bill to a team member that successfully jumped backwards over the bill.

Variations If you like this style of activity, we invite you to read:

Bet You Can't Do This! - Impossible Tricks to Astound Your Friends, 2002, Sandy Ransford, Macmillan Children's Books, London, UK ISBN 0-330-39772-9 Fun stunts, tricks and challenges.

Hints and Clues Try jumping backwards!

Teambuilding
Puzzles

98. Just One Word
Sometimes the solutions are right in front of us!

Some puzzles are made more difficult because we often 'interpret' what we think the instructions are rather than completely listening to the directions as provided.

Using the eleven letters shown at the right, you should be able to create just one word.

Supplies You can use index cards with the above block letters clearly printed on each card. (The letters in the title of this activity.)

Teachable Moments Carefully listening to instructions before beginning can be the difference between a successful completion to a project or challenge and a lengthy and frustrating experience. Conversely, when a team is struggling, what can a facilitator, team leader, teacher, counselor, mentor or coach do to assist the team? How else could the original instructions have been presented to increase the opportunity for a successful outcome? Obviously, the manner in which we attempt to communicate directly effects the quality and interpretation of our words.

Variations Instead of index cards, you can also use letter tiles borrowed from your favorite word board game, wooden letters from a craft or hardware store, large paper letters created using a word processor and a personal computer, and even children's building blocks with the correct letters present.

Hints and Clues The answer is just one word.

99. Concentration
This Puzzle Has Rhythm!

For those with musical talent, timing, or the ability to concentrate, this activity should be a snap!

> *When I was about 10 years old, my entire family (aunts, uncles, cousins, grandparents, and parents) would all gather together about once a month and play, talk, eat and enjoy each other's company. In the evening just before sunset, while the adults were off talking, my cousins and I would amuse ourselves outside playing flashlight tag and ghost in the graveyard. When it was too dark to play anymore, and no one wanted to start a long board game or play cards, we would play a game we called "concentration." Over the years, it seems as though the basic rules of the game changed a bit, but the rhythm and motions were always the same. The best part of the game was that it didn't take long to explain, there was no need to keep score, each round took only a minute or two and everyone could play (even Stephanie, my youngest cousin, who is probably reading this right now and laughing).*

> Jim Cain, Memories from my Youth

Our family's version of Concentration involves what today is known as 'whole brain learning' and incorporates the ability of one side of the brain (movement) with an ability from the other side of the brain (memory recall and speech). Thirty years ago, we had no idea that we were on the cutting edge of learning theory. We were just having fun!

Concentration - The Original Version - Sitting in chairs in a circle, players learn the basic rhythm and movements of the game. Everyone begins by placing their palms face down and slapping both knees at the same time. Then clap both hands together once. Next snap the fingers on your right hand, and finally, snap the fingers on your left hand. This is the basic pattern: Slap, Clap, Right Snap, Left Snap. Keep practicing this rhythm in 4/4 time, until you can do it without thinking. Then have the entire group number off, from one to the total number present and remember their own number.

You can keep the other side of your brain busy with some linguistical gymnastics. You will need to speak the words, in this case numbers, on the 'downbeat' of each measure of the rhythm. Each round begins by saying the word concentration twice to the beat of the rhythm... con (slap), cen (clap), tra (right snap), tion (left snap), followed immediately (on the downbeat of the next measure) with two numbers. The first number is the number of the person starting this round, the second number is the number of the person they are 'sending' the control of the game to. The right and left hand finger snaps provide a 'thinking pause' during the game to allow the next person to prepare their thoughts. A typical round might go like this:

Motion	Slap	Clap	Right Snap	Left Snap
Words	con	cen	tra	tion
	con	cen	tra	tion
	one	four	(pause)	(pause)
	four	nine	(pause)	(pause)
	nine	two	(pause)	(pause)
	two	nine	(oops! game over)	

There are three potential errors that can stop this game in a heartbeat. The first error is sending control of the game back to the same person that sent control to you. So 'nine-two' and then 'two-nine' above is the first style of fatal error. The second style of error is failing to speak on the correct beat of the rhythm. You must give your own number on the first beat of the measure (slap), followed immediately by another person's number on the second beat of the measure (clap). The third and final fatal error is made by keeping the rhythm, but saying a number that is not present in the group. Perform any one of these errors and the game is over with the faulting party given control to begin the game again.

Categories - This second version of Concentration, which we called Categories, most likely came about because the older cousins couldn't remember the rules for the original version, though everyone seemed to remember the rhythm and motions. Someone begins the round by stating what category they are looking for (automobiles, days of the week, good books, animals, etc.) The person to their right is next, and so on around the circle. Instead of starting each round with the phrase 'concentration', this version begins with 'categories,' like this (next page):

Motion	Slap		Clap	Right Snap	Left Snap	Person #
Words	cate		gories	(pause)	(pause)	1
	names		of	(pause)	(pause)	1
	things	to	eat	(pause)	(pause)	1
	peach		pie	(pause)	(pause)	2
	dough		nuts	(pause)	(pause)	3
	banana		split	(pause)	(pause)	4
	flat		tire	(oops! game over)		5

There are two potential errors that stop this version of the game. The first error is saying anything which does not fit in the category. In the case above, anything which is inedible is probably going to stop the game (although silliness was one of the things we most enjoyed about this activity!) The second error is failing to speak on the correct beat of the rhythm.

Supplies None, although chairs make for a much more comfortable setting than standing or sitting on the floor.

Teachable Moments You can use the original version as a get acquainted activity, especially if you use names instead of numbers. Categories can be used to teach any subject which can be expressed as a list. The following are all potential 'categories:' vocabulary words, synonyms, corporate core values, the twelve cranial nerves, farm animals, foreign language words and numbers, the problem solving sequence, library books, favorite colors and types of automobiles. Think of the 'lists' that your audience would know and use some of these to create your own teachable moment.

Variations We never played Concentration as an elimination game, although you probably can. If you play our original version (with numbered players) as an elimination game, you will need to decide if you plan to renumber the remaining players each round, or allow each person to keep their number for the duration of the game. Since childhood, I have heard of other versions of this game from summer camp counselors and youth

leadership workers. Some refer to Concentration as 'Head Elephant' or 'Big Booty.' The motions and words change to match the audience, but the central theme of a rhythm and alternating control of the game remains.

Rather than using words in the game of Concentration, each person can create their own hand signal. Speaking on the first and second beat of every measure is then replaced with performing your own personal hand signal on the first beat, and the hand signal of the person you are passing control of the game to, on the second beat.

Hints and Clues You will need to practice the rhythmic movements of Concentration until you can perform these without thinking about them. You'll also need to memorize at least two different player's numbers for the original version.

*"Welcome every problem as an opportunity.
Each moment is the great challenge, the best thing that ever happened to you.
The more difficult the problem, the greater the challenge in working it out."*
Grace Speare

100. Ciphers and Codes
A Modern Day Rosetta Stone

Everything is not as it appears. There is an important message here for your team. Can you decipher it?

T E A S O V C H G E C

E E R O S T Y M M H O

P O E N L R R E I E 4 X 8

Supplies Paper and pencils or pen will be helpful. You will need a cylinder or tube for the variation shown below, along with a long paper or fabric ribbon.

Teachable Moments   There is certainly no lack of the 'ah-hah!' phenomenon here, especially when you are able to decode a message. You might try using your company's mission statement, credo, core values or motto as a message to be decoded, and presented in 'common speak.'

Variations There is a rich history of the ciphers and codes used throughout the world. You will find another one on the last page of this book. You'll need to look for patterns, helpful clues and perhaps experience just a bit of plain luck.

   If you take the cipher from above, and write this on a strip of paper ribbon wrapped around a cylinder with four letters per revolution, you may find the answer you seek.

Hints and Clues Standard encryption methods switch letters or alter the order they are presented in. Can you think of any way to rearrange the letters shown to form a coherent message?

For more information about ciphers and codes, read:

Code Breaking - A History and Exploration, 1999, Rudolf Kippenhahn, The Overlook Press, Woodstock, NY USA ISBN 1-58567-089-8

Secret Codes, 1996, Robert Jackson, Running Press, Philadelphia, PA USA ISBN 0-7624-1351-4

Digital Fortress, 1998, Dan Brown, St. Martin's Press, New York, NY USA ISBN 0-312-99542-3

"The only interesting answers are those which destroy the questions."
Susan Sontag

"The things we never challenge are the things that never change."
Songwriter and Folk Singer
James Keelaghan, Turn of the Wheel

"I imagine good teaching as a circle of earnest people sitting down to ask each other meaningful questions. I don't see it as the handing down of answers. So much of what passes for teaching is merely a pointing out of what items to want."
Alice Walker

Solutions
Shown Here in Order of Puzzle Number

1 - For 2B or Knot 2B, the solution can be found by picking up any one of the ropes. For The Missing Link, just pull the two loops apart to see if they are linked or not. For Not Knots, simply pull the ends of the rope to see if it does form a knot, or not!

2 - Handcuffs and Shackles. While facing your partner, pass the center of your rope handcuffs towards you and into the triangular opening near their right wrist, then over their hand, and back underneath their wrist loop. Now, if you pull gently on your rope handcuffs, they will separate from your partner. This is the ONLY techniques that will work through a chain link fence or keyhole with your partner's assistance. In larger groups, use this same approach with the person on your right first and then your left. Surprisingly, the same technique works for pairs, trios and very large circles too.

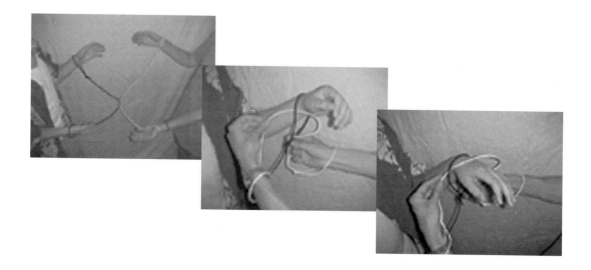

3 - 3 Cubed - The first step to successfully solving this puzzle is to place the container cube at a slight incline on top of the cube lid. This allows each of the placed balls to stay in position. You should be able to completely fill the container with nine balls per level using this technique.

4 - The Labyrinth - You can construct your own labyrinth for personal reflection using the resource books listed in this activity. The team labyrinth is best solved by steady communication. After leaving the labyrinth, participants are no longer allowed to speak so the location of their last message becomes a useful beacon for other team members.

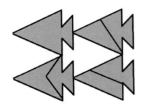

5 - Arrowheads - There are sufficient pieces to construct four arrowheads. The missing fifth arrowhead occupies the interior space when the other four arrowheads are placed together as shown.

6 - People Movers - The solution for PM5 is shown here. For the other puzzles, you'll need to discover your own solutions.

PM1 - 15 moves are required to complete this puzzle with three participants per side. The same style of moves used for this puzzle can be used for PM1.5 and PM2.

PM1.5 24 moves are required for four participants per side and 35 moves for five participants per side.

PM2 - The T and Y configurations are provided as a variation for those groups that may have experienced the standard 'in-line' formation.

PM3 - The M and E formations allow for the possibility of making mistakes or errors and still correcting them before moving on. The M configuration is a bit easier than the E puzzle.

PM4 - The Double Diamond configuration requires a minimum of 46 moves to complete.

PM5 - The four paired moves are shown here.

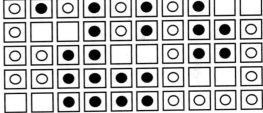

7 - Tangrams - Visit your library to find a collection of Tangram shapes to make. To explore diversity issues, use each of the four patterns to create various shapes and see which ones are unique to certain patterns. The Diversity Quilt Tangram is theoretically possible, but still quite difficult. If you discover a solution, please send us a photo and we will include it in the next edition of this book.

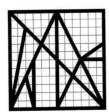

8 - The Archimedes Puzzle is considered to be one of the oldest puzzles in the world. You can use the 14 shapes in this puzzle to make a variety of geometric patterns, similar to a Tangram.

9 - Switching Corks - If you start this activity holding onto the two corks with the fingers of your right hand pointed up and the fingers of your left hand pointed down, you can easily touch your thumbs to the opposite hand's cork. Next, fold your right middle finger over the top, until it makes contact with the opposite hand's cork. Then, fold your left middle finger up towards the opposite hand's cork. Now simply slide your two hands apart.

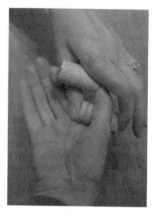

10 - Rock Around the Clock - While it is possible to rotate the circle with everyone remaining in contact, it is not easy. Instead, invite the group to sit on the ground with their legs extended towards the center of the circle and their feet still touching. From this position, it is often obvious to groups that they can simultaneously scootch around the circle, using their hands to lift their bodies, while keeping their feet in contact.

11 - Plenty of Room at the Top - You can stack at least a dozen nails on top of a single nail by building the structure shown.

12 - Building Connection - You can 'connect' the two towers together with only a single nail, if the first thing you do is bring the two towers closer together. Likewise, you can connect two groups together, with less resources, in less time, if the first thing you do is bring the two groups closer together.

13 - How Deep is the Well? While your wooden block may have different length nails or bolts and different depths of holes, the final configuration should look a bit like this.

14 - T.H.E. Puzzle

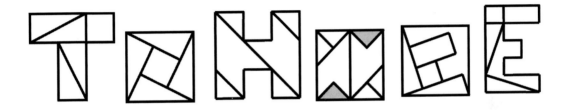

15 - The PVC Network- There are many possible solutions to this puzzle. If you start with short tubes and the four-way cross connectors, then add more tubes and the T connectors next, you should be able to complete the task.

16 - Plumber's Delight - You will need to analyze your own plumbing system to determine which valves must be opened or closed for the flow condition you desire. As an example, the two-dimensional version shown in puzzle #16 requires four valves to turn off the flow. The three-dimensional PVC house version requires eight valves to turn off the outlet flow.

If you lack the hardware and water supply for these versions, consider drawing a water system, filled with connectors, valves and pipes, and presenting this drawing to your team to solve as a pencil and paper challenge.

17 - Inside Out - Participants often use their hands to balance themselves or other members of the group, or crawl on their hands and knees to exit the circle. While this is a violation of the rules, a better question might be to ask, why did they interpret the rules in this manner and how can I, as a teacher or trainer, give better rules in the future to avoid this situation?

18 - The Electric Box - A good solution for your team is to consider in advance what size the opening will be and who is best suited to this particular geometry.

Teambuilding Puzzles

19 - Matchstick Puzzles and More

A. Add one stick to the V to make it into a square root sign.

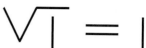

B. Remove one stick from the equal sign and add it to the plus sign to make it into the number four (4), leaving the equation 141 - 11.

C. Add the two sticks at the beginning to make a V, forming the Roman numeral eight (VIII).

D. Use the nine sticks to spell out the word TEN. Use these same nine sticks to make twenty-eight in Roman numerals (XXVIII).

E. Four similar sized equilateral triangles and one very large one. Place the three moving sticks upwards to form a pyramid which contains a total of four equilateral triangles.

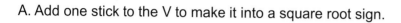

F. You can spell out the word "one" by taking away the base of the second square and then moving the right side of the third square to make an "e" - leaving "one square."

G. Take away the sides of the first square. Make the base vertical in the first square to create the letter T. Place the top of the second square vertically in the center to create the letter W. Which leaves TWO.

H. Remove the top and top left stick from the first rectangle. Move the right top stick from the third rectangle to the first to form a lower case letter d. Move the lower left stick from the third rectangle and place it horizontally in the third rectangle to form the letter s. Which leaves DOS, or two, in Spanish.

I. Use the twelve paper clips to form four square by collaboration.

J. With the eleven sticks you are holding, you can spell out the word NINE.

K. You can create eight small and two large squares.

L. You can rotate two of the roof lines to make the house face the other direction.

M. Use these nine sticks in three-dimensional space to form a double pyramid. The midplane equilateral triangle is shaded in gray.

N. Turn the two sticks of the dog's face to make the dog look the other way.

O.

P. A CUBE

Q. Use the twelve sticks to make a three-dimensional cube which contains six squares.

20 - Slow Burn - The last match to burn, is located just to the left of the square in the upper right hand corner of the puzzle. It is shown here as a black match (see arrow). Every other match (all 47 of them) will burn before this one ignites. There are no matches that do not catch fire. As a safety reminder, <u>DO NOT ATTEMPT TO PERFORM THIS PUZZLE WITH ACTUAL MATCHES!</u>

21 - Houses and Utilities - It is fairly easy to make <u>most</u> of the early connections for this puzzle, but the final few are much more difficult. The final connection itself cannot mathematically be made to work, so an alternative and creative solution is proposed below. The final connection   passes through one of the utilities which, although it does not break the stated rules, does require a bit of 'outside-the-box' thinking

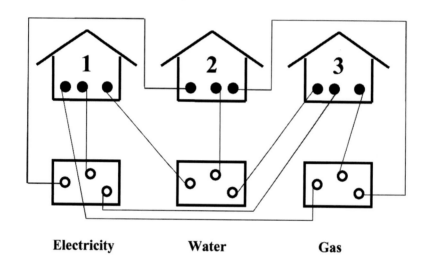

22 - Making Connections - Each of the puzzles presented is possible.

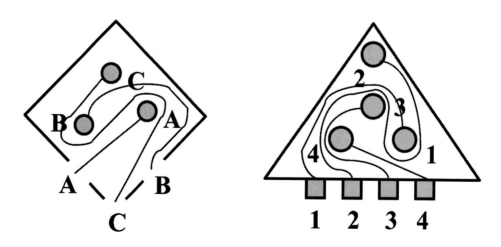

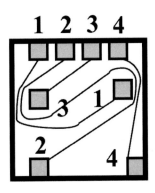

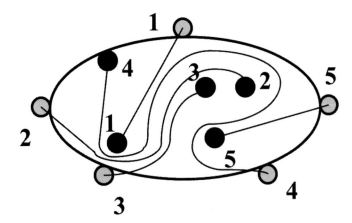

23 - Heads or Tails

A. Stack the two end coins
in the position shown.

B. Stack the bottom coin on the center coin.

C. First stack two coins at each corner location to create five coins per side. Next stack three coins at each corner location to produce a square with six coins per side.

D. Each of the following squares has five coins on each side.

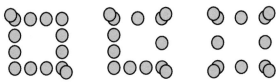

E. Place one coin on the left side of the line heads up. Place another coin on the right side of the line, tails up. Place the third coin upright on the line with the head facing towards the left side and the tail facing towards the right side.

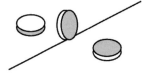

F. Place the ten coins in the pattern of a five pointed star with four coins in each line.

G. The word 'touching' is key to the instructions for this coin puzzle. Take the right most coin in the second horizontal row and use it to push each of the other coins in this row to the right one position. Then place this coin at the leftmost end of the row. Do the same with the rightmost coin in the fourth horizontal row. You will now have the same side of each coin showing in each of the vertical columns.

H. Sorting Things Out - The solution to this coin puzzle is shown in People Movers (#6), earlier in this section.

24 - Drink Up! If you create a check mark profile with your straw, slide it into the bottle, and allow the short leg of the check mark to wedge itself against the sloping inside top portion of the bottle, you will be able to lift the bottle off the table (as shown at right).

25 - Pigs & Pens - Two styles of solutions are possible. Type one solutions include those answers with pens inside of pens, but where pens do not cross boundaries. Type two solutions (on the following page) are comprised of answers where pens can intersect, connect, and cross boundaries.

Type One
Solution

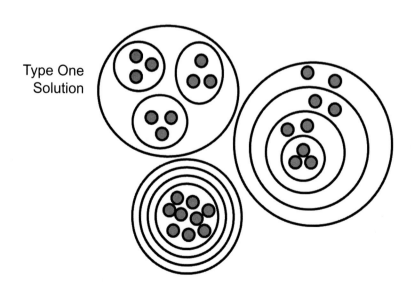

Type Two
Solutions

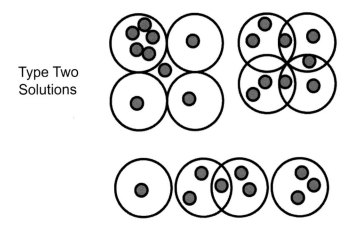

26 - Sheep & Pens - Placing one sheep in each of the four corner pens and four sheep in each of the remaining pens follows the inspector's recommendations and keeps the center pen unoccupied.

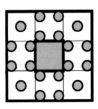

27 - Modern Hieroglyphics

A. Scrambled Eggs
B. Traveling Overseas
C. Forum
D. Line up in alphabetical order
E. Water (H2O)
F. Just Between You and Me
G. The End of 'The World'
H. More Often than Not
I. Long time no see

J. Blanket
K. Look both ways before crossing
L. A little bit more
M. Apartment
N. Eraser
O. Tennis shoes
P. Hang in there
Q. Tunafish
R. Room for one more

S. Brian Underwood Andover, Ohio
T. The start of 'Something Big'
U. Tooth Decay
V. Just under the wire
W. Banana Split
X. Tennessee
Y. Love at first sight
Z. A bad spell of weather

28 - A Quick Study - Part I - The letters of the alphabet organized by those with straight lines only (M), those with curved lines only (O), and those that are mixed (straight and curved) (B). Part II - Letters of the alphabet organized by those that are open (F), and those that have enclosed areas (Q). Part III - Letters of the alphabet organized by the number of pen strokes or lines necessary to produce each letter (M = 4, N = 3, T = 2, S = 1). The numbers are similarly organized in Parts I, II and III. The Bonus numbers puzzle presents each of the numbers in alphabetical order.

29 - Pangrams, contain every letter of the alphabet. The 'near miss' pangrams are missing an 's' in the first sentence, a 'j' in the second sentence, and a 'v' in the third sentence.

30 - Back & Forth - These unusual sentences are known as palindromes and spell the same sentence backwards and forwards. 'Madam, I'm Adam' is the same when spelled backwards (except for punctuation, obviously). The eleven palindromes within the article include the ten palindromes listed plus the third line of the title. You'll find another interesting backwards spelling if you look at the teaching assistant's name and title, in reverse.

31 - Magic Carpet - Although it is possible to twist the carpet and turn it over as a single 'team,' it is far easier to collaborate with other local groups and share the available resources. Transferring a few members to another carpet, flipping your own carpet and then returning the favor for other groups makes for a quick, easy and collaborative solution compared to a competitive one.

32 - Pencil Pushers - The major difficulty is the total amount of time required to place the pencil beyond the line. Climbing over other participants and remaining in push-up position for any length of time is quite a physical challenge. If a team were to be in place behind the line, and then pivot (like a windshield wiper) or crawl straight forward in a line, and then retreat, this would minimize the amount of time and physical exertion beyond the line.

33 - Bite the Bag - There is no trick here. This is simply a matter of physical balance and ability.

34 - The 15th Object - Knowledge is Power - The various forms of this puzzle all rely on discovering the 'key' objects to control (to take) to win the game. With 15 objects, taking 1, 2 or 3 objects per turn, it is important to control (take) the second, sixth and tenth object. For 16 objects with the same rules, it becomes the third, seventh and eleventh objects controlling the outcome of the game. Which objects control the game with 14 total objects present?

35 - The Tower of Hanoi - Try beginning with three disks at first. Once you learn the procedure for this number, try four, and then five.

The number of moves required to complete the tower of Hanoi is a function of the number of disks present. You can calculate the number of moves from the following equation, where N is the number of disks:

$$(2 \text{ raised to the power N}) - 1 = (2^N) - 1 = \text{The Number of Moves}$$

The chart below provides the number of moves for disks from one to ten.

Number of Disks	Number of Moves	Number of Disks	Number of Moves
1	1	6	63
2	3	7	127
3	7	8	255
4	15	9	511
5	31	10	1023

If you move one disk every five seconds, how long would it take to move a stack of ten disks?

First of all, it will require 2^10-1 moves, or 1024-1 = 1023 moves.

1023 moves x 5 seconds per move = 5115 seconds = 85.25 minutes
which is the same as: 1 hour, 25 minutes and 15 seconds.

36 - Just Passing Through - There are at least two different cutting techniques that greatly enlarge an opening in an index card, shown here. Each pattern turns the index card into a giant circle (see the picture on the next page).

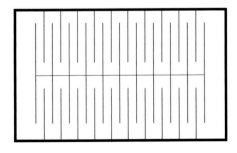
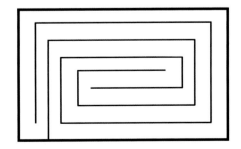

Just Passing Through

37 - Pipe Chimes - The lengths for the middle octave of a piano are given. Additional lengths can be calculated from the provided equation based upon the note frequency (which can often be found in music theory and physics books). If you number each pipe chime, you can simplify writing music for group performances by just using the number rather than musical notes.

38 - Pyramid Power - With the rope you can tie a loose knot around the perimeter of the pyramid, about mid-height, and quickly pull it tight, lifting the pyramid at the same time. Or, you can use the rope, stick and ball all in the following manner. Place any of these objects below the pyramid, between the two hinged boards and the third 'holding' board. Gently press against the two hinged boards until the third board drops slightly. Next allow this third board to wedge below the hinge, and lift vertically.

39 - The Great Golf Ball Pyramids - Use one 2x3 ball section together with the 1x4 section. Make a second identical piece from the other 2x3 section, together with both of the 1x2 sections. Now place these two pieces together so that the 2x3 sections are touching, but each piece is turned 90 degrees to each other.

40 - Paper Pyramids - Make your own pieces by cutting and folding paper. Form the tetrahedron (pyramid) by placing the square face of each piece together with the rest of each piece rotated at 90 degrees to the other. Form the cube by placing the points opposite the square bases all together.

41 - SNAP - By leaning inward and removing most of the stretch (stress) within the elastic band, the team should be able to let go and place the band near the center of the target.

42 - Blind Square - Creating four equal lengths of rope can be accomplished by folding the rope in half twice and placing a person at each of the corner locations.

43 - Shape Up - Some shapes are easier to create if the first thing your group does is untie the knot.

44 - The Corporate Maze - You can choose any continuous pattern through the maze that you like. One example is shown here.

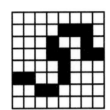

The Chasing Sheep puzzle is very unusual. Unless the sheep runs into a corner, the farmer can NEVER catch their own sheep. However, by working together on one sheep at a time, both farmers can help each other catch both sheep. A perfect lesson in teamwork.

45 - Pentominoes are the twelve two-dimensional shapes that can be constructed from 5 cubes that have been joined together. The definitive work on this puzzle is: Polyominoes - The Fascinating New Recreation in Mathematics, 1965, Solomon Golomb, Charles Scribner, New York, USA

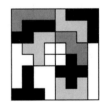

A few interesting configurations of Pentominoes are shown here. The first can be made with the Corporate Maze, and is an 8x8 square with the middle four spaces unoccupied. The second structure, made from Pentominoes of five cubes each, is thought to be impossible to construct from the twelve basic pentominoes.

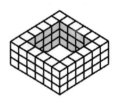

46 - Five Rooms and One Extension Cord is a lesson in topology. No matter where you begin, you will not be able to pass through each wall only once and still pass through each wall segment. The first illustration below is one example of an attempt that falls short. You'll notice that two wall segments are untouched. A next solution which meets this criteria is shown below, although some may argue that it breaks a few unwritten rules in the process.

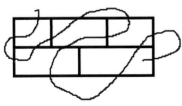

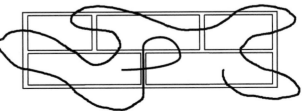

47 - True North - Having an accurate compass, map or GPS unit are essential.

48 - The Human Knot - There are three likely final configurations from the Human Knot puzzle. The group can create one large circle, or two separate circles, or two interlocking circles. For truly difficult knots, a visit from the Knot Doctor can be the only resource to success.

49 - Line Up - Sign language, hand gestures, body language and other forms of non-verbal communication are helpful in this activity. Knowledge of specific subjects such as mathematics, planets, Roman numerals or Morse code can also be useful.

   To teach environmental issues related to the amount of time necessary for various forms of trash to decompose, Mike Anderson provides his students with the following information on individual index cards. The Line Up Challenge is for them to stand in the order they believe these items will decay.

Item Writing on Index Card	Answer (not written on the index card)
Traffic Ticket	2 to 4 weeks
Cotton Rag	1 to 5 months
Manila Rope	1 to 14 months
Bamboo Pole	1 to 3 years
Wool Sock	1 year
Painted Wooden Stake	3 years
Tin Can	100 years
Aluminum Can	200 to 500 years
Plastic 6-pack Ring	450 years
Glass Bottle	Undetermined

50 - Paint Stick Shuffle - Be sure to know the questions in advance. This will assist you in placing the paint stirring sticks in a pile before the group arrives. If you use long dowel rods instead of paint sticks, you can also play a king size version of pick-up sticks as part of the challenge.

51 - Seven Boxes of Bolts - Arrange the seven boxes of bolts in a line and remove one bolt from box one, two bolts from box two, three bolts from box three, and so on. The total number of bolts weighed will be 1+2+3+4+5+6+7, or 28. The weight of a nondefective bolt

is 1.0 pounds and a defective bolt is 0.9 pounds. If the 'bad' bolts are in box three, the total weight of all the bolts will be three times 0.1 pounds under the expected weight of 28 pounds, or 27.7 pounds. A chart calculating these weights is shown below.

Box Number	Number of Pieces = N	Delta N x 0.1	Total Weight (Pounds)
1	1	0.1	27.9
2	2	0.2	27.8
3	3	0.3	27.7
4	4	0.4	27.6
5	5	0.5	27.5
6	6	0.6	27.4
7	7	0.7	27.3

52 - A Problem of Weight - With eight containers - Place three containers on the left side of the balance, and three on the right. If the scale balances, the light container is one of the two left. If the balance tips, the higher side possesses the lighter container. If it is one of the two containers left, place one on each side of the balance, and the answer is revealed. If it is one of the three on one side of the balance, remove the rest, place one on the left, one on the right, and leave one in front. If they balance, it is the one in front. If they do not, it is the one on the higher side of the balance.

　　For nine containers - place three on the left side, three on the right side, and three in front. If the scale balances, the light container is one of the three in front. Of the three that contain the lighter container, place one on the left side of the scale, one on the right side, and one in front. If they balance, it is the one in front. If they do not balance, it is the one on the higher side of the balance.

53 - Count Six - There are several techniques for improving the performance of your team. First, you can divide the task. For example, you can organize your team so that half perform the left arm movement only and the other half provide the right arm movement only. Or, one person can perform the 'one' movement with both arms. The next person can perform the 'two' movement. And so on. Don't forget, the original challenge was to show proficiency in performing this task as a team. No mention was made that every person had to demonstrate the pattern all by themselves.

　　If you would like to individually improve your ability to perform the Count Six pattern, we recommend that you quickly think 'left hand - right hand' as you count from one to six. In　this way, you quickly cover each hand movement independently instead of literally trying to perform two tasks at once.

54 - Coiled Rope - This puzzle will be slightly different each time. Move slowly, avoid knots and encourage communication.

55 - The White Board Puzzle - You can find whiteboard material at a large hardware store.

56 - Giant Jigsaw Puzzle - You will find assembling this puzzle a simple task with your eyes open, but considerably more challenging for a group when their eyes are closed.

57 - An Unusual Jigsaw Puzzle - two of the pieces fit only when turned to the opposite side from the rest of the pieces. This puzzle was one of two cut out at the same time using a bandsaw. The two boards were joined together in multiple places with masking tape and then cut into several pieces. When complete, two of the pieces were switched between puzzles, creating the one shown in the illustration of Puzzle 57. For information about where to find this type of puzzle, see the Teamwork & Teamplay website at: www. teamworkandteamplay.com Click on the Teambuilding Puzzles icon.

58 - The Whole Story - The scrambled quotation at the bottom of the page is:

The road to wisdom? Is plain and simple to express.
Err and err and err again, but less, and less, and less.
Attributed to Piet Hein

59 - Tongue Twisters - Visit www.uebersetzung.at/twister for almost 3000 tongue twisters in 105 different languages. Red leather, yellow leather. Truly Rural.

60 - Shaping the Future - The six pieces can be used to form each of the outlines shown.

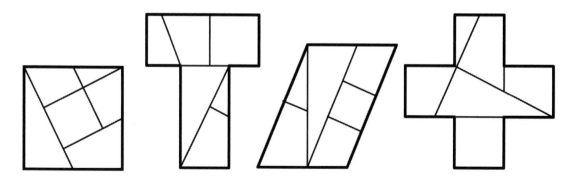

Teambuilding Puzzles

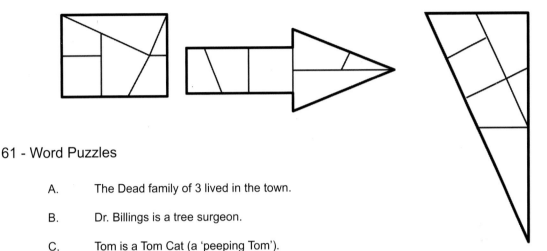

61 - Word Puzzles

A.   The Dead family of 3 lived in the town.

B.   Dr. Billings is a tree surgeon.

C.   Tom is a Tom Cat (a 'peeping Tom').

D.   The queen was a 'queen' sized bed that was not replaced for five years.

E.   Sandy and her brother were skin diving and came across a school of piranha fish.

F.   Taylor had been cut from a professional sports team and then picked up by another team shortly after.

G.   Baxter Knox was the family puppy who chewed and ruined the leather couch.

H.   It was a car pool.

I.   A Chicken and a Half. 1.5 chickens lay 1.5 eggs in 1.5 days. One chicken lays one egg in 1.5 days. This means that 12.5 chickens, can lay 12.5 eggs in 1.5 days. To lay 37.5 eggs would require 12.5 chickens 3 x 1.5 days, or 4.5 days.

62 - We invite you to find the answers to the questions from "A Strange Day" yourself. Email your answers to: jimcain@teamworkandteamplay.com, and we'll verify if you have discovered the right facts. Good Luck. If you just can't wait, we invite you to solve the final puzzle in this book, entitled "One For The Road," and you'll find the answers there as well.

63 - Changing Sides - It is surprisingly possible to switch sides in both the hand held and king size versions of this puzzle. The first person near the central hole moves towards the hole, passing under the bight (rope talk for the central loop that goes around the two central ropes). Once they are standing near the hole, they coerce the bight around the back of the 2x6 and through the hole. By passing sufficient rope through this hole, it will be possible to pass through the bight to the other side. Now return the bight back through

the hole and step into the other side. The rope is now ready for the second person to journey to the other side. Move slowly, avoid knots and be especially careful when any team member is moving along the ropes near the central hole.

You may want to give each participant a handsize version of the puzzle to work out for themselves before connecting them to the king size version.

64 - Classical Knot Theory - There are three possible solutions to this task. The first and true solution is to cross your arms prior to picking up the rope. When you uncross your arms, you'll find that an overhand knot is tied in the rope. A second solution is possible by picking up the middle and one end of the rope and, while still holding these positions, tie an overhand knot in the free end of the rope. The third technique, which involves some 'slight of hand' magic skill, is illustrated here. This technique requires a bit more work and some practice to make this version look authentic. Begin by holding the rope  as shown, with about 4 inches of rope over the top of each hand. The illustrations shown below are pictures of what your hands should look like as you execute this trick. This, however, is not an easy trick to visually explain here. If you would like a more complete explanation, look up Jim Cain at his next conference appearance and he would be glad to show you this trick in detail.

After grasping the rope, loop the left hand over the right hand to form a "window" with the rope. Next, pass the left hand through this window behind the part of the rope marked "A" and then back out of the window. Now move the left and right hands away from each other.

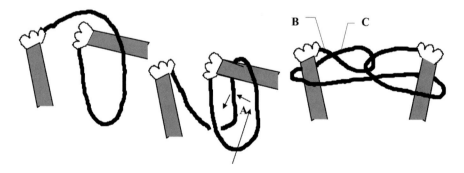

If you pull the left and right hands apart now, no knot. The secret move is to take the left hand and switch the position where it is holding the rope from the segment marked B to the segment marked C. This is accomplished by dropping the center of the rope downward and moving the contact point with the left hand from the end of the rope to about 1 foot inward (i.e. from point B to point C). The result is an overhand knot.

65 - The Placemat Puzzle - The real challenge of this activity is having exactly the right number of objects or puzzle pieces for the size group you have. If your group size is unknown, use simple objects that you can easily change the quantity such as playing cards or dominoes.

66 - Making Contact - Twelve tennis balls can be made to contact one central tennis ball. Three on the upper level, six surrounding the ball at the middle level, and three more at the bottom level. Four tennis balls can contact each other.

Wooden Blocks or Cubes - Would you believe that twenty similar sized cubes can be placed in contact with one central cube? Seven in the base level, six surrounding the cube at the middle level, and seven more in the upper level. Four cubes can be in line contact with each other. Can you find a technique to include more?

Sticks - The first illustration shows one technique for placing six sticks in contact with each other. The second illustration shows a possibility for seven sticks. If you use foam noodles, you can create contact with eight or more sticks because noodles are flexible and they bend.

Coins - It is possible to place five coins in contact with each other. Two coins for the base. One coin resting on these two base coins. Now place two coins vertically, as shown. Complete the task by tipping these vertical coins towards each other so that they touch each other at the top. You now have five coins in contact with one another.

People - As a facilitator, be sure to define appropriate contact, such as shaking hands, for the culture of people you are leading. Appropriate contact differs with nationality, race and culture. Be sure you know the respectful limits of your team's ability to connect.

67 - Nothing Can Divide Us. There are 25 prime numbers between 1 and 100. They are: 2, 3, 5, 7, 11, 13, 17, 19, 23, 29, 31, 37, 41, 43, 47, 53, 59, 61, 67, 71, 73, 79, 83, 89, and 97. The number 1, by the way, is not typically considered a prime number.

68 - Where Do You Stand?   Answers for the four configurations initially presented are shown below. The final configuration is impossible since the center location touches each of the other locations.

69 - Adaptation or Extinction - One technique that meets the requirements for safety is for the entire team to sit on the floor, with just their feet within the boundary of an island.

70 - The Fence - By moving just two corner posts rather than three, the farmer's new pasture looks like this.

Original Pasture Configuration ·······

New Pasture Configuration ▬▬▬

You can produce a triangular pasture that is half the area of the present pasture, without moving any corner posts.

71 - Land of Lakes - Increase the size of each lake.

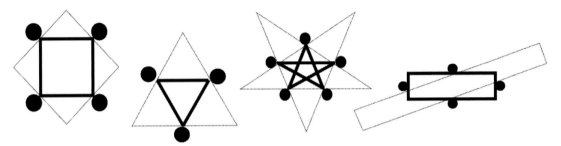

The first three geometries do not require filling in any of the previous pond. The rectangular pond does. The circular pond requires a bit more thinking. You could dig the pond twice as deep, which increases the volume by a factor of two. Or, you could wait until winter, and pile up ice till it is as high as the lake is deep doubling the amount of water (although most of it is frozen). What other creative solutions can you think of?

72 - Making Connections - The more the members of your team share, the greater the opportunity for the ball of string to make it completely around circle.

73 - The Bridge - Is based on a concept of Leonardo Da Vinci. The sketch here illustrates one possible configuration.

Balance - During the writing of this book, we discovered that the bridge pieces can also be used for the nail activity, Plenty of Room at the Top. The photograph shows one configuration that works.

74 - Three Kinds of Memory - Perform the visual memory marathon last as this style of memorization is typically the strongest.

75 - Matchmaking - Pictures, objects and words can be placed on the bottom of each board in pairs (2) or even trios (3) to make a 'match.' The acoustic version incorporates different objects within recycled plastic film canisters to produce different sounds. For this case, two or three canisters can carry the same objects.

76 - Changing Directions - Three People are all that is needed to make the arrow point the other way, as shown in the sketch below.

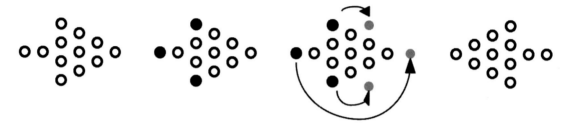

77 - Island Hopping. As shown, it is impossible to cross each bridge only once and end up on the same island as you began your journey. Your team needs to build or remove some bridges.

Close All the Doors - You could argue that if you start in the supply closet (top middle) and weave your way in an out of doors until you pass into the room at the upper left, you could leave through the outside left door and close the top door on your way past. But this approach doesn't meet the required rule that Joe 'pass through' each of the doors. As shown, the challenge cannot be met. Removing two doors in the upper left room would resolve this situation. Can you find   other possibilities?

78 - Line Up the Glasses - Pour the contents of the fifth glass into the second glass and then return the now empty fifth glass to its original location

79 - Mathematical Magic - for each puzzle, just turn the entire sign (equations) upside down.

80 - Parking Cars - It is impossible to place 31 dominoes on a chess board where the two opposite corners have been removed. Why? Because each domino requires one red and one black square, and with opposite corners missing from the chess board, there are insufficient red or black squares to satisfy this mathematical requirement.

81 - The Tower - Building the maximum perimeter base typically leads to the tallest structure.

82 - A Single Drop of Water - It is possible to place 30-50 drops of water on a standard U.S. Penny.

83 - Extreme Origami - If you begin with a standard 8.5 x 11 inch pieces of writing paper it is very difficult to achieve seven folds. Try working with a full sheet of flip chart paper. You just might be able to do it. If you start with an index card, you'll be lucky to get five folds.

84 - Arm Wrestling - You can win the most candy by each cooperating, rather than competing. This win-win scenario requires both contestants to relax and work together to quickly rotate their arms back and forth. A win-win scenario for Cross the Line involves both partners offering to change sides, without force.

85 - Finding Your People - You can find the perfect collection of colorful wooden shapes from Training Wheels, Inc., www.training-wheels.com or call 1-888-553-0147
    We highly recommend the Robert Fulghum story 'The Mermaid.'

86 - I'm In Games

Silly Tilly Williams	She likes things with double letters (books but not magazines)
Johnny Whoops	Fold your hands together at the end
The Moon Is Round	Use your LEFT hand
Black Magic	It is the item that comes after a black object
Crossed or Uncrossed	Watch the person's legs (crossed or uncrossed), not the scissors
Magic Writing	Use the stick to tap out vowels (a = 1 tap, u = 5 taps). The first letter of any other word, phrase or sentence is the next consonant. For example, "listen carefully." Tap, tap, tap, tap. "Very carefully." Tap, tap. Spells out L-O-V-E.
Polar Bears & Ice Holes	Ice holes are the dots at the exact center of any face, and are found on the one, three and five sides. Polar bears surround the ice hole dots, and so are found on the three (2 polar bears) and five (four polar bears) sides only. The two, four and six sides do not represent ice holes or polar bears.

Card Tricks	Six Cards - You hold your thumb over the remaining cards in the deck, at the position of the correct card.
Nine Books	The location you point to on the very first book, is the location of the correct book. So pointing at the center of any other book, indicates that the center book is the correct one.

87 - 63, 64, 65 - The puzzle is originally cut from a square 8x8 pattern, producing 64 square units of area. The 65 unit rectangle actually has one square unit missing from the diagonal center line. The 63 unit configuration actually has more area in each rectangular region than counting the blocks would indicate. In this case 64 square units, rather than 63. Calculating the area of each of the four individual pieces will provide an exact answer, even if your team is visually confused.

88 - Parade - Various forms of cooperative movement and carrying others is acceptable. However, it is possible to move the distance simply by log rolling along the ground, using zero feet!

89 - First Flight - One possible solution that works well is for a group of 3-5 participants to place their paper against a wall, with each of the four paper edges slightly folded away from the wall (which makes the paper look like a small serving tray) and then to alternately use their breath to keep the paper against the wall and off the floor.

90 - Your Move - From Anthony Curtis of Adventure Designs (www.adventure-designs.com) A total of 70 points for each team, 140 points total, is possible if the wild card balls are used to benefit both teams, as shown in the illustration.

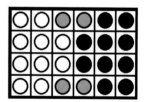

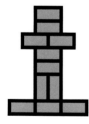

91 - Inuksuit - Balancing stones takes a steady hand and calmness. If at first you don't succeed, breathe, and try, try again.

92 - The Big Cover Up - Run, look, run some more, communicate, run, catch your breath.

93 - A Circle of Connection, participants just need to share their interests, hobbies and talents until another member of the group shares one of these with them.

94 - The Square - Slide one board to form a square at the intersection of all other boards. You can also place this same board as shown in the second illustration to create the number four, which is a perfect square (2x2=4, or 2^2=4).

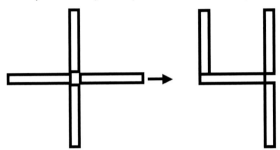

95 - Team Labyrinth - Everyone needs to move slowly, pull together and use teamwork.

96 - The Puzzle Cube - A portable spider web that can be assembled in five different sizes of cubes and can be used to create the equipment for 10 other team activities.

97 - Jumping George - Just one of those things you can either do, or you can't. Jumping backwards works for some people.

98 - Just One Word - Spells out exactly that, "Just One Word."

99 - Concentration - slap, clap, right snap, left snap

100 - Ciphers & Codes - Together Everyone Accomplishes More

Mencken's Metalaw

*"For every human problem,
there is a neat, simple solution;
and it is always wrong."*
H. L. Mencken

Modifying Puzzles for Teams

How to Turn a Puzzle Solving Session
Into a Group Experience

1. Take a simple visual puzzle and require the group to achieve consensus before revealing the solution. For example, puzzle #1, 2B or Knot 2B is a simple visual tangle puzzle. But this simple puzzle becomes very valuable when used as a tool to talk about consensus, buy-in, collaboration, accountability and working together as a team.

2. Require everyone in the group to demonstrate the solution, not just a single person. For example Handcuffs and Shackles or Switching Corks can both be demonstrated by the entire group with some valuable teaching and sharing between group members.

3. Apply some additional limitations to the puzzle. For example, the Tangram activity for building a square is easily accomplished by one person. By only allowing participants the time they can hold their breath in the construction zone, more team members are given the opportunity to contribute.

4. Use simple, familiar equipment and props in new ways. Plenty of Room at the Top (puzzle #11), the PVC Network (puzzle #15) and Switching Corks (puzzle #9) utilize familiar objects, but require new, unusual and sometimes unexpected solutions.

5. Substitute or modify the materials required. For example, the Matchstick Puzzles (puzzle #19) included in this book can obviously be performed with small matchsticks. Why not increase the size of this puzzle, and substitute 10 foot (3 meter) long PVC tubes instead? Now you'll have a puzzle that will take more than one person to complete.

6. Utilize different learning styles. We suggest you read the book: Multiple Intelligences in the Classroom, 2000, Thomas Armstrong, ASCD, Alexandria, VA USA ISBN 0-87120-376-6. This book provides excellent templates, ideas and suggestions for reaching participants using a variety of techniques. Apply these various techniques to the puzzles you choose from this book. This will insure that you create a healthy balanced diet of styles and skills from the puzzles you have chosen.

7. Start with a purpose in mind. If you have a specific training need (such as problem solving, decision making, ethical behavior in the workplace, collaboration vs. competition, communication or teamwork), look for a puzzle that will reinforce this concept. You'll soon find that the puzzles themselves are not the 'end' but rather the tool that opens the door to meaningful discussions about the subject you present.

8. Keep the puzzle the same, but modify the group. Provide additional challenges to the group. Such things as time limitations, limited resources, limited vision or hearing, incomplete rules or puzzle presentation, mobility limitations, communication delays or other changes during the solution process often remind participants of similar events encountered in their daily lives. These become teachable moments in themselves.

9. Encourage communication and connection between participants. Choose puzzles that provide the opportunity for discussion, interaction and collaboration whenever possible.

10. Break the puzzle into smaller pieces and make each member of the group responsible for one component of the solution. For example, the Giant Jigsaw Puzzle in this book can be performed blindfolded with each person holding a piece of the puzzle initially. Where Do You Stand?, True North and Handcuffs and Shackles are just a few examples of teambuilding puzzles that build upon individual contributions to assist the total group's success.

Additional Ideas:

"To feel that one has a place in life solves half the problems of contentment."
George Woodberry

*"Experience is a great advantage. The problem is
that when you get the experience, you're too damned old to do anything about it."*
Jimmy Connors

One question you may have related to solving puzzles is how to transform a basically cerebral and often solitary experience into a group project that is active: mentally, physically and socially. Luckily, we have found the perfect technique for turning almost any collection of puzzles or challenges into an interactive group experience. Our thanks to Greg Huber, President of Challenge Discovery in Richmond, Virginia USA for allowing us to share this wonderful and unique technique that he created as part of the CONQUEST teambuilding program. You can learn more about CONQUEST by visiting the Challenge Discovery website at: www.challengediscovery.com.

In a nutshell, 'The Great Puzzle Quest' begins by inviting group members to locate and collect a variety of PVC pipes and connectors, along with some tubular climbing webbing and construct an emergency rescue litter with which the team will transport one of their own members. During transport, the team encounters a variety of puzzles and challenges along the way. By solving these challenges, the team effectively 'cures' the afflicted group member, restoring their hearing, speech, sight and eventually mobility. This technique encourages connection, empathy, and creative group problem solving, and requires physical, mental and social skills to successfully complete the quest. All-in-all, a perfect combination of skills for the scholastic classroom, corporate board room, adventure-based learning environment, or summer camp activity field.

On the following pages, you'll find a detailed description of how to utilize this very portable technique for your next group. The PVC rescue litter, this book, and many of the puzzles described here can be purchased at Training Wheels, Inc. Visit their website at: www.training-wheels.com or call them, 1-888-553-0147

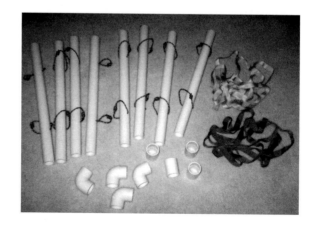

Please read the following information carefully before attempting to utilize this technique for your teambuilding event. Recommendations for group size, equipment requirements, safety information and other essential programming ideas are provided here. If you have any additional questions, please feel free to contact Jim Cain for more information, at:

Jim Cain
Teamwork & Teamplay
468 Salmon Creek Road
Brockport, NY 14420 USA
Phone (585) 637-0328
jimcain@teamworkandteamplay.com
www.teamworkandteamplay.com

The Great Puzzle Quest

The Great Puzzle Quest has been divided into the following five sections:

1. Basic Information
2. Gathering the Components of the Rescue Litter
3. Construction of the Rescue Litter
4. Puzzles and Challenges
5. Optional Final Debriefing Session

Section 1. Basic Information

The PVC rescue litter used in The Great Puzzle Quest is constructed of 1-1/2 inch diameter Schedule 40 PVC tubing and connectors which are available at most hardware or plumbing supply stores. For safety considerations, construction of each litter by teambuilding groups should be supervised with a final inspection before use. While group sizes may vary, a minimum group size of 11 adults per litter (one passenger and ten lifters), or 13 teenagers per litter (one passenger and 12 lifters) is recommended. This is also a reasonable size group for solving some of the problems and challenges presented during the Great Puzzle Quest.

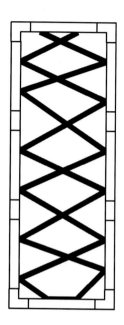

The quest begins with the group attempting to locate and then collect the necessary components of their rescue litter. As shown here, the PVC litter consists of the following components:

4   1-1/2" PVC Corner (90 Degree Elbow) Connectors

4   1-1/2" PVC Straight (Union) Connectors

8   1-1/2" PVC Tubes with Rope Attachment Points

2   15 foot long Tubular Webbing Segments

It is important for each PVC tube segment to be fully inserted into each of the connectors, and for the two tubular webbing segments to be attached to each of the rope attachment points of the rescue litter with secure knots at each end.

Section 2. Gathering the Components of the Rescue Litter

To provide a higher level of challenge, or for thematic teambuilding programs, several challenges can be provided for each group attempting to locate and obtain the various components of their rescue litter. While 25 different activities are suggested here, there are dozens more available from the teambuilding books listed in the References and Resources section of this book (Teamwork & Teamplay, and Affordable Portables, for example). We recommend at least three different challenges to obtain the complete set of components for each rescue litter, or as few as limited time permits.

1. Map & Compass Orienteering, Geocaching and/ or GPS Navigation can be used to locate specific components. You'll need a detailed map of the local area and the appropriate navigational tools (compass, scale, tape measure, GPS device, etc.). A good reference for this style of challenge is: The Complete Idiot's Guide to Geocaching, Jack Peters and Staff of Geocaching.com, 2004, Alpha Books, New York, NY USA ISBN 1-59257-235-9

2. The Complete Story Team members are given strips of paper with an assortment of information, clues and hints, which they must place in order. These clues can be presented in the form of riddles, limericks, stories or maps. One of our favorite versions is to write a colorful story on the front of blank puzzle pieces (available at many craft and stationery stores) and the clues to finding the puzzle pieces on the back. Once the group has completed the 'easy' puzzle on the front side, they can turn the puzzle over to reveal additional clues on the reverse side.

3. Broken Token Clues Team members are each individually presented with part of a clue, but must find one or two additional team members to complete their hint. While these can be written on paper, you can also use more creative media, such as carved wood, jewelry or stones.

4. Roll On A subset of team members from each group uses a 2 foot by 4 foot 'raft' of 3/4" thick plywood, 1 inch diameter dowel rods four feet long with rubber tips and half a dozen 2-3" in diameter PVC tubes to roll over a flat surface from a starting position to the storage location of several PVC components, and back again. Dropping a component in transit could result in the loss of that component.

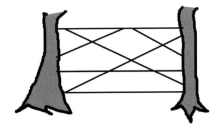

5. The Spider's Web
A few members of each team are asked to pass through a large-scale spider's web without touching it in the process, retrieve several components and then return through the web using a different path.

6. The Puzzle Cube As an extremely portable version of the spider web, the Puzzle Cube (puzzle #96 in this book) presents a challenge as groups attempt to pass through the cube without tipping it off balance. Components of the rescue litter can be obtained by each team member successfully passing through the cube.

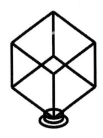

7. The Human Ladder One team member is asked to traverse a horizontal ladder made from 1-1/2 inch hardwood dowels, 36 inches long, and held at each end by a member of the team. They traverse in one direction to recover the two segments of tubular climbing webbing and then return to the starting location. The climber crawls on their hands and knees to traverse the ladder.

8. Golf Ball Crossing 2-3 team members use a 2 foot by 4 foot 'raft' of 3/4" plywood that 'floats' on several dozen golf balls to cross a flat paved surface. 1 inch diameter dowel rods, four feet long with rubber tips, are used as push poles for those on each raft.

9. Magic Carpets With each team on their own plastic tarp, shower curtain, or tablecloth, the entire team attempts to flip over their 'magic carpet' without lifting up any team member, and with no member of the team touching the ground or floor. Successfully flipping the tarp over wins the team several components of the rescue litter. Another variation includes presenting clues on the reverse side of the magic carpet. When the group successfully flips over the carpet, they can read the information on the other side.

10. Message in a Bottle This technique requires the group to find or be given a unique corked bottle with a message, map or series of clues inside. The collection of rescue litter components then becomes a search based upon this information. As an alternative, a recorded message, cassette tape, videotape, website address, CD or DVD recording can be included with information and clues related to finding the rescue litter components. Each of these message styles can be altered to fit a specific adventure theme.

11. Stilts Individual team members can use wooden stilts or tin can stilts to traverse a short distance, retrieve valuable components and then return with this equipment via another route.

12. Word Search Groups can find clues of where key rescue litter components have been hidden by finding words in a seek 'n find word grid. You can build your own word puzzle at: www.puzzlemaker.com.

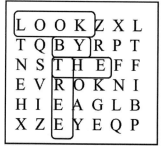

13. Puzzle Warm-Up Groups can obtain components for their rescue litter by successfully completing some warm-up puzzles, ice breakers and get acquainted activities (such as learning the names of each member of the group, finding commonalties, solving individual puzzles, etc.).

14. Boardwalking Several team members board a pair of wooden 2x6's with several ropes attached. The group uses these boards to 'walk' to a region where they can recover the components of their rescue litter.

15. Just a Little Bit Farther Team members find themselves on one side of a perimeter line with the rescue litter components on the other side. Each team member is responsible for retrieving one of the needed components on the other side of the line. Components are placed so that those items first retrieved can be used to reach other items which are located somewhat farther away.

16. The Pot of Gold The entire team attempts to use a minimum of resources (such as short ropes, coat hangers and clothespins) to retrieve the components of their rescue litter from the center of a 20 foot (6 meter) diameter rope circle without touching the ground inside the circle.

17. Deep Sea Diving The entire team assembles on one side of a line or boundary (dry land) and all rescue litter components are placed at a considerable distance on the other side of the line or boundary (which represents the underwater side). The goal is for each participant (as an underwater rescue diver) to recover and bring back one piece of the rescue litter. This task can be made more physically challenging by asking that all divers hold their breath as long as they are on the other side of the line (underwater).

18. Go Fly a Kite Attach index card clues to the string of a high flying kite. As the group winds in the kite string, each clue can be detached. The final clue can be attached to the kite itself.

19. Go Fish! Attach a series of laminated (waterproof) notes to a fishing pole line with a large sinker at the end (forget the hook). Invite the group to reel in the line and discover the clues along the way. A second version is to cast a plastic toy fish or food storage container attached to the far end of the line. For each preliminary task performed by the group (learning each other's names, creating a group cheer, making a group flag or pennant, deciding on a group name, etc.), one person is allowed either a fixed number of winding turns on the fishing reel or a fixed time to wind in as much fishing line as they can. When the plastic fish or small storage container is retrieved, the group can begin to search for the rescue litter using the clues provided.

20. Challenge Course Elements If the Great Puzzle Quest is performed as part of a challenge course experience, teams can obtain components of their rescue litter by successfully completing various rope course elements or reaching key handholds on climbing walls.

21. Mysterious Writing Here is an encoded message technique that you can use to pass clues and hints along to team members. Begin by wrapping a piece of white tubular climbing webbing around a PVC cylinder (2-4 inches in diameter). Next, write the message of your choice, one letter per segment.

When the webbing is removed from the cylinder, the message appears as a random collection of letters. Only by wrapping the webbing around the appropriate cylinder can the message be correctly read.

Present the team with the webbing coded message and several pieces of PVC tubing and let them discover which cylinder is the one required to decode the message or hint.

22. The Wild West Team members take turns to try to 'rope' various components of their rescue litter using a genuine lariat throwing rope, typical of the style used by rodeo riders and western cowboys. It can be helpful to partially assemble several of the PVC pieces together or even to create a rodeo 'animal' for this event. An excellent reference for this activity is: Ranch Roping with Buck Brannaman - A practical guide to traditional roping, 2000, A. J. Mangum, Western Horseman Inc., Colorado Springs, CO USA ISBN 0-911647-54-6.

23. Lillypads Team members attempt to cross a short distance of hypothetical water using small boards, carpet squares (outdoors), large index cards or sheets of paper (indoors). If at any point a board or ca rd is touching the floor or ground, but is not being touched by a team member, that board or card is swept away by the rapid current of the hypothetical river.

24. River Crossing Using a collection of lightweight wooden 4x4's, the entire team attempts to cross a collection of stone or block 'islands' using the 4x4's as portable bridges. Various components of the rescue litter can be placed on these islands or on the other side of the imaginary river.

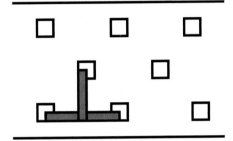

25. Blind Navigation Blindfolded team members work with sighted partners to traverse a playing field scattered with miscellaneous objects, including components of the rescue litter. They each attempt to locate and retrieve one of the components necessary to complete the litter without coming in contact with any other objects or fellow teammates. Sighted partners can offer only verbal commands to those blindfolded, to assist them in their search.

Section 3. Construction of the Rescue Litter

After obtaining all the components necessary, each team assembles their rescue litter. These components include the various PVC connectors and tubes, and an assembly instruction card with the following detailed instructions and illustrations:

Now that you have collected the necessary components for your rescue litter, you are ready to begin assembling this essential device.

Step 1 - Take an inventory of the parts you have obtained. You should have:
   A. Four 90 degree elbow connectors
   B. Four straight union connectors
   C. Eight tube segments with cord attachment locations
   D. Two segments of tubular climbing webbing
   E. One assembly instruction card

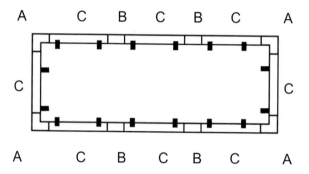

Step 2 - Begin by assembling the PVC frame as shown in the illustration. The completed frame will be three pipe segments long and one pipe segment wide. It is important for each PVC tube segment to be fully inserted into each of the connectors, and that the cord attachment locations on each tube segment are located towards the inside of the frame.

Step 3 - Attach the two tubular webbing segments to the PVC frame through each of the two cord attachment locations on each tube segment. The webbing pattern will resemble the pattern made by shoelaces. Secure each piece of webbing with secure knots at each end.

Step 4 - Inspection - When completed, each PVC tube segment should be fully inserted into each connector. Webbing segments must pass through each of the cord attachment locations and be securely knotted at each end.

Step 5 - Before placing a passenger into the rescue litter, instruct the team to lift the litter and verify that it has been correctly assembled. There should be at least 10 adult or 12 youth lifters, with at least four lifters on each of the long sides, and one or two lifters on each end.

> *Note: If for any reason one of the PVC tubes or connectors of the rescue litter becomes disconnected during this activity, simply lower the passenger to the ground and reconnect the tubes and connectors as required before continuing.*

Step 6 - You are now ready to enter the next phase of the Great Puzzle Quest. Ask for a volunteer member of your team to be transported. Lift this person using the now assembled rescue litter and transport them to the first puzzle location. The person being transported in the rescue litter can exhibit a variety of conditions requiring the attention of the group. Successfully solving challenges and puzzles will restore this person's capabilities. For example:

> Limited Vision (blindfolds, sunglasses, goggles or eyes closed)
> Limited Hearing (industrial hearing protection, ear muffs, headphones)
> Limited Speech (no verbal communication)
> Minimal Speech (speaking only YES or NO, speaking only NUMBERS)
> Lack of Tactile Response (heavy gloves or mittens)
> Limited Mobility (no arm, hand or facial gestures)
> Ability to Trade Places (passenger can trade places with ANY lifter)

You can also require EVERY member of the group to be transported at some time during the event.

Section 4. Puzzles and Challenges

At this point, your team is ready to begin finding and solving puzzles. You can utilize any of the puzzles presented in this book. We recommend a collection of puzzles that will require a variety of talents and skills to complete, as well as engaging every member of the team. You'll find an inventory of puzzles along with their teachable moments and associated team skills in the main activity section of this book. We recommend some of the following puzzles for the great puzzle quest:

2B or Knot 2B	Magic Carpet	Where Do You Stand?
Handcuffs and Shackles	The 15th Object	The PVC Network
Arrowheads	Golf Ball Pyramids	The Bridge
Tangrams	Shape Up	Line Up
Inside Out	Chasing Sheep	Finding Your People
Matchstick Puzzles	Count Six	I'm In Games
Modern Hieroglyphics	The Giant Jigsaw	A Circle of Connection

There are some additional challenges that can be fun to include in the Great Puzzle Quest. These challenges include: throwing and catching foam boomerangs, dance movements, singing together as a group, balancing on one foot, juggling, writing backwards, balancing rocks (or eggs) on their pointed end, or athletic challenges, such as sinking a long putt or throwing a ball through a distant hoop.

You can also provide additional challenges to a puzzle by requiring the group to retrieve the puzzle before attempting to solve it. The puzzle can be affixed to a climbing wall or other challenge course elements, scattered around a conference room or classroom or even fixed to the ceiling. It could also be set afloat in a boat or raft on a small lake, posted to a website or be presented in a foreign language.

As an example, here is a technique that requires a team to retrieve the puzzle before they can solve it.

Team members gather around a large rope circle and hold onto various strings that are attached to a small platform in the center of the circle on which a puzzle resides. By successfully transporting this puzzle from its original location to the 'solution zone' it is possible for the group to approach and solve it.

Section 5. Optional Final Debriefing Session

As an optional closing activity for the Great Puzzle Quest, invite team members to discuss what they have learned during their quest. Include opportunities to discuss teachable moments, valuable skills, new abilities and useful insights experienced during the quest, and where each person might use these skills in the future.

For more information about teachable moments and activities for debriefing and reviewing effectively with teams, we encourage you to read: A Teachable Moment - A Facilitator's Guide to Activities for Processing, Debriefing, Reviewing and Reflection, 2005, Jim Cain, Michelle Cummings and Jennifer Stanchfield, Kendall Hunt Publishing Company, Dubuque, IA USA

Additional Ideas:

"Focus 90% of your time on solutions and only 10% of your time on the problem."
Anthony J. D'Angelo
The College Blue Book

"It isn't that they can't see the solution. It is that they can't see the problem."
G. K. Chesterton
Scandal of Father Brown (1935)

The Back Nine
Enjoy a Round of Puzzle Golf

Here is an exciting way to enjoy solving puzzles as both a team activity and as a competitive event. This version of golf can be played indoors, outside, and even in moving vehicles.

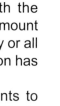

Foursomes are organized and set about to solve a series of nine different puzzles that have been placed around the room or open field. Golf pennants or flags can be used to identify puzzle location. Each puzzle includes an information sheet with the challenge clearly explained. The score for each hole is the amount of time necessary to successfully complete the puzzle by any or all members of the foursome. Timing begins once the information has been read aloud by a member of the team.

After completing each puzzle, return all components to their starting position so that the next foursome will be able to immediately begin working.

Supplies For this version of a team puzzle challenge, you will need nine different puzzles plus one additional puzzle as a tie breaker. Teams are organized in foursomes (four players per team). It is best to allow some space between puzzles so that foursomes do not interfere or reveal answers to the members of other teams. Scoresheets are required for each team. Stopwatches or some form of timer at each puzzle location, or for each team, are also required. You can place each puzzle in a box or envelope, with directions, to further conceal it from other teams.

Variations Many ideas for games of puzzle golf can be taken from golf course and tournament variations including: scramble start, best ball, speed golf, the driving range, and concepts such as a hole in one, double bogie, sand traps, and others. Foursomes do not need to solve the puzzles in order and may pass by a group that is struggling with a particular puzzle.

There are several puzzles in this book that use golf balls and other sport props. If you would like to continue the golfing theme, we recommend these puzzles for various holes on your puzzle golf course: 3 Cubed, The Great Golf Ball Pyramids, Making Contact, and People Movers (with blocks of wood and golf tees instead of people). Other great choices for Puzzle Golf puzzles include: Arrowheads, Plenty of Room at the Top, Matchstick Puzzles, Modern Hieroglyphics, Human Knot, Matchmaking and Just One Word.

**Teambuilding
Puzzles**

Hints and Clues For more ideas about golfing, read:

Golf for Dummies, 1999, Gary McCord, For Dummies Publishers, ISBN 0-7645-5146-9.

The Complete Idiot's Guide to Golf, 2002, Michelle McGann and Mike Purkey, Alpha Publishers. Available in digital book form from www.amazon.com.

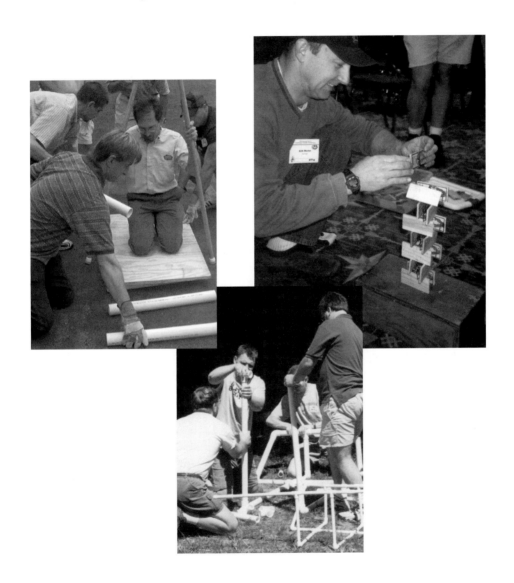

The Puzzle Party
Social Recreation

I attended a conference a few years ago where one room contained dozens of toys, games and other social recreation props, including a table filled with a wide variety of puzzles and challenging objects. During the conference, participants would attend regular workshops in various locations, but always found themselves drawn back to this particular room (of course it helped that the coffee pot and snacks were also in this room). By the end of the week, many folks had experienced nearly every puzzle and had begun working together to solve the more difficult ones. Some spectators would offer suggestions and hints, while others just watched on in amazement. The puzzle table became one of the favorite destinations of the conference.

To create your own puzzle table, you'll need plenty of visually interesting and challenging puzzles and games. Large tavern puzzles, colorful cubes, and many of the object puzzles in this book are good candidates for the table. You may want to include pictures of each puzzle along with instructions. You can also provide a 'solution manual' if you choose, or simply let those that solve each puzzle become a useful resource to other puzzlers.

Some of our favorite puzzle table puzzles include: Handcuffs and Shackles, Arrowheads, People Movers with wood blocks and golf tees, Plenty of Room at the Top, Matchstick Puzzles using new pencils instead of matches, Coin Puzzles, Modern Hieroglyphics, The Great Golf Ball Pyramids, Shaping the Future, Line Up the Glasses, Ciphers and Codes, and Parking Cars.

Make It - Take It - Solve It - Keep It

A variation of the puzzle table is to provide equipment for making your own puzzles. In a well defined space, place a finished model of each puzzle. In another nearby location provide paper, scissors, cardboard, wood blocks, balls, nails and other simple props so that puzzlers can create their own puzzles based on the models provided.

Some of our favorite puzzles are also easy to build. These include Handcuffs and Shackles, Arrowheads, Tangrams, Switching Corks, Plenty of Room at the Top, T.H.E. Puzzle, Matchstick Puzzles using toothpicks instead of matches, Coin Puzzles, Modern Hieroglyphics, The 15th Object, Tower of Hanoi, The Great Golf Ball Pyramids, Pentominoes, Shaping the Future, Classic Knot Theory, 63 / 64 / 65, Just One Word, Pipe Chimes and the Placemat Puzzle.

You can even provide sufficient puzzle equipment to create an entire puzzle kit. We call this our 'make it and take it' workshop. Enjoy!

You may occasionally want to group puzzle challenges by specific categories, thereby creating your own list of favorites. Here is a brief listing of powerful activities that explore the following themes and create teachable moments.

Visual, Auditory & Kinesthetic Techniques

Visual	Three Kinds of Memory, 2B or Knot 2B
Auditory	Tongue Twisters, The Whole Story, Just One Word
Kinesthetic	Switching Corks, People Movers, Inside/Out, Count Six

Small Groups, Triads, Dyads	Handcuffs & Shackles, Rock Around the Clock
Large Groups	Finding Your People, I'm In Games, Word Puzzles
Warm-Up Activities	Handcuffs & Shackles, Modern Hieroglyphics
Diversity / Inclusion	Finding Your People, Diversity Tangram Quilt
Adapting to Change	Adaptation or Extinction, Shaping the Future, Changing Directions, Pyramid Power
Creative and Artistic Techniques	Just Passing Through, Land of Lakes
Athletics	Pencil Pushers, Bite the Bag, The Great Puzzle Quest, The Puzzle Cube, Inuksuit (balance), Jumping George
Personal Contact	Human Knot, Magic Carpet, Handcuffs & Shackle
Goal Setting	Magic Carpet, Drops of Water
Humorous and Fun	Modern Hieroglyphics, Tongue Twisters
Thought Provoking	Finding Your People, I'm In Games, A Strange Day
Rope Tricks	2B or Knot 2B, Not Knots, Classic Knot Theory, The Missing Link, The Coiled Rope, Blind Square
Hardware and More	Plenty of Room at the Top, PVC Network, 7 Bags of Bolts Plumber's Delight, Houses & Utilities, Pipe Chimes
Common Dollars and Common Sense	Heads or Tails, Jumping George, Extreme Origami
Farmers and Animals	Chasing Sheep, Pigs & Pens, Sheep & Pens, The Fence

Fun and Games	Modern Hieroglyphics, Handcuffs & Shackles, Bite the Bag
Geometry, Shapes and Patterns	Shape Up, Golf Ball Pyramids,
Simple Equipment	Matchstick Puzzles, Heads or Tails, The 15th Object
Creativity	Just Passing Through, Matchstick Puzzles
Construction Activities	PVC Network, The Bridge, T.H.E. Puzzle, The Giant Jigsaw
Corporate Philosophy	Electric Box, Building Connection, Corporate Maze
Non-Visual (Blindfolded)	Blind Square, Finding Your People, The Giant Jigsaw
Alphabets and Number Systems	A Quick Study, Nothing Can Divide Us, Pangrams
Talking, Listening and Communicating	Tongue Twisters, The Whole Story
Cultural Awareness	Diversity Tangram, I'm In Games
Unusual Questions	A Strange Day, Word Puzzles
Unity, Community and Connection	A Circle of Connection, Sharing Connection
Communication	Talking Tangrams, How Deep is the Well?
Resource Management	Tangrams, PVC Network, The Fence
Make It and Take It	Handcuffs, Pyramids, Modern Hieroglyphics
Teachers	Just One Word, Switching Corks, Palindromes
Engineers	PVC Network, The Square, Plenty of Room at the Top
Athletes	Pencil Pushers, Bite the Bag, Count Six
Mike's Favorites	The Bridge, Three Cubed, Modern Hieroglyphics, Tangrams, The Tower, White Board Puzzle, Making Contact, Line Ups, People Movers, Just One Word

Jim's Favorites	2B or Knot 2B, Not Knots, Arrowheads, PVC Network, Slow Burn, Modern Hieroglyphics, The 15th Object, Closing All the Doors, Inuksuit, The Puzzle Cube, SNAP!
Chris' Favorites	Word (lateral) Puzzles, Matchstick Puzzles, SNAP, Count 6, Human Knot, Coiled Rope, Blind Square, Giant Jigsaw Puzzle, Corporate Maze
Tom's Favorites	2B or Knot 2 B, Corporate Maze, Drop of Water, Labyrinth, PVC Network, Tangrams

"Never let a problem to be solved become more important than a person to be loved."
Barbara Johnson,
The Joy Journal

Changing the Rules of the Game
Ideas for Adapting Puzzles for your Team

Here are a few dozen techniques for adapting your favorite puzzles and turning them into teambuilding puzzles. We begin by developing a brief list of criteria for a suitable teambuilding puzzle. First, it should be the kind of puzzle or challenge which requires more than a single person to accomplish. You may need to modify or adapt the original puzzle to meet this criteria. Secondly, it should create a teachable moment for the group. Thirdly, it should require the kind of team skills needed by the team in their home environment. Next, it should create solutions which require a variety of learning styles, techniques and creative problem solving methods - so as to encourage learning and growth. Finally, it should be engaging, active, portable, valuable and fun.

To transform your favorite puzzle into a tool that creates teachable moments for your team, here are a few suggestions:

Ask your students to modify the puzzle they just experienced for a new outcome. Try using a different set of equipment for the same puzzle. If the puzzle is initially small, consider making it very large (if matchsticks are involved, switch to PVC tubes, yardsticks, dowel rods or pencils - if coins are involved, switch to dinner plates, hula hoops, flying disks or very large coins). For any puzzle that takes place in a straight line, consider switching to a circle, and vice versa. Replace paper and pencil puzzles with wood and markers, replace rope with string, dowel rods or 2x4's. Modify the objects used in the puzzle, especially if you can incorporate objects familiar to your audience. If words show up on various pieces of puzzle equipment, change them to reinforce the concepts you wish to introduce to the participants. Employ a time limit. Reduce the equipment to microscopic size, and yes, bring a microscope. Use every style of learning possible, including multiple intelligences and emotional intelligence. Whenever possible, incorporate movement and activity. Use stories to introduce each puzzle. Simplify the instructions. Try out each puzzle on a pilot audience, before the real thing. Don't be afraid to modify what is not working. Always keep an element of surprise or fun as part of each puzzle.

In order to adapt the puzzles found in this book, we considered some of the following possibilities:

How could this puzzle be used with teams larger than 50 members?
How could this puzzle be used in the dark?
How could this puzzle be used underwater?
How could this puzzle be used in zero gravity?
How could this puzzle be used during an interview?

How could this puzzle be used without speaking?
How could this puzzle be used without breathing?
How could this puzzle be used over the telephone?
How could this puzzle be used over the Internet?
How could this puzzle be used with culturally diverse audiences?
How could this puzzle be used with audiences with special needs?
How could this puzzle be used in a canoe or inflatable raft?
How could this puzzle be used in an elevator?
How could this puzzle be performed in less than 5 minutes?
How could this puzzle be used with limited resources?
How could this puzzle be used without using your hands?
How could this puzzle be used without using your thumbs?
How could this puzzle be used with family groups?
How could this puzzle be used with sport teams?
How could this puzzle be used during a staff meeting?
How could this puzzle be used by pre-school children?
How could this puzzle be used in a foreign country?
How could this puzzle be taken on an airplane?
How could this puzzle be made smaller?
How could this puzzle be made very, very, large?
How could this puzzle involve more people in the solution?
How could this puzzle be used for a different teachable moment?
How could this puzzle be used outdoors?
How could this puzzle be used on the wall or ceiling?
How could this puzzle be used in the rain? Snow? Winter?
How could this puzzle be used to introduce the next one?
How could this puzzle be used during a keynote presentation?
How could this puzzle be introduced by a member of the team?
How could this puzzle be taken a step farther?
How could this puzzle be solved as a homework problem?
How could this puzzle be solved in a more active manner?
How could this puzzle be modified for small teams?
How could this puzzle be constructed for free?
How could this puzzle be used with no equipment at all?
How could this puzzle be performed with simple props we already have?
How could this puzzle be performed with different equipment?
How could this puzzle be performed with equipment familiar to the team?
How could this puzzle be introduced without language?

Adapted from a story shared by
Denny Elliott at 4-H Camp Ohio

One Sunday afternoon, Mom decided to run few errands, leaving her husband and their seven year old son together at home. Dad had a few projects to do that day including finishing up some paperwork. As he sat working at the dining room table, his son played noisily nearby and managed to interrupt his poor Dad at least once every five minutes. After thirty minutes of accomplishing almost nothing, Dad was ready to pull his hair out. "I've got to find something for Junior to do so that I can get some work done!"

As he gazed over at the Sunday newspaper, a plan formed in his head. He quickly glanced through the paper until he found a large picture on one of the pages. In this case, a full color illustration of the earth. He removed this page from the paper and began tearing it into smaller pieces. After finishing this task, he presented his son with the puzzle and invited him to put the world back together. "That should keep him busy for a while," he said, and went off to finish his paperwork.

But within five minutes, his son was back. "I'm done Papa," said the boy. Now this father always thought that he had a pretty smart son, but was skeptical that he could have finished the puzzle in such a short time.

When he stepped into the living room however, he found that the puzzle was indeed completed, and in the correct order. "How did you finish this puzzle so quickly?" he asked his son. As the boy spoke, he began turning over each piece of the puzzle. On the reverse, there was a full page photograph of his favorite professional sports team. "You see Dad, if you can get your team to come together, then the rest of the world comes together too!"

A slightly annotated bibliography of references,
resources and interesting reading.

Creative Puzzle Solving and Problem Solving References

Brain Fitness @ Work - Unlock Your Mind's Potential and Achieve Peak Performance, 2003, Judith Jewell, Hamlyn, London UK ISBN 0-600-60721-6. A personal workout plan for your brain that is sure to help you solve the puzzles in this book.

Creative Growth Games - 75 Fascinating Games to Expand Your Imagination and Unleash Your Originality, 1977, Eugene Raudsepp and George P. Hough, Jr., Perigee Books, New York, NY USA ISBN 0-399-50415-X.

Four Colors Suffice - How the Map Problem Was Solved, 2002, Robin Wilson, Princeton University Press, Princeton, NJ USA ISBN 0-691-11533-8.

How Would You Move Mount Fuji? - How the World's Smartest Companies Select the Most Creative Thinkers, 2003, William Poundstone, Little, Brown and Company, Boston, MA USA ISBN 0-316-91916-0. Some of the most creative thinking puzzles, and solutions, ever.

Kepler's Conjecture - How some of the greatest minds in history helped solve one of the oldest math problems in the world, 2003, George G. Szpiro, John Wiley & Sons, Hoboken, NJ USA ISBN 0-471-08601-0.

Pumping Ions - Games and Exercises to Flex Your Mind, 1988, Tom Wujec, Doubleday, Toronto, Canada ISBN 0-385-25113-0.

Test Your Creative Thinking, 2004, Lloyd King, Kogan Page, London, UK ISBN 0-74944-004-X.

The Mind Workout Book - Over One Hundred Exercises to Train Your Brain to the Peak of Perfection, 2003, Robert Allen, Collins & Brown, London, UK ISBN 1-84340-101-0. An interesting theory - using games, puzzles and exercises to improve your memory, creativity, communication, mind development and problem-solving skills.

Why Not? How to Use Everyday Ingenuity to Solve Problems Big and Small, 2003, Barry Nalebuff & Ian Ayres, Harvard Business School Press, Boston, MA USA ISBN 1-59139-153-9.

Visual Puzzle References

Errata: A book of Historical errors, 1992, A.J.Wood and Hemesh Alles, Green Tiger Press, New York, NY USA ISBN 0-671-77569-3. A great way to discuss chronological history.

Picture Puzzle Mysteries - Whodunits You Can See, 2003, Rolf Heimann, Sterling Publishing, New York, NY USA ISBN 1-4027-0262-0. Stories and pictures combined for the perfect searching puzzles.

Re- Zoom, 1995, Istvan Banyai, Puffin Books, New York, NY USA ISBN 0-14-055694-X.

Something's Not Quite Right, 2002, Guy Billout, David R. Godine Publisher, Jaffrey, NH USA ISBN 1-56792-230-9. A beautifully illustrated collection of images with something unusual in each and every one.

The Mysteries of Harris Burdick, 1984, Chris Van Allsburg, Houghton Mifflin, Boston, MA USA ISBN 0-395-35393-9 Have your students write a story to accompany this interesting collection of images.

Zoom, 1995, Istvan Banyai, Puffin Books, New York, NY USA ISBN 0-14-055774-1
If you remove the binding from this book, or the book Re-Zoom, you'll have a story-telling sequence with pictures that makes for an interesting 'put-the-puzzle-back-in-order' activity.

Puzzle Collections

There are a literally thousands of interesting puzzle books today. Just visit your local library or bookstore and you are sure to find a shelf full of books on puzzles and games. While there are far too many to list here, a few stand out from the rest, and we recommend these to the avid puzzle enthusiast. These books have dozens of photographs of some historically significant puzzles, as well as more modern creations from around the world.

New Book of Puzzles - 101 Classic and Modern Puzzles to Make and Solve, 1992, Jerry Slocum and Jack Botermans, W.H.Freeman and Company, New York, NY USA ISBN 0-7167-2356-5.

The Book of Ingenious & Diabolical Puzzles, 1994, Jerry Slocum and Jack Botermans, Times Books, New York, NY USA ISBN 0-8129-2153-4.

Creative Puzzles of the World, 1995, Pieter Van Delft and Jack Botermans, Key Curriculum Press, Berkeley, CA USA ISBN 1-55953-116-9.

Sliding Piece Puzzles, 1986, Edward Hordern, Oxford University Press, Oxford, UK ISBN 0-19-853204-0. A thorough investigation of puzzles with sliding pieces.

Tangram - The Ancient Chinese Shapes Game, 1976, Joost Elffers, Penguin Books, New York, NY USA ISBN 0-1400-4181-8.

The Greatest Puzzles of All Time, 1988, Matthew J. Costello, Dover Publications, Mineola, NY USA ISBN 0-486-29225-8.

The Jigsaw Puzzle - Piecing Together a History, 2004, Anne D. Williams, Berkley Books, New York, NY USA ISBN 0-425-19820-0.

Miscellaneous Puzzles and Interesting Reading

Bet You Can't Do This! - Impossible Tricks to Astound Your Friends, 2002, Sandy Ransford, Macmillan Children's Books, London, UK ISBN 0-330-39772-9.

Careers for Puzzle Solvers & Other Methodical Thinkers, 2002, Jan Goldberg, VGM Career Books, New York, NY USA ISBN 0-658-00181-7.

Games With Codes and Ciphers, 1994, Norvin Pallas, Dover, NY ISBN 0-486-28209-0.

The American Sign Language Puzzle Book - The Fun Way to Learn to Sign, 2003, Justin Segal, Contemporary Books, New York, NY USA ISBN 0-07-141354-5.

The Art of the Maze, 2000, Adrian Fisher and George Gerster, Seven Dials, London, UK ISBN 1-84188-025-6.

The Colossal Book of Mathematics - Classic Puzzles, Paradoxes and Problems, 2001, Martin Gardner, W. W. Norton, New York, NY USA ISBN 0-393-02023-1.

The Puzzle Instinct - The Meaning of Puzzles in the Human Life, 2002, Marcel Danesi, Indiana Unversity Press, ISBN 0-253-34094-2

Never Odd or Even and Other Tricks Words Can Do, 2005, O. V. Michaelson, Sterling Publishing, NY, USA ISBN 1-4027-2896-4

The Compleat Cruciverbalist - Or How to Solve and Compose Crossword Puzzles for Fun and Profit, 1981, Stan Kurzban and Mel Rosen, Van Nostrand Reinhold, New York, NY USA ISBN 0-442-25738-4. A very complete collection of ideas and suggestions for composing crossword puzzles.

The Knot Book: An Elementary Introduction to the Mathematical Theory of Knots, 1994, Colin Adams, W. H. Freeman, New York, NY USA ISBN 0-7167-2393-X. A simple introduction to some rather complicated theory.

The Wooden Puzzle Book - 40 Wooden Puzzles and Their Solutions, 2002, Rea Gibson, Forest Hill Studio, Mount Forest, Ontario, Canada ISBN 0-9689539-1-3. A great book for the woodworker.

Wonder of Numbers - Adventures in Mathematics, Mind and Meaning, 2001, Clifford A. Pickover, Oxford University Press, New York, NY USA ISBN 0-19-515799-0.

Additional References of Merit

Another Fine Math You've Got Me Into. . ., 1992, Ian Stewart, W. H. Freeman, New York, NY USA ISBN 0-7167-2341-7.

Games 101, Eva Curlee Doyle, *Training and Development*, Volume 55, Number 2, February 2001, page 16+.

Games, Set & Math - Enigmas and Conundrums, 1989, Ian Stewart, Basil Blackwell, Cambridge, MA, USA ISBN 0-631-17114-2.

Why People Play, 1973, Michael J. Ellis, Prentice Hall, Englewood Cliffs, New Jersey, USA ISBN 0-13-958991-0. Read this and understand how to make learning and education fun again.

Multiple Intelligences in the Classroom, 2000, Thomas Armstrong, ASCD, Alexandria, VA USA ISBN 0-87120-376-6. Read this book to explore other training, teaching and learning styles appropriate for your audiences.

The Complete Idiot's Guide to Geocaching, Jack Peters and Staff of Geocaching.com, 2004, Alpha Books, New York, NY USA ISBN 1-59257-235-9. You can use information from this book to assist you in planning your own GPS version of The Great Puzzle Quest.

Teambuilding Books of Merit

Affordable Portables, 1998, Chris Cavert, FUNdoing Publications, Flagstaff, AZ USA www.fundoign.com   Teambuilding activities and building plans.

Affordable Portables 2, 2010, Chris Cavert, Wood N Barnes Publishing, Oklahoma City, OK USA www.wnbpub.com

A Teachable Moment, 2005, Jim Cain, Michelle Cummings and Jennifer Stanchfield, Kendall Hunt Publishers, Dubuque, IA USA Activities and techniques for processing, debriefing, reviewing and reflection. Interesting activities for bringing out the best moments from any activity, including teambuilding, puzzles, and other moments in life.

Feeding the Zircon Gorilla, 1995, Sam Sikes, Learning Unlimited Publishers, Tulsa, OK USA ISBN 0-9646541-0-5. Teambuilding ideas and more.

Games for Teachers, 1999, Chris Cavert, Laurie Frank & Friends, Wood 'n Barnes Publishers, Oklahoma City, OK USA ISBN 1-885473-22-2. Learn how to bring teambuilding into the classroom.

Journey Toward the Caring Classroom - Using Adventure to Create Community in the Classroom and Beyond, 2004, Laurie Frank, Wood 'n Barnes Publishers, Oklahoma City, OK USA ISBN 1-885473-60-5. If you have always wanted to know how to create unity in your classroom, here is the book on the subject.

Raptor, 2003, Sam Sikes, Learning Unlimited Publishers, Tulsa, OK USA   ISBN 0-9646541-7-2. Teambuilding ideas and a few puzzles, too.

Teamwork & Teamplay, 1998, Jim Cain and Barry Jolliff, Kendall Hunt Publishers, Dubuque, IA USA ISBN 0-7872-4532-1. One of the most extensive collections of teambuilding activities, and teambuilding references ever assembled, including building plans, sequencing information and much, much more.

The Revised and Expanded Book of Raccoon Circles, 2007, Jim Cain and Tom Smith, Kendall Hunt Publishers, Dubuque, IA USA www.kendallhunt.com (1-800-228-0810) ISBN 0-7575-3265-9. Hundreds of activities (including puzzles) using only a single, simple prop.

Teambuilding Puzzles

The Empty Bag, 2004, Chris Cavert and Dick Hammond, FUNdoing Publications, Arizona USA ISBN 0-9746442-1-8. Community and teambuilding activities with no props at all!

Essential Staff Training Activities, 2009, Jim Cain, Clare-Marie Hannon and Dave Knobbe. Kendall/Hunt Publishers, Dubuque, IA USA www.kendallhunt.com (1-800-228-0810)

"Idealism increases in direct proportion to one's distance from the problem."
John Galsworthy

Resources and Vendors of Puzzle and Teambuilding Equipment

MindWare 2100 Country Road C West Roseville, MN 55113 www.mindwareonline.com 1-800-999-0398 Hundreds of puzzles, puzzle books, games and interesting, tactile stuff.

Training Wheels, Inc., Colorado USA www.trainings-wheels.com 1-888-553-0147. Tools and equipment for adventure-based learning and processing.

Teambuilding Puzzles

Websites and Internet Resources
A slightly annotated bibliography of internet resources.

Try using the following words when using an internet search engine: puzzles, games, challenges, teambuilding, teamwork, groupwork, mathematical recreations and creative problem solving.

www.puzzles.com	Excellent Internet resource for teachers/trainers, includes
www.education.puzzles.com	lesson plans, dozens of PDF downloadable files, and links
www.puzzleplayground.com	sites with teaching standards and other valuable information
www.mathpuzzles.com	Bringing the best math puzzle resources on the web
www.thinks.com/puzzles	An interactive site with word problems, logic puzzles and brain teasers
www.puzzlepalace.com	An Internet store for very creative hand-crafted puzzles that will challenge even the most advanced puzzlers
www.mazemaker.com	Internet website of labyrinth and maze designer Adrian Fischer
www.fundoing.com	Chris Cavert's website, filled with activities
www.teamworkandteamplay.com	Jim Cain's website, activites, articles and pictures
www.IATFconnect.com	Tom Heck's website and internet newsletter site
www.lwtd.com	Mike Anderson's website
www.learningunlimited.com	Sam Sike's website, with creative activities and ideas
www.sportime.com	Sportime's website, with hundreds of teaching ideas
www.challengeworks.com	Modern Hieroglyphics cards and teambuilding gear
www.justropes.com	A resource for ropes, string and cordage for teambuilding activities
www.alljigsawpuzzles.co.uk	One of the larges Internet jigsaw puzzles stores ever

www.puzzlers.org	If you are really (and we mean really) into puzzles, join the National Puzzlers' League
www.scientificpsychic.com	An Internet collection of optical illusions and logic problems
www.puzzlemaker.com	A Discovery School site - Make your own word search puzzles here
www.tangrams.ca	A comprehensive resource for tangram enthusiasts. Features downloadable documents, references & a 'make your own' guide.
www.johnrausch.com	An amazing Internet site. See the IPP puzzle design competition link. The handmade puzzles are extraordinary.
www.lateralpuzzles.com	Loads of puzzles, book sources, and links to other great puzzle sites.
www.opticalillusions.com	
www.vision3d.com	
http://dspace.dail.pipex.com/Sloane/	Paul Sloane's Internet website. Lateral thinking puzzles galore.
www.reachoutmichigan.org/ funexperiements/quick/thaum.html	Learn how to build a thaumatrope.

*"Computers can figure out all kinds of problems,
except the things in the world that just don't add up."*
James Magary

*"Every generation thinks it has the answers,
and every generation is humbled by nature."*
Phillip Lubin

**Teambuilding
Puzzles**

Additional Quotations
of Problem Solving

"I believe that a scientist looking at nonscientific problems is just as dumb as the next guy." Richard Feynman

"The direct use of force is such a poor solution to any problem, it is generally employed only by small children and large nations." David Friedman

"To solve the problems of today, we must focus on tomorrow." Erik Nupponen

"I can teach anybody how to get what they want out of life. The problem is that I can't find anybody who can tell me what they want." Mark Twain

"When solving problems, dig at the roots instead of just hacking at the leaves." Anthony J. D'Angelo, The College Blue Book

"The problem is not that there are problems. The problem is expecting otherwise and thinking that having problems is a problem." Theodore Rubin

"It would be naive to think that the problems plaguing mankind today can be solved with means and methods which were applied or seemed to work in the past." Mikhail Gorbachev

"Science is the search for truth - it is not a game in which one tries to beat his opponent, to do harm to others. We need to have the spirit of science in international affairs, to make the conduct of international affairs the effort to find the right solution, the just solution of international problems, not the effort by each nation to get the better of other nations, to do harm to them when it is possible." Linus Pauling, No More War!

"Solutions- The first step toward a cure is to know what the disease is." Latin

"Solutions are not the answer." Richard Nixon

"Scientists are the easiest to fool. They think in straight, predictable, directable, and therefore misdirectable, lines. The only world they know is the one where everything has a logical explanation and things are what they appear to be. Children and conjurers—they terrify me. Scientists are no problem; against them I feel quite confident." Zambendorf, Code of the Lifemaker, by James P. Hogan

"I was always puzzled by the fact that people have a great deal of trouble and pain when and if they are forced or feel forced to change a belief or circumstance which they hold dear. I found what I believe is the answer when I read that a Canadian neurosurgeon discovered some truths about the human mind which revealed the intensity of this problem. He conducted some experiments which proved that when a person is forced to change a basic belief or viewpoint, the brain undergoes a series of nervous sensations equivalent to the most agonizing torture."   Sidney Madwed

"Man is not a machine... Although man most certainly processes information, he does not necessarily process it in the way computers do. Computers and men are not species of the same genus... However much intelligence computers may attain, now or in the future, theirs must always be an intelligence alien to genuine human problems and concerns."   Joseph Weizenbaum

"The problem with the cutting edge is that someone has to bleed."   Zalman Stern

"The greatest and most important problems of life are all fundamentally insoluble. They can never be solved but only outgrown."   Carl Jung

"The wise man doesn't give the right answers, he poses the right questions."   Claude Levi-Strauss

"The only interesting answers are those which destroy the questions."   Susan Sontag

"Computers are useless. They can only give you answers."   Pablo Picasso

"Life is made up of constant calls to action, and we seldom have time for more than hastily contrived answers."   Learned Hand

"The purpose of art is to lay bare the questions which have been hidden by the answers."   James Baldwin

"To endure oneself may be the hardest task in the universe. You cannot hire a wise man or any other intellect to solve it for you. There's no writ of inquest or calling of witness to provide answers. No servant or disciple can dress the wound. You dress it yourself or continue bleeding for all to see."   Frank Herbert

A Note of Thanks

During the preparation and printing of this book, several friends, colleagues and fellow facilitators provided assistance, activities, ideas, editing, suggestions and encouragement, and for this we are extremely grateful. To our first-line reviewing team, Allison Phaneuf, John Berkeley, Monique Klein Swormink, Greg Huber and Kirk Weisler, we owe a debt of gratitude and a free copy of this book. To the many contributors that have so willingly shared their best ideas, puzzles and activities, thank you for allowing us to again share these with the rest of the world.

We would like to thank Kenya Masala and Sam Sikes for all their pre-press help and all those adventurous players who came out for picture parties - especially the Pinerock Camp staffers. And, thanks to Susana and John, for the valuable picture contributions.

We have done our best to acknowledge and credit the sources of unique puzzles and teachable moments presented in this publication. If you are aware of any reference or acknowledgment that we have failed to adequately provide the proper credit for, please let us know so that we can include this information in a future edition.

The Teambuilding Puzzle Team

Now that you have one of the most innovative puzzle and teambuilding books ever written, you might be interested to know that for each of the authors, this is only a small portion of the skills, talents and knowledge they possess and share. And the word share is important here. In the past decade, Mike, Jim, Chris and Tom have presented hundreds of workshops, conference sessions, train-the-trainer programs and staff development events throughout North American and around the world.

If you would like to create some enthusiasm with your team, host a workshop on the activities in this book, have your summer camp staff trained in The Great Puzzle Quest, include these activities as part of a corporate training program, include multiple intelligence activities in your classroom, lead a make-it and take-it workshop or take your next conference social hour to a higher level, we would like to help.

You can find out more about our work by visiting our websites. Please contact any of us for more information about Teambuilding Puzzles, teambuilding programs and active learning. You'll find contact information on the following pages.

About the Authors

Mike Anderson

Mike Anderson is a tattoo collecting father of three. As a California native who now lives in the beautiful Green Mountain State it is safe to say that Mike has lived all over (CA, MT, SC, IN, NJ and VT). Anyway, Mike first walked on the adventure play scene as a complete novice over 15 years ago; his first ropes course experience was on Adrian Kissler's Grass Valley course in 1991. Since then Mike has been lucky enough to associate with and be mentored by some of the industry's biggest and most respected leaders. Beginning in college Mike made it a priority to work exclusively in all areas related to adventure play, community building and team development. After all, you have to have felt the power of adventure play to be passionate about it.

Mike holds a Bachelors degree in Recreation Administration from CSU Sacramento and a Masters degree in Education from Monmouth University. Mike is author of the Interact Curriculum, co-author to Teambuilding Puzzles and Setting the Conflict Compass (available spring 2009) as well as a contributor to numerous other texts on adventure play including the Book on Raccoon Circles, A Teachable Moment, The More the Merrier, Affordable Portables 2 as well as two science based texts.

Mike focuses much of his time on the advancement of adult teams and adult learners. Mike has presented workshops on associated topics and many others all across the USA and internationally and has delivered pre-conference and general session workshops at many of the adventure and challenge industry's largest conferences including the Association for Challenge Course Technology, the American Camp Association, Teachers of Experiential and Adventure Methodologies, the International Alliance for Learning and the Association of Experiential Education. Mike has presented workshops in 31 states, in 5 countries on 3 continents.

Mike is the creator of many classic teambuilding exercises including the Table Web, Adventure Puzzle, Image Chips, the raccoon activity Believe it or Knot, Decomposition Line, as well as Phobia and the Web We Weave. Mike is also responsible for the adaptation of Cup Stacking to a teambuilding activity.

Mike Anderson, M. Ed
Owner, Campbell Anderson Holdings, LLC
The Petra Cliffs Group
Mike Anderson & Associates
Petra Cliffs Climbing Center
SumMAT Camp
Mountaineering School
Petra Cliffs Adventure Travel
Bolton Adventure Center

**Teambuilding
Puzzles**

Jim Cain

Dr. Jim Cain is the author of five adventure-based teambuilding texts: Teamwork & Teamplay, which received the Karl Rohnke Creativity Award presented by the Association for Experiential Education (AEE); The Book on Raccoon Circles; A Teachable Moment; Essential Staff Training Activities; and this book, Teambuilding Puzzles. He is the owner and creative force behind Teamwork & Teamplay - The Adventure-Based Training Company, a Senior Consultant for the Cornell University Corporate Teambuilding Program, and a former Executive Director for the Association for Challenge Course Technology (ACCT). Jim makes his home in Brockport, NY. He holds four engineering degrees including a Ph.D. in Mechanical Engineering from the University of Rochester. Dr. Cain frequently serves as a visiting professor and staff development specialist on subjects ranging from experiential education using adventure-based and active learning activities to corporate leadership, recreational dancing and games leadership, and from structural engineering and chaos theory to his Ph.D. research topic, powder mechanics. In the past 5 years, he has presented programs and workshops in 46 states and 17 countries and generally has more teambuilding toys and a library of adventure-based and active learning books larger than that of many developing nations. He also is an avid collector of puzzles, games and other props for social recreation and active learning.

Jim Cain, Ph.D.
Teamwork & Teamplay
468 Salmon Creek Road
Brockport, NY 14420 USA
Phone (585) 637-0328
Email: jimcain@teamworkandteamplay.com
Website: www.teamworkandteamplay.com

Chris Cavert

Chris has been active with groups of all ages for over 30 years. He is an award winning author and an international trainer and speaker in the area of Experiential Adventure-Based programming and focuses on how activities within this field help to develop and enhance pro-social behaviors, especially with youth populations.

Chris holds a Physical Education Teaching Degree from the University of Wisconsin-LaCrosse and a Masters Degree in Experiential Education from Minnesota State University at Mankato specializing in curriculum development. He is the author of six books and the co-author of five more, including: the E.A.G.E.R. Curriculum; Games (& other stuff) for Group, books 1 & 2; Affordable Portables: A Workbook of Activities and Problem Solving Elements; What Would It Be Like?: 1001 Anytime Questions for Anysize Answers; Ricochet - and Other Fun Games with an Odd Ball; Games (& other stuff) for Teachers (with Laurie Frank); 50 Ways to Use Your Noodle: Loads of Land Games with Foam Noodle Toys and 50 More Ways to Use You Noodle: Loads of Land and Water Games with Foam Noodle Toys (with Sam Sikes); Are You More Like: 1001 Colorful Quandaries for Quality Conversations (with Susana Acosta); and The EMPTY Bag: Non-Stop, No-Prop Adventure-Based Activities for Community Building (with Dick Hammond).

Chris' books focus on sharing activities that help educators in many different fields, utilize experiential/adventure-based education to encourage pro-social behaviors in the groups that they work with. Some of Chris' first writings were published in the best selling *Chicken Soup for the Soul* series books by Jack Canfield and Mark Victor Hansen and some of his activities have been published in books by Karl Rohnke, Laurie Frank, Jim Cain & Barry Jolliff, and Simon Priest, Sam Sikes & Faith Evans.

Chris Cavert, Ed.D.
FUNdoing
Email chris@fundoing.com
Website www.fundoing.com
Check the FUNdoing website
for additional contact information.

Tom Heck

Tom Heck is president and founder of the International Association of Teamwork Facilitators (IATF) which trains and supports the work of teamwork facilitators, coaches, trainers, supervisors, managers and team leaders on five continents. Through the IATF Tom develops and leads professional development programs, which promote a "coach appraoch" to working with and leading teams.

In addition to offering virtual (distance learning) training through the IATF, Tom has developed a series of multi-media training CDs, audio programs, books and teambuilding games that support the work of teamwork facilitators worldwide.

Tom has interviewed more than 60 of the top leaders in the teambuilding industry including Stephen M.R. Covey, Dr. Ken Blanchard, and Jack Canfield with these audio interviews appearing at www.IATFconnect.com.

The most powerful (and effective) teachers Tom has ever had are his two children who are hleping him get a PhD in life. Tom loves his family and friends and enjoys playing banjo, building catapults, and riding bikes.

Tom Heck
President and Founder
International Association of
Teamwork Facilitators
Phone (828) 348-4677
Email: tom@IATFconnect.com
Website: www.IATFconnect.com

Teambuilding Puzzles

Index

Information in this book is indexed alphabetically below,
Followed by the page number on which this information appears.

Teambuilding Puzzles

One for the Road

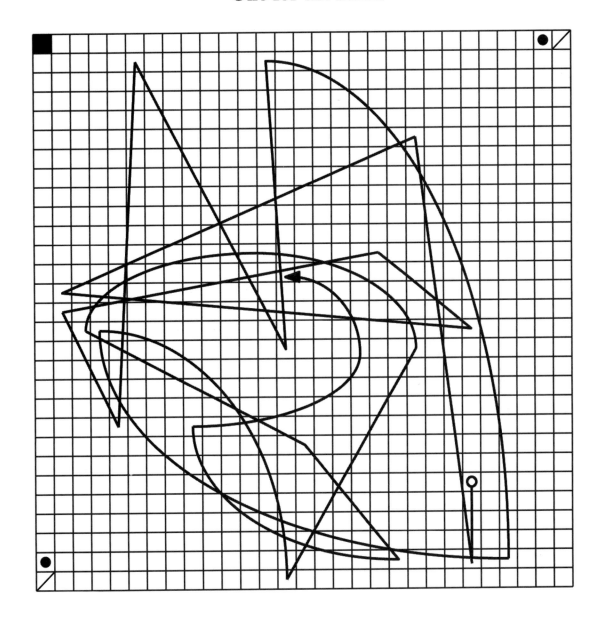

Teambuilding Puzzles

The following books from author Jim Cain are available from Kendall Hunt Publishing

Teamwork & Teamplay by Jim Cain and Barry Jolliff. Winner of the Karl Rohnke Creativity Award from the Association for Experiential Education. One of the best teambuilding resource books ever, with 417 pages of essential adventure-based learning ideas, activities and reference materials.
ISBN 978-0-7872-4532-0

The Revised and Expanded Book of Raccoon Circles by Jim Cain and Tom Smith. Two hundred group activities using only a piece of tubular climbing webbing. Raccoon Circles have become 'the world wide webbing!'
ISBN 978-0-7575-3265-8

Teambuilding Puzzles by Jim Cain, Chris Cavert, Mike Anderson and Tom Heck. One hundred puzzles for teams that build valuable skills authored by four of the most innovative authors in the teambuilding world.
ISBN 0-978-0-7575-7040-7

A Teachable Moment by Jim Cain, Michelle Cummings and Jennifer Stanchfield. One hundred and thirty processing, debriefing, reviewing and reflection techniques essential for every group leader and facilitator.
ISBN 978-0-7575-1782-2

Essential Staff Training Activities by Jim Cain, Clare Marie Hannon and Dave Knobbe. Tips, activities, ideas and suggestions for making your staff training active, engaging, memorable, effective and fun!
ISBN 0-978-0-7575-6167-2

Kendall Hunt Publishing Company
4050 Westmark Drive
Dubuque, Iowa 52002 USA
Phone 1-800-228-0810 or (563) 589-1000
Fax 1-800-772-9165 or (563) 589-1046
orders@kendallhunt.com
www.kendallhunt.com

Teambuilding Resources
from Tom Heck

Teambuilding Puzzles

Duct Tape Teambuilding Games by Tom Heck. Fifty fun activities to help your team stick together. Using one roll of regular, inexpensive duct tape, you can easily lead teambuilding games that teach skills such as leadership, trust, cooperation, creativity, problem solving and confidence. Duct Tape Teambuilding Games provides detailed lead-it-yourself instructions for team leaders, trainers, coaches, facilitators, and educators of all kinds. Includes access to a password-protected website where you can view video clips of all 50 Duct Tape Teambuilding Games in action. 300 pages
ISBN 978-1-60743-908-0

Purchase the book here:
International Association of Teamwork Facilitators
www.IATFconnect.com
Phone: 828-665-0303

International Association of Teamwork Facilitators (IATF) provides volumes of free teambuilding and leadership development resources including free teambuilding game write-ups and videos, free audio interview recordings with teambuilding masters, free leadership skills TeleSeminars, and so much more. When you sign up for the free IATF teambuilding ideas e-newsletter you'll instantly receive the free teambuilding games e-book entitled "Top Four High Impact Team & Leadership Development Activities" by IATF President & Founder Tom Heck. Access all the free IATF teambuilding resources now here: **www.IATFconnect.com**